The Cheyenne Wars Atlas

by

Charles D. Collins, Jr.

Combat Studies Institute
United States Army
Combined Arms Center
Fort Leavenworth, Kansas

Cover Photos: Lt. Col. George Armstrong Custer as he looked during the Washita campaign of 1868 and Cheyenne Chief Black Kettle. Both photos courtesy of the Washita Battlefield National Historic Site, National Park Service website. Used with permission.

Published by Books Express Publishing
Copyright © Books Express, 2012
ISBN 978-1-78266-016-3

Books Express publications are available from all good retail and online booksellers. For publishing proposals and direct ordering please contact us at: info@books-express.com

Foreword

"A century of Indian warfare should have taught us much about dealing with a people who did not fight in conventional ways, and our military tradition might reasonably have been expected to reflect the lessons thus learned."

— Indian Wars Historian Robert M. Utley

The genesis for the publication of The Cheyenne Wars Atlas goes back to June 1992. It was then that the Combat Studies Institute (CSI) conducted the first Sioux Wars Staff Ride for Brigadier General William M. Steele, Deputy Commandant of the US Army Command and General Staff College (CGSC). The next year, CSI expanded the staff ride into a full elective course for the college and supported the course with the publication of the Atlas of the Sioux Wars (First edition, September 1992). The atlas, a work compiled by Dr. William Glenn Robertson, Dr. Jerold E. Brown, Major William M. Campsey, and Major Scott R. McMeen, represented a modest effort to rectify the omission of the Indian Wars in the West Point atlas series by examining the Army's campaigns against the Sioux Indians on the Northern Plains. In 2006, CSI published a second edition of the *Atlas of the Sioux Wars* with updated narratives and full color maps. That atlas has since served as an educational reference for hundreds of students of US Army campaigns against the Sioux during the conduct of dozens of Sioux Wars staff rides.

The Sioux War Staff Ride proved very successful as both a college elective class and a unit staff ride. Then in 2006, CSI was faced with a challenge when CGSC restructured its curriculum for two courses each year. The summer startup class continued to conduct elective periods in the spring. This allowed those students to participate in the field study of the Sioux Wars Staff ride in late May/early June, one of the best times of the year to visit the rolling hills of the campaign area in Montana and Wyoming. However, the elective period for the winter startup class fell into late fall and early winter, a less than ideal time to bus across the Northern Great Plains. Nevertheless, CGSC students continued to ask for the opportunity to participate in an Indian Wars staff ride. Therefore, CSI began to explore options for another Indian Wars staff ride that would be more favorably executed in late fall and early winter.

Popularity of the course was not the only motivation to develop a second Indian Wars staff ride. There is a firm commitment within CSI that the relevance of the Indian Wars to today's Army is even more evident than it was in 1992. Therefore, we wanted to ensure that both CGSC classes had the opportunity to participate in an Indian Wars staff ride. The Indian campaigns are replete with valuable lessons for the professional soldier. Today's soldiers find themselves, as did the frontier regulars of the 19th century, on an asymmetric battlefield with an enemy whose culture and fighting styles are vastly different from their own. A study of the Indian Wars offers the opportunity to compare, contrast, and discover the threads of continuity linking the Indian campaigns with the unconventional warfare of the 21st century. A serious study of the period also allows today's professionals to examine the importance of military commanders addressing cultural awareness as a key operational planning factor. Frontier Army commanders frequently failed to address cultural awareness as an important operational planning factor which lead, at times, to unforeseen consequences on the battlefield.

In 2007, the Institute developed a staff ride that examined General Winfield Scott Hancock's 1867 expedition against the Cheyenne in Kansas (Part II of this atlas). The end result was an excellent staff ride concentrating on cultural awareness issues which frustrated the Army's attempt to compel peace through negotiation. However, the staff ride lacked the breadth and scope needed for a full college course. Thus, our interest turned toward Major General Philip H. Sheridan's 1868 winter campaign against the Cheyenne. In this campaign, Sheridan launched three converging columns into what is now western Oklahoma with orders to put into practice a technique of total war in which he targeted entire Indian villages for destruction. His strategy was that even if an advancing column did not find the hostile Indians, their advancing movement would help to drive the Indians into the other columns. His field commanders managed to surprise and overrun Indian villages in the war's two most significant engagements: the battles of Washita (November 1868) and Soldier Spring (December 1868). The destruction of these two villages was a major loss for the Southern Plains tribes; they could no longer count on the vastness of the territory or harsh winter conditions to protect them from the soldiers. The Southern Plains tribes acknowledged the futility of the struggle and eventually resigned themselves to life on the reservation, and a temporary (transient) peace settled upon the land for the space of four years.

Sheridan's 1868 Winter War was well-suited to the staff ride's three-phase methodology: preliminary study phase, field study phase, and integration phase. The conflict was operationally and tactically complex: unfamiliar terrain, logistics, and cultural issues dramatically affected the engagements. Ample sources of both primary and secondary material are available to support a rigorous preliminary study. The ground targeted for the field study has retained good historical integrity and includes: Camp Supply, Lieutenant Colonel George Armstrong Custer's route to the Washita River, the Washita Battlefield, portions of Major Andrew Evans' approach march along the North Fork of the Red River, and the Soldier Spring Battlefield. The staff ride's third phase, the integration phase, was also easily facilitated by the scenario. The tactical and operational dilemmas faced by Sheridan's soldiers are similar to those faced by US soldiers fighting today in Iraq and Afghanistan. The staff ride allows participating students to reflect with ease upon the similarities and to learn from the experiences of the 19th-century soldiers. Consequently, at least in part, we fulfill Robert Utley's admonition for our Army to reflect upon the *"lessons thus learned."* CSI—*The Past is Prologue!*

Acknowledgments

I wish to acknowledge the many people who made the publication of this work possible and thank them for their efforts. First, I express my gratitude to all of the personnel involved in researching, interpreting and preserving the various battlefields and sites associated with this atlas. This group includes many National Park Service (NPS) personnel, State Historical Site personnel, privately owned museums, and land owners. The staffs at the Fort *Larned National Historic Site* and the Washita *Battlefield* National Historic Site were especially helpful. I offer my special thanks to Rangers George Elmore and Felix Revello at Fort Larned and to Rangers Kathryn Harrison and Joel Shockley at the Washita Battlefield. Mr. Bob Rea at Fort Supply, an Oklahoma State Historic Site, was also key to the success of the project and amazingly patient in providing both insights and material which assisted greatly in my research. His careful editing and recommendations on both the Washita maps and Soldier Spring maps were invaluable. Others I wish to recognize and thank include Leo E. Oliva and William Chalfant, both gifted authors on the Cheyenne Wars. Mr. Oliva gave me a personal tour of the key sites associated with the Hancock Expedition of 1867, and his books on the Kansas Forts were very useful. Mr. Chalfant willingly shared his vast knowledge of the Hancock campaign and executed significant factual editing on much of the early Hancock War narratives and maps. Also, Ms. Ardith Hendrix, at the Wray Museum in Wray, Colorado, provided priceless information in understanding the terrain at the Beecher Island historic site. I know there are many others who have provided help. But unfortunately, in the four years I have worked on and off this project, I have failed to record all the names of those who assisted me and sincerely beg their forgiveness.

Second, I would like to thank the many historians who have researched and published so many great works on this exciting period in our country's history. Without their efforts, my modest endeavor would not have been possible. The atlas's bibliography shows the many publications that I used in my research. However, I would be remiss if I did not note some of the outstanding works that I especially depended upon: Jerome Greene's *Washita*, Richard Hardorff's *Washita Memorie*s, Robert Utley's *Frontiersmen in Blue* and *Frontier Regulars*, and William Leckie's *The Military Conquest of the Southern Plains*.

Third, I would also like to thank the Combat Studies Institute leadership and my colleagues at the institute. Our director, Dr. William Glenn Robertson, has mentored me for many years in the study of the Indian Wars. His original development of a Sioux Wars Staff Ride at the US Army Command and General Staff College was the genesis of the idea to do a Cheyenne Wars Staff Ride. I must also thank Mr. Robert Ramsey, the Staff Ride Team Chief, for allocating the time to finish the project and gently nudging me along to get it done. Special thanks to Lieutenant Colonel (R) Kevin Kennedy for helping me with the first reconnaissance to the campaign area. I greatly value the ideas and insights provided by Doctors Curtis King and Rick Herrera on our second major research trip to the area. Kevin, Curt, Rick, and I spent many hours walking the ground in Kansas where General Winfield Scott Hancock's troops campaigned in 1867 and in Oklahoma where General Phillip H. Sheridan's soldiers campaigned in 1868. Without doubt, their contributions were instrumental to the success of the first iteration of the Cheyenne War Staff Ride at the college which we executed in September 2009 and to the development of this supporting atlas.

Fourth, I must thank my two editors: first, my wife, Judy, who made the careful initial edit of my very rough first drafts and continually encouraged clarification and other needed improvements, and, of course, Jody Becker, Combat Studies Institute editor, who diligently polished the final draft into a professional package for publication.

Last, on a personal note, I offer my heartfelt thanks to my family for always supporting me through my many staff rides and research trips not only to the Cheyenne Wars battlefields, but to many other historical sites across our nation. Such great opportunities and experiences are hard for me to think of as "work."

Charles D. Collins, Jr.
Historian, Combat Studies Institute

Contents

Foreword

Acknowledgements

I. Background

Map 1. The Southern Plains
Map 2. The Cheyenne 1850
Map 3. The Cheyenne Campaign of 1857
Map 4. The Treaty of Fort Wise
Map 5. Trouble in Colorado
Map 6. The Cheyenne War of 1864
Map 7. The Sand Creek Massacre
Map 8. The Treaty of the Little Arkansas

II. Hancock's War

Map 9. An Unsteady Peace
Map 10. A Failure in Cultural Awareness
Map 11. Confrontation Hill
Map 12. The Village at Pawnee Fork
Map 13. The Futile Chase
Map 14. Lookout Station
Map 15. The Unnecessary War

III. Sheridan's Summer War

Map 16. Sheridan Takes Command
Map 17. The Sully Expedition
Map 18. Forsyth's Scouts
Map 19. The Battle of Beecher Island
Map 20. The Beaver Creek Skirmishes
Map 21. Sheridan's Winter Campaign Plan

IV. The Fight at the Washita

Map 22. The March to Camp Supply
Map 23. 19th Kansas Cavalry
Map 24. Camp Supply
Map 25. General Sheridan's Decision
Map 26. The March to the Canadian River
Map 27. Custer's Gamble
Map 28. Movement to Contact
Map 29. Tactical Pause
Map 30. Plan of Attack
Map 31. Dawn Attack
Map 32. Custer's Command Post
Map 33. Unforeseen Circumstances
Map 34. A Brevet or a Coffin
Map 35. Total War
Map 36. Custer's Victory
Map 37. Retreat to Safety

V. The Fight at Soldier Spring

Map 38. Sheridan Continues the Campaign
Map 39. The North Fork of the Red River
Map 40. Christmas Morning Decision
Map 41. Opening Shots at Soldier Spring
Map 42. Major Tarlton Overruns the Village
Map 43. Evans' Victory
Map 44. Sheridan's Campaign, 26 December 1868 – 19 February 1869
Map 45. Custer Again, March-April 1869

VI. The Republican River Expedition

Map 46. Trouble on the Republican River
Map 47. The Spillman Creek Raid
Map 48. The Republican River Expedition
Map 49. The Pursuit
Map 50. The Battle of Summit Springs
Map 51. The End of the Cheyenne War

Appendix A: The 7th US Cavalry

Appendix B: Army Logistics

Bibliography

About the Author

Notes

I. Background

1. The Southern Plains

The Southern Plains of the 19th century were a broad expanse of generally level and almost treeless, semiarid terrain covered by thick prairie grass. The expanse stretched northward from the Rio Grande River to the Platte River and westward from the 98th meridian to the Rocky Mountains. It encompassed today's Kansas, eastern Colorado, Oklahoma, Texas, and portions of Nebraska and eastern Wyoming. The Plains supported an abundance of wildlife including antelope, bison, and deer. The bison, or American buffalo, was the most significant of all the Plains animals. Travelers noted in astonishment, *"The whole plain, as far as the eye could discern, was covered by one enormous mass of buffalo."*[1] It is believed the buffalo originally ranged from Texas to Canada and from the Rocky Mountains all the way to the Atlantic Coast. Although their ancestral home covered the entire Great Plains, their prime grazing grounds were on the Southern Plains between the South Platte and Arkansas Rivers. The buffalo was essential to the Plains Indian's way of life. It yielded meat for food, hides for clothing and shelter, and bones for utensils and tools. Even dried buffalo droppings, "buffalo chips," provided a burnable fuel.

Despite the abundance of wildlife, it was a harsh land suffering from a lack of water with an average annual rainfall of less than 20 inches. In addition to the drought-like climate, the Plains endured the constant buffeting of erratic winds. In the summer months, hot southerly winds created almost furnace-like conditions. Then, from early fall until late spring, cold northern winds swept across the land. These *"northers"* could bring on rapid drops in temperature, and many times brought with them deadly blizzards. Despite these conflicting conditions, plentiful resources on the one hand and unforgiving climatic conditions on the other, the land of the Southern Plains was considered a worthy prize. In the mid-19th century, five Indian tribes claimed the Southern Plains as home. The Comanche, Kiowa, and Kiowa-Apache had migrated into the region in the early 18th century. The Cheyenne and Arapahos were new to the area, having more recently arrived during the 1830s. White emigrants began moving into the region in the 1850s. Ironically, the fight for the Southern Plains was not so much a contest of indigenous Native Americans against the white invaders, but more of a conflict between two vastly different emigrant cultures.[2] The determination of the Southern Plains tribes to retain control of the land and preserve their way of life, in opposition to an equal determination on the part of the white man to possess the land, led to an unyielding conflict between the two cultures.

The Cheyenne people made up one of the largest tribes in the region during the mid 19th century. Prior to the 18th century, the Cheyenne lived in the Great Lakes region until stronger tribes in that area forced them westward. Over time, the Cheyenne migrated toward the Black Hills and the Platte River valley. Eventually, the massive herds of buffalo roaming the plains lured a branch of the tribe southward across the Platte River into the Arkansas River valley of today's southern Colorado and Kansas. By the mid 1800s, the Cheyenne had totally abandoned their sedentary agricultural traditions and completely adopted the nomadic buffalo-hunting culture. They replaced their earthen lodges with tepees, and their diet changed from agricultural products to mainly buffalo meat. The Cheyenne flourished in the Arkansas River region up into the late 1840s. War between the US and Mexico in 1846, brought increased traffic onto the Santa Fe Trail, but most travelers passed unmolested through the Cheyenne territory. However, the discovery of gold in California brought hordes of miners through the Cheyenne lands. The gold prospectors were only passing through, but without realizing it, they brought cholera to the Southern Plains in 1849; the disease was devastating to the Cheyenne and may have killed more than half the Southern Cheyenne population.

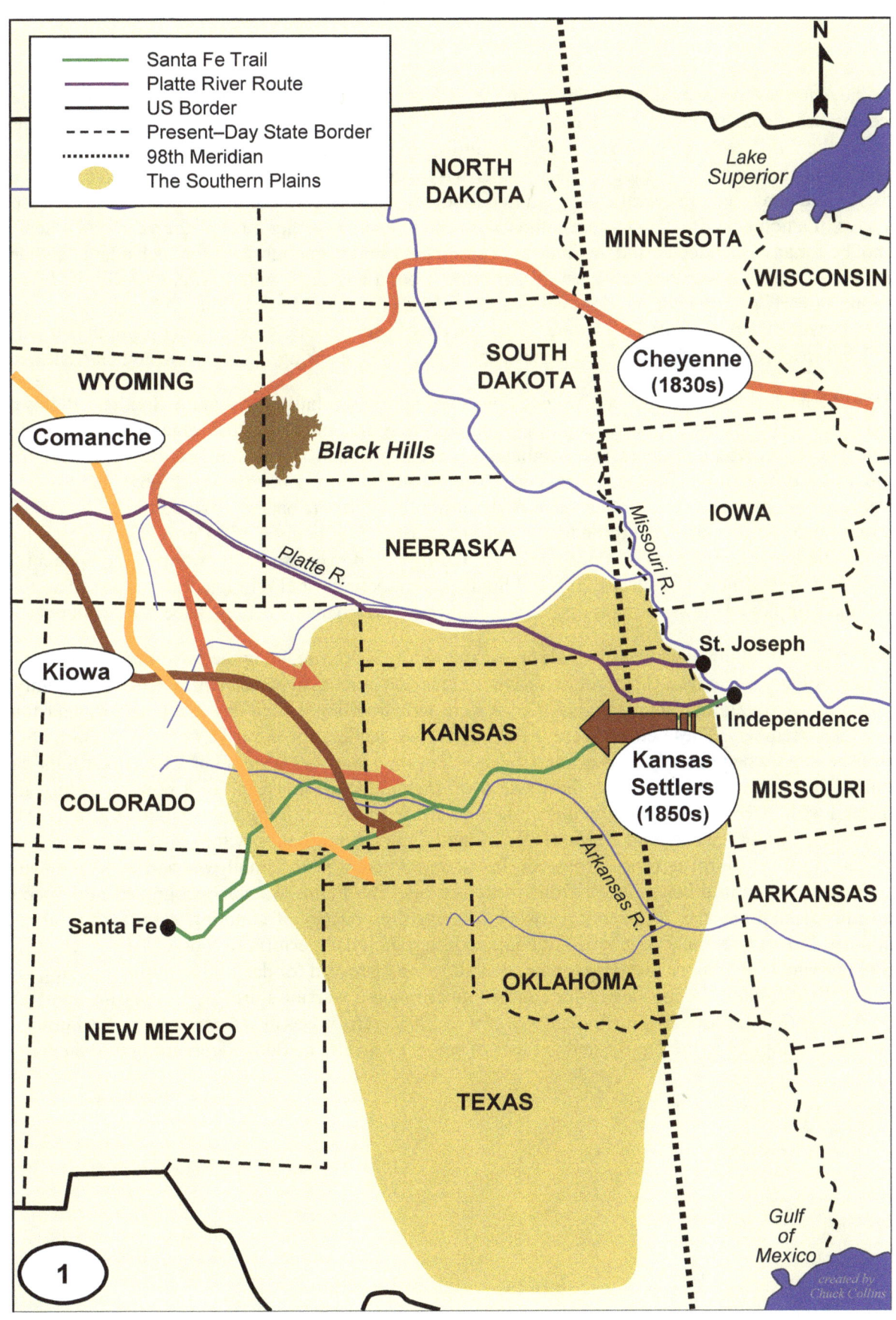

2. The Cheyenne

The Cheyenne society was democratic in nature with a social structure built upon the family. They had a reverence for individual freedoms tempered by a respect for the needs of the people. In the Cheyenne tribal organization, the family was the basic social unit. A family grouping, called a kindred, began with the lodge of the family head, branched out with the lodges of his other wives, and again with the lodges of the daughters and their husbands. A band consisted of several closely related kindred. There were 10 main bands and several lesser bands. The demands of a nomadic life did not permit the Cheyenne to camp together most of the year, and when they did, it could not be for any extended period. A single area could not provide enough food for such a large gathering, and their vast herds of ponies would quickly eat all the grass around any large village site. Usually the bands joined in late spring or early summer for religious celebrations and a communal buffalo hunt. After the hunt, each of the bands would scatter for the winter. By October, the bands might scatter into even smaller groupings to ensure that available local resources were sufficient to survive the winter. In the spring, the cycle would start all over again.

The Southern Cheyenne were never a large nation. The eight-and-a-half bands on the Southern Plains probably numbered about 3,500 people. Of those, perhaps 60 percent were female, and of the remaining 1,400 males, about 20 percent would have been children and another 20 percent old men. Most likely, there was never more than about 850 warriors for all the Southern Cheyenne. Their leaders were not vested with absolute power. Instead, they governed through the power of influence and persuasion. Each of the bands provided four chiefs who, in turn, selected four head chiefs considered to be the wisest in the tribe. This council of 44 provided the civil leadership of the tribe. The council acted as court and judge for the tribe and exercised authority over movement, locating campsites, determining times and places for tribal hunts, and directing tribal religious ceremonies. The four chiefs from each band employed the same authority within their respective bands when the tribe was scattered.

Warfare was the traditional pathway to male honor and status. Therefore, integrated within the tribal organization were various military societies. These societies were clubs or social groups responsible for community service and the training of young men into warriors. There were four traditional societies. Each society had four chiefs elected by their members. These chiefs were the principal war leaders for the tribe or, more commonly, the war leaders for the band when the tribe was scattered. The Cheyenne warriors were some of the best light cavalry in the world. Before extensive contact with the white man, their weapons consisted of a bow, war club, and lance. Over time and with increased contact with the white man, firearms became common weapons for them. The Plains Indians had their own unique style of warfare. Occasionally, the tribe or bands within the tribe conducted warfare against other tribes to control territory. However, it was more common for small war parties to conduct raids to steal horses or cattle from other tribes or from white settlers. The Plains warrior recognized no noncombatants and would not hesitate to slay an enemy. However, it was the concept of counting coup and obtaining honor that dominated Indian warfare. The practice of coup counting included performing brave deeds such as killing an enemy and scalping him. A more prestigious coup was showing disregard for danger or simply touching or striking an opponent. The number of coups a warrior counted determined a warrior's prestige among his peers. Avoiding casualties was another key aspect of the Indian way of war. Each warrior was also a provider for his family. The loss of a warrior was crippling to the family, and the loss of several warriors could be devastating to the band or tribe.[3]

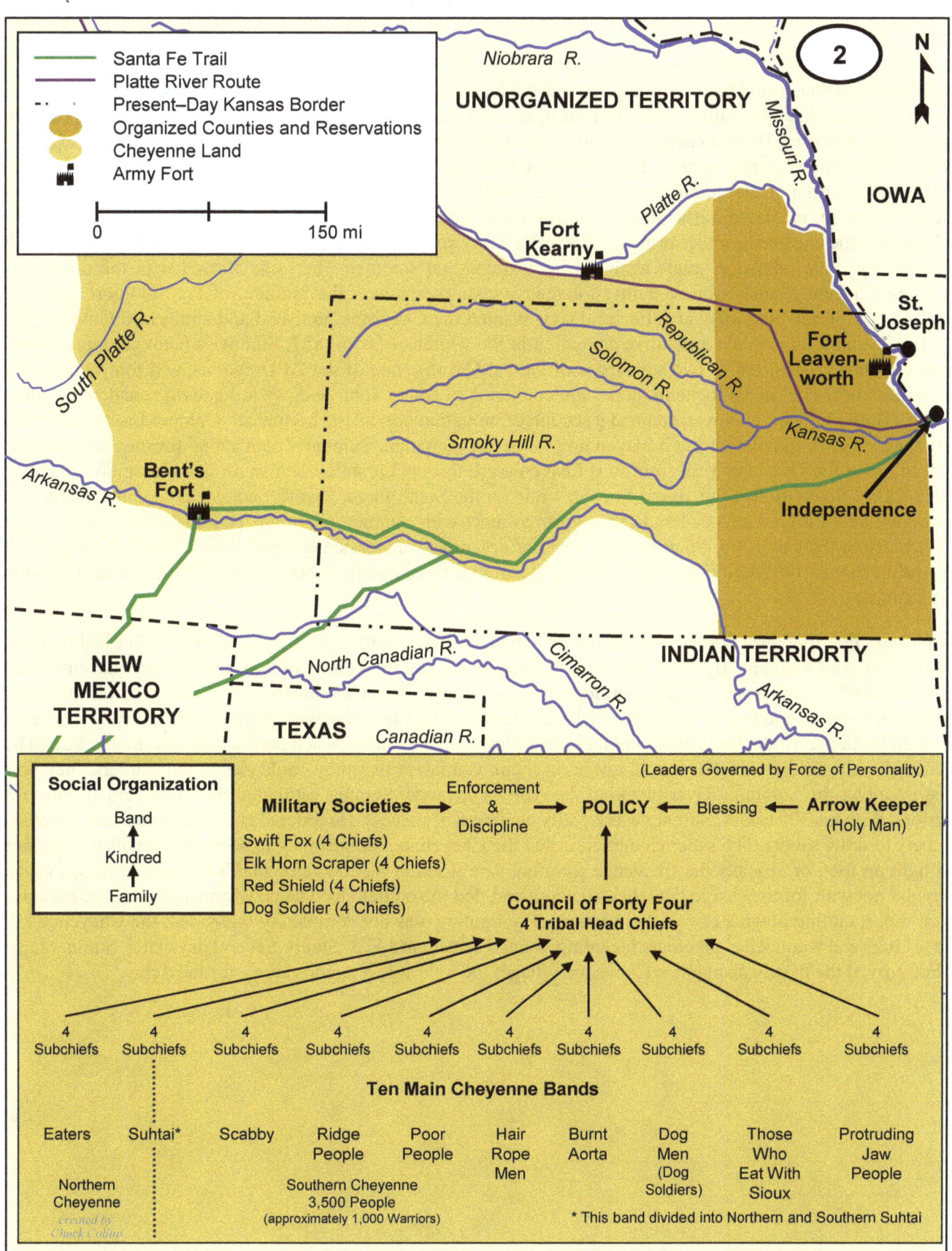

3. The Cheyenne Campaign of 1857

The United States government anticipated that the increasing influx of emigrants moving across the Great Plains through Cheyenne land would eventually lead to conflict. It attempted to forestall problems with the Cheyenne through negotiations. Those negotiations led to the Fort Laramie Treaty of 1851. The goal of the treaty was to avoid confrontation by moving the Cheyenne away from the white settlements and emigrant trails. The treaty set aside land in northern Colorado for the Cheyenne. Initially, it was successful in promoting peace between the two cultures. Even so, increased traffic along the Kansas and Nebraska overland migration routes prompted Cheyenne raids against the emigrants in the spring of 1856. The Army struck back against the Indians, which, in turn, resulted in more Cheyenne retaliatory raids against wagon trains that summer. The raids slowed with the onset of fall when the Cheyenne bands came together for their winter camps near the junction of the Solomon and Smoky Hill Rivers. But Secretary of War Jefferson Davis wanted the Cheyenne punished and authorized Colonel Edwin V. "Bull" Sumner to conduct a punitive campaign in the winter of 1856-1857. Sumner's main column, under his direct command, consisted of two squadrons of the 1st Cavalry, one of the 2d Dragoons, and four companies of the 6th Infantry. The second column, under the command of Major John Sedgwick, had two squadrons of the 1st Cavalry. Both of these columns contained a section of mountain howitzers. Lieutenant Colonel Joseph E. Johnston commanded the third column, but it played no role in the campaign. Sumner's plan called for the main column to proceed along the Overland Trail from Fort Leavenworth to Fort Laramie, then south into Colorado uniting with Sedgwick's column at the ruins of old Fort St. Vrain on the South Platte River[4]. Sedgwick's column was to move down the Santa Fe Trail into Colorado then north to meet with Sumner's column. The link-up was set for 4 July 1857. Early in the campaign, Sumner's squadron of dragoons was reassigned to Colonel William Harney's Utah expedition against the Mormons. They were replaced with three additional companies of the 6th Infantry out of Fort Laramie.

During their marches, Sumner and Sedgwick covered a large portion of the Central Plains but had no contact with the elusive Cheyenne. By July, Sumner and Sedgwick had united their columns and turned eastward into the heart of the Cheyenne lands. On the morning of 29 July, scouts reported Indians ahead. Sumner left the infantry and artillery behind and then pushed ahead with the cavalry. The Cheyenne were aware of the Army's presence and prepared for battle. Under the direction of their medicine men, they had washed their hands in a small lake and been assured that the soldiers' bullets would not harm them. Confident that they could defeat the soldiers, they boldly lined up along the Solomon River blocking the Army's advance. Sumner estimated their numbers at 300 to 350 warriors. With his 300 troops, Sumner was equally confident of success. He ordered charge sounded and directed his troopers to draw sabers. The saber charge unsettled the Cheyenne. Perhaps they expected the cavalry to dismount and fight on foot, or possibly the Cheyenne were not sure whether the medicine man's blessing applied to sabers. They did not wait for the charge but wheeled about and fled the battlefield. The cavalrymen chased the Indians for seven miles, cutting down a few of the warriors. The fighting was not completely one-sided; the Cheyenne killed two soldiers and wounded eight others including young Lieutenant J.E.B. Stuart. Several days later, Sumner located and destroyed the hastily abandoned Cheyenne village; the fight was a major victory for the Army.[5]

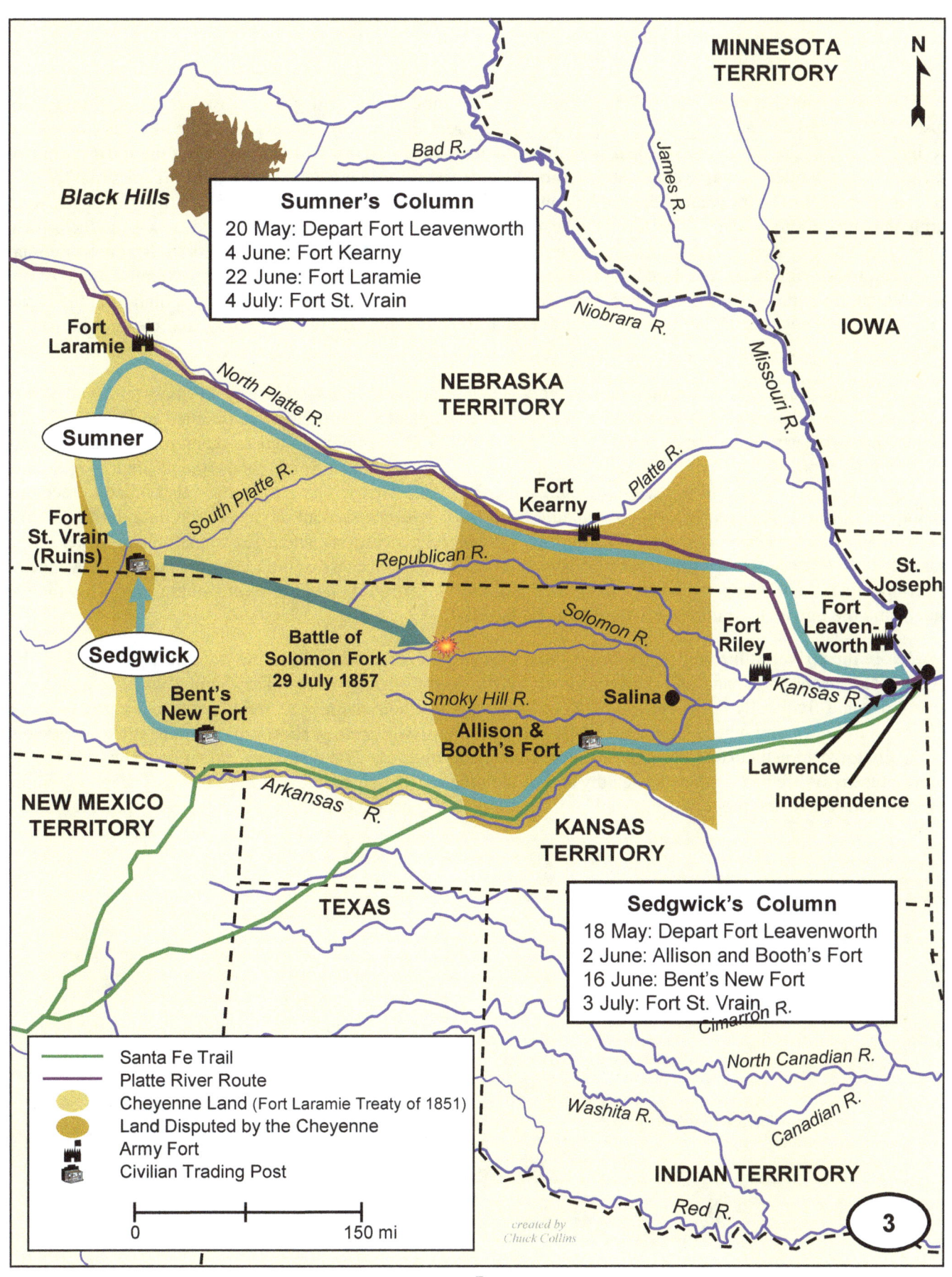

4. The Treaty of Fort Wise

The Cheyenne Campaign of 1857 restrained the Cheyenne for several years. However, the Colorado Gold Rush of 1858 doomed any hope of lasting peace when great numbers of settlers and gold seekers moved onto the Indian lands. The miners established several settlements in Colorado with Denver being the most prominent. Unfortunately, the new towns were established on land promised to the Cheyenne in the Fort Laramie Treaty of 1851, and the Coloradoans wanted the Indians out of the region. Some Cheyenne leaders, with Chief Black Kettle being one of the more influential, believed the best course of action was to voluntarily move away from the growing white population centers. Black Kettle and other peace advocates signed the Treaty of Fort Wise on 18 February 1861. The treaty significantly reduced the Cheyenne lands and provided a meager compensation payment of only $450,000 to the Indians. The Fort Wise treaty was unfairly advantageous to the new white population of the region. It removed the Cheyenne from the heavily settled areas, which were also the best lands, and cleared the way for Congress to officially establish the Colorado Territory.

Most of the government negotiators and the Cheyenne peace chiefs were acting in good faith and naively hoped the fruits of their efforts would be a lasting peace. Tragically, the treaty was doomed to failure primarily because neither party understood the other's culture. The US Government failed to recognize that a few peace chiefs did not represent the will of all, or even a majority of the Cheyenne. Some bands, the militant Dog Soldiers Band being the most adamant, refused to recognize the Fort Wise Treaty. The government also failed to recognize the importance of the Cheyenne people's nomadic freedom. The establishment of reservation boundaries on a map was foreign to them. They had followed the buffalo for several generations, and a few signatures on paper did not erase the Cheyenne people's will to roam. Equally foreboding to the success of the treaty, neither the Cheyenne nor government negotiators understood how overwhelming the white migration to the West would become nor did they understand the impact their numbers would have on the land.

Before the arrival of the whites, the only boundaries recognized by the Cheyenne were those imposed by their own limited means to expand and those enforced by the might of other tribes. They hunted buffalo within their boundaries and frequently raided across the boundaries against their enemies to steal horses and gain honor. The Cheyenne did not comprehend how the overpowering wave of white emigration moving onto their lands would eventually force upon them fixed boundaries across which the white man would tolerate no raiding. Nevertheless, the Cheyenne way of life had produced a healthy and productive society, an enviable culture that they were determined to retain. This brave and proud people would not be compelled to accept the white man's changes upon their culture without a fight.

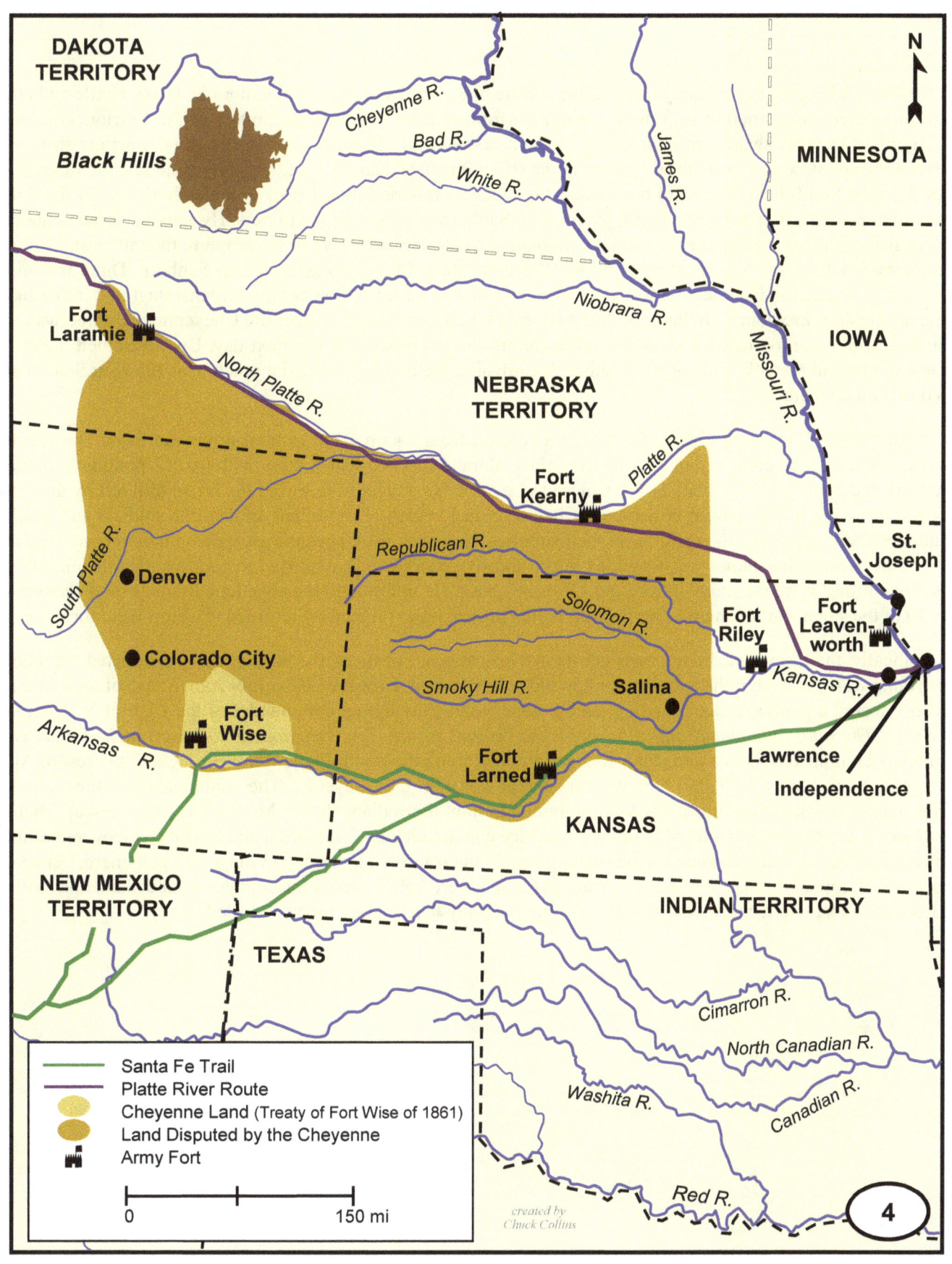

5. Trouble in Colorado

By 1864, it became increasingly challenging for the two cultures to coexist in Colorado. Black Kettle and other Cheyenne peace chiefs tried to stop their young men from raiding. Nevertheless, many of the warriors continued to participate in raids against emigrants and isolated homesteads. Then in early April 1864, warriors from two Cheyenne bands stole 175 cattle from ranches in the Bijou Basin, and another raiding party stole several mules from a ranch on the South Platte River. In both cases, the ranchers reported their losses to the authorities. On the South Platte, Lieutenant Clark Dunn led a patrol from Camp Sanborn in pursuit of the raiders. His small column contained 40 men from Companies C and H of the 1st Colorado Cavalry. His orders were to recapture the mules and capture the raiders. On 12 April, he caught up with the Cheyenne about 20 miles east of Camp Sanborn. Dunn was more interested in retaliation than negotiation, thus any hope of a peaceful settlement quickly disintegrated into a fight. In the skirmish at Fremont's Orchard, he lost two men killed and two wounded; the Cheyenne had three warriors wounded. Dunn then retreated without the mules or any Indian prisoners. The next day, Dunn resumed the chase but lost the trail in the cold and snowy weather. Meanwhile, the raiders attacked a ranch near Junction Station and killed two ranch hands.

To the south, Lieutenant George Eayre led a column from Camp Weld to hunt down the Bijou Basin cattle thieves. His command consisted of 54 men from the Colorado Independent Battery with two 12-pounder mountain howitzers and 26 men of Company D, 1st Colorado Cavalry. He doggedly followed the broad trail left by the cattle for eight days and finally caught up with the Cheyenne on 15 April. The Indians spotted the soldiers and quickly abandoned their lodges and the majority of their supplies. However, the Cheyenne escaped with their pony herd and most of the cattle. One soldier was wounded in the abortive encounter. Eayre tried to continue the pursuit, but his horses and mules were worn down from the 120-mile chase. He returned to the abandoned village after recovering only 19 of the stolen cattle. There he burned the Indian property and reluctantly returned to Camp Weld for resupply.

Ironically, the Cheyenne did not consider themselves at war. For them, the raiding was an expected practice of their young warriors even if the tribal leadership did not endorse it. However, Governor John Evans of the Colorado Territory feared a general Indian uprising, and Colonel John Chivington, commander of the District of Colorado, believed, *"The long anticipated difficulties with the Indians in this Territory appear to have reached a crisis."*[6] Marauders continued to harass and steal from the ranches along the South Platte River throughout the rest of April convincing Evans and Chivington they were indeed at war with the Cheyenne. The commanders of the Colorado camps and forts dispatched numerous small columns to hunt the Indians down. Most were unsuccessful. Then in early May, a detachment of Colorado volunteer cavalry commanded by Captain Jacob Downing discovered a small Cheyenne village at Cedar Canyon. In the ensuing attack, the soldiers captured the village and pony herd, but again, most of the occupants managed to escape. Army casualties were light with several soldiers wounded but none killed; the Cheyenne lost two teenage boys killed watching the pony herd and two women killed.

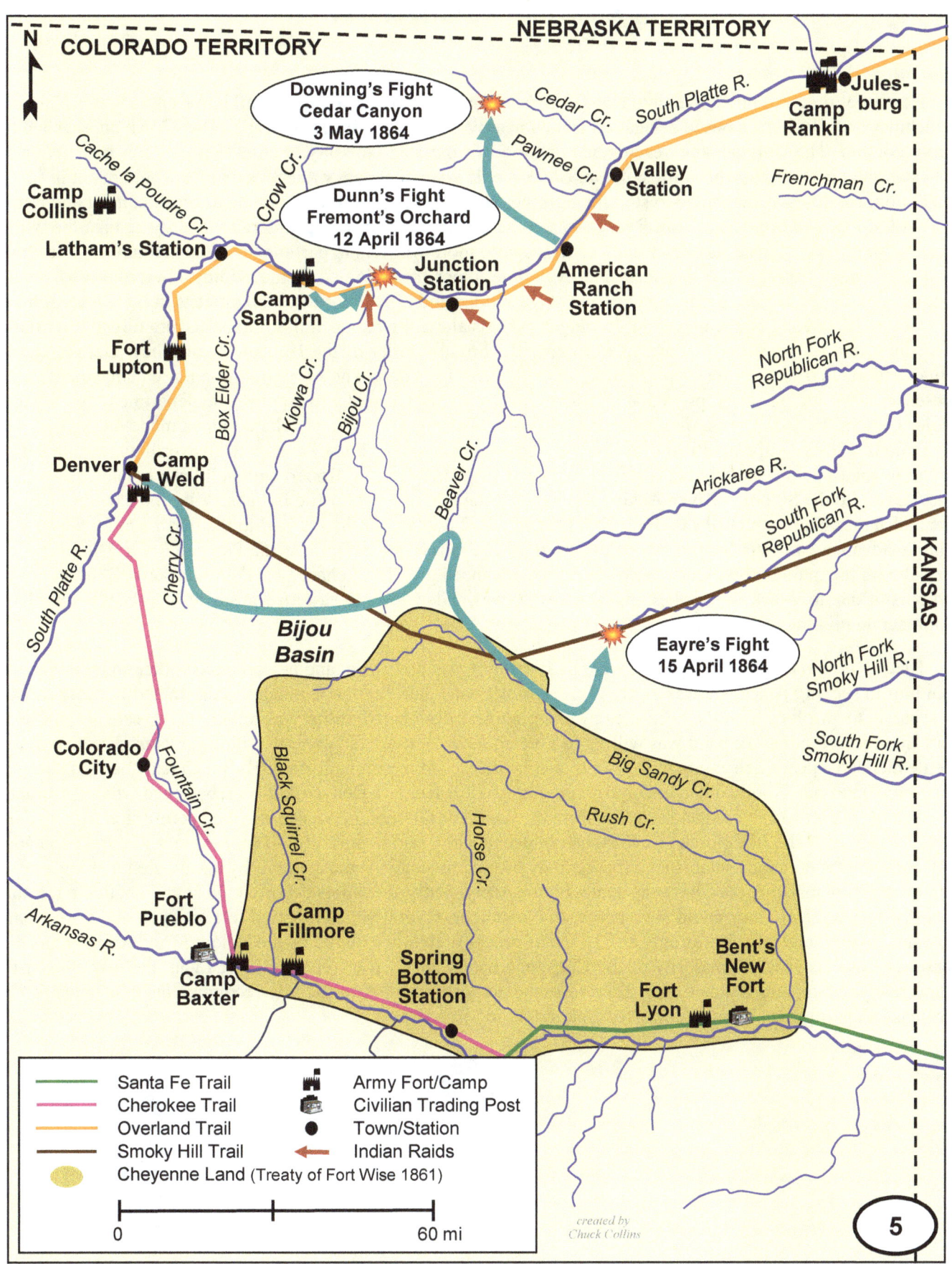

6. The Cheyenne War of 1864

Hostilities quickly spilled over into Kansas. In May, Eayre followed an Indian trail into Kansas with a Colorado detachment. On 16 May, a peace delegation from a nearby Cheyenne Village on Big Timber Creek approached the Army column. The Coloradoans treacherously shot down the lead emissary, a chief named Lean Bear. Warriors then swarmed in to engage the Army column. Black Kettle knew that heavy Army casualties would result in severe retaliation. He quickly intervened to stop the fighting. His actions allowed the soldiers to break contact and retreat to Fort Larned. The murder of Lean Bear incensed the Cheyenne, and they countered violently against the whites throughout the region. The success of their raids inspired more warriors to participate in the marauding. The chiefs could no longer restrain their warriors, and over time, other tribes joined in the raiding. Over the next several months, the hostile Indians disrupted mail and stage service and killed more than 50 citizens in Nebraska, Kansas, and Colorado. In Kansas, the unendurable weight of raids along the Saline and Solomon Rivers forced the frontier settlement line to recede to the east. In Colorado, the brutal murder of the Hungate family near Denver caused panic, and much of the territory's population fled to Denver for safety. The Army did little more than expand Army presence in the region which proved an ineffectual deterrent to the raids. In August, the department commander, Major General Samuel Curtis, dispatched several columns from Fort Larned. The columns made no contact with the Indians. Curtis's only significant success was the establishment of Forts Zarah and Ellsworth which opened the emigrant routes again. In early September, Curtis and Brigadier General Robert Mitchell led a column south from Fort Kearny to the Solomon River. Again there was no contact with the hostile Indians. A second expedition under General James Blunt marched east from Fort Larned on 22 September then turned to the north. On 25 September, Blunt's advance party clashed with warriors from a large Cheyenne camp near the Pawnee River. Blunt's timely arrival with the main body rescued the beleaguered advanced guard and chased off their attackers. Blunt broke off the pursuit due to a lack of supplies and, soon after, was called back to eastern Kansas to help beat back a large Confederate raid into Missouri.

Black Kettle recognized his people were in a war they could not win, and he convinced other council chiefs to join him in seeking peace. He was aware of Governor Evans' late June proclamation that invited friendly Indians to separate themselves from the hostilities by camping near designated military installations. He sent emissaries to Fort Lyon relaying that his band was willing to give up their captives and comply with the Evans' directive. Black Kettle then led a peace delegation to Denver to meet with the Governor. Unfortunately, much had changed since the June proclamation. Colorado had endured a summer of violence, and Denver had been besieged when the Indians blocked the movement of food and supplies from the East. The Governor had also received permission from Federal authorities to raise the 3d Colorado Cavalry, a volunteer cavalry regiment of *"100-day men."* In short, the population of Colorado was no longer interested in peace; they wanted revenge. At the council, Evans avoided making a peace commitment by insisting the Cheyenne deal with the Army. Sadly, the chiefs departed the council believing, if they reported to Fort Lyon, they could have peace. In November, several bands reported to Fort Lyon and set up camp on Sand Creek. Tragically, it was only an illusion of peace. With much duplicity, the Colorado and Army authorities reasoned that, because the majority of the Cheyenne bands declined to report to Fort Lyon, the war against the Cheyenne and Arapaho was not over. Therefore, the authorities did not officially recognize the Cheyenne at Fort Lyon as being at peace. The stage was set for a horrifying tragedy.

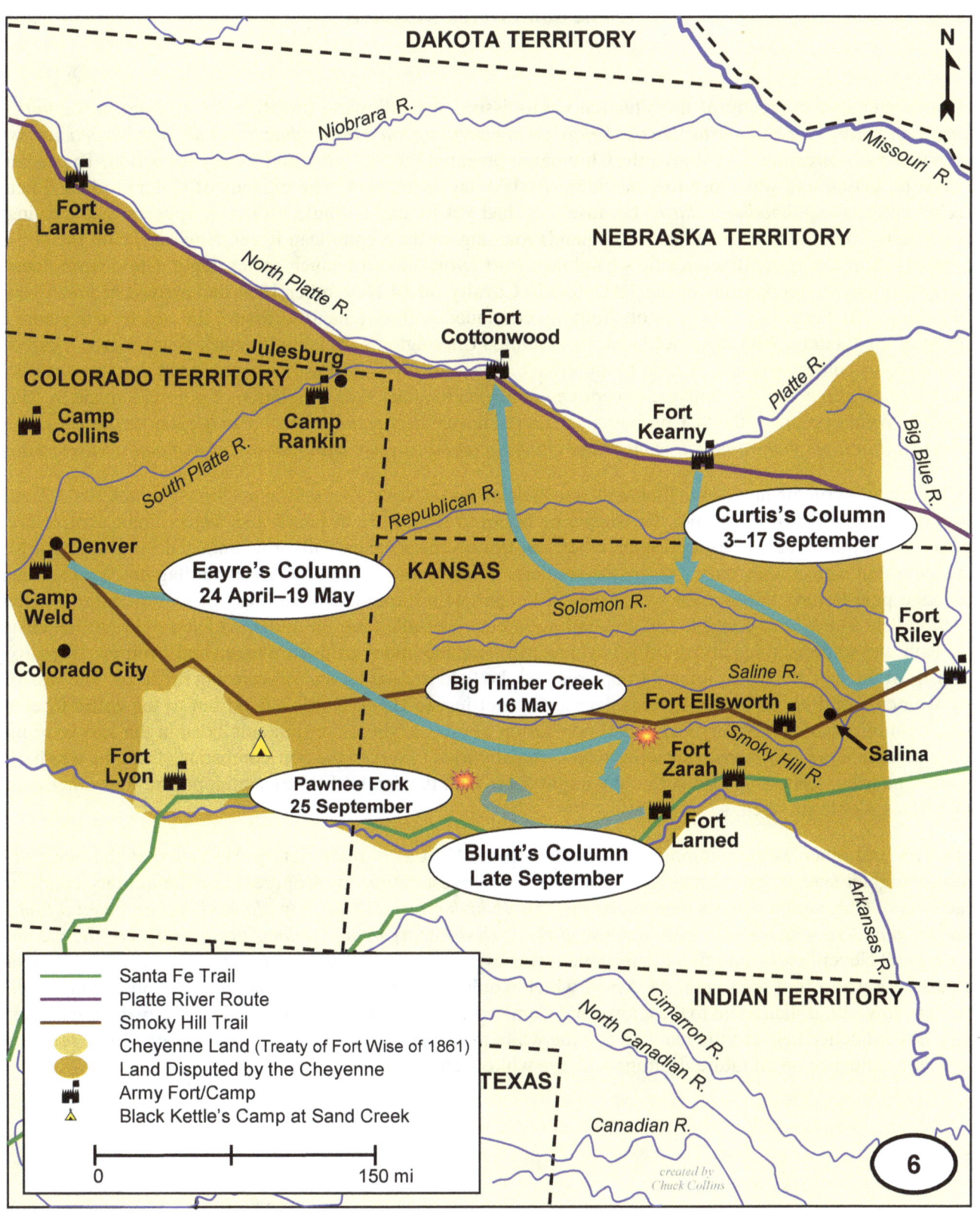

7. The Sand Creek Massacre

Compounding the tragedy of the situation Curtis issued the following directive, *"I want no peace until the Indians suffer more… It is better to chastise before giving anything but a little tobacco to talk over. No peace must be made without my directions."*[7] Meanwhile, Chivington prepared the 3d Colorado Cavalry for action. The regiment had seen no action and was close to concluding its 100-day enlistment. The citizens of Colorado had ridiculed the regiment as the *"Bloodless Third"* because they had yet to slay a single Indian. It appears that Chivington had considered operations against the hostile bands roaming on the Republican River. However, with the 100-day enlistments soon to expire, Black Kettle's band near Fort Lyon offered a much easier target. Chivington departed Denver with the 3d and portions of the 1st Colorado Cavalry on 14 November 1864 and arrived at Fort Lyon on 28 November. At Fort Lyon, Major Scott Anthony continued with one hand to assure the nearby Cheyenne and Arapaho of their safety. With the other hand, he sustained Chivington's decision to attack Black Kettle's camp; he even offered to guide the attack column to the village. Several officers at Fort Lyon protested that, because Black Kettle was acting in good faith with the government, the plan to attack was a violation of promises made by Majors Edward W. Wynkoop and Anthony. Chivington countered it was *"right and honorable to use any means under God's heaven to kill Indians that would kill women and children, and damn any man that was in sympathy with Indians."*[8]

Chivington's column moved out that night and at dawn on 29 November was in position to attack Black Kettle's village of about 700 people. Again, the Cheyenne believed they were at peace and were caught completely by surprise. White Antelope, a leading council chief, ran toward the soldiers with arms upraised begging the soldiers not to shoot but was quickly cut down by the soldiers. Black Kettle hoisted an American flag and a white banner on a lodge pole hoping the soldiers would accept his people's surrender. Regardless of their attempt to submit, the *"Bloodless Third"* had come to kill and had no intention of allowing the Indians to surrender. In the ensuing blood bath, the soldiers killed about 200 Cheyenne and Arapaho, many of them women and children. Intensifying the horror of the day, the undisciplined troops roamed the field mutilating and desecrating the dead. The loss of so many women, children, and warriors was devastating not just to Black Kettle's band but to the entire Cheyenne tribal community which probably had a total population of only 3,000 at the time. Included in the loss were many prominent members of the warrior societies who heroically tried to screen the non-combatants from the wrath of the soldiers. The tribal leadership also suffered a major blow with the death of White Antelope and four other council chiefs; Black Kettle survived.

Denver and other western communities celebrated the fight as a great victory. However, as the news of the wanton slaughter spread, most Americans were outraged. Investigations by Congress and the military condemned the actions of Chivington and his men declaring, *"He [Chivington] deliberately planned and executed a foul and dastardly massacre which would have disgraced the veriest* [most] *savage among those who were the victims of his cruelty."*[9] Nevertheless, no official punishment was ever enacted upon any member of Chivington's command. The massacre was a foul stain upon the Army, which would haunt the leadership in all future operations. Colonel Jesse Leavenworth, Indian agent to the Kiowa and Comanche, was of the opinion that this atrocity destroyed the last vestige of confidence between the red man and the white man. For the Cheyenne, the specter of Sand Creek would have a dark influence on all future dealings with the white man.

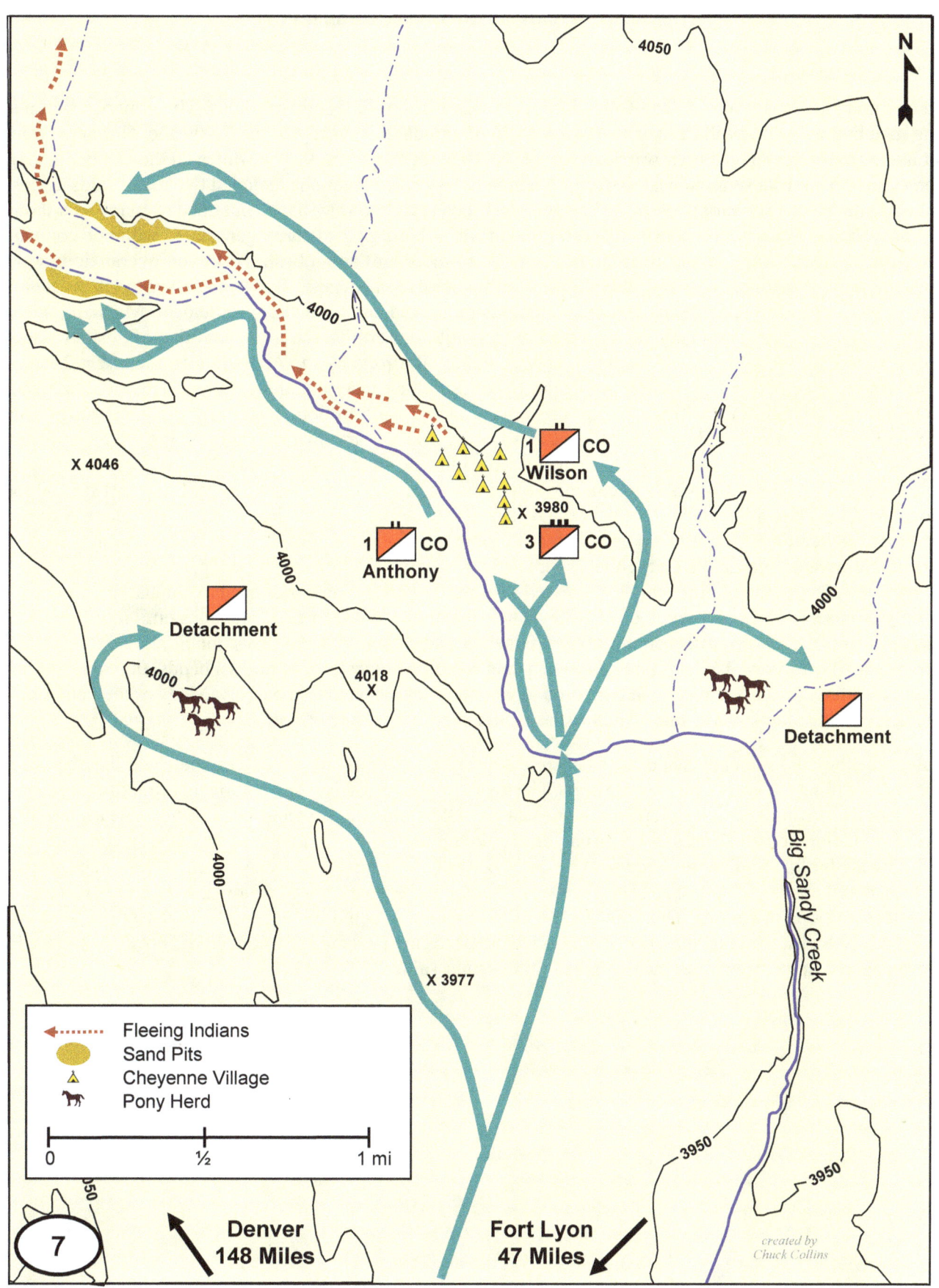

8. The Treaty of the Little Arkansas

The immediate result of the Sand Creek Massacre was war on the Southern Plains. The previous summer the young men had defied the will of their chiefs in conducting raids. Now many of the Cheyenne, Northern Arapaho, and Lakota chiefs encouraged their warriors to exact revenge for Sand Creek. The whites on the frontier in Kansas, Colorado, and Nebraska suffered heavily from Indian raids. Significant actions included two major raids against the small community of Julesburg, Colorado. The first on 7 January 1865 may have contained as many as a thousand Cheyenne, Sioux, and Arapaho warriors. Julesburg had a small army post nearby garrisoned with one company of cavalry. In the attack, the Indians attempted to lure the soldiers into an ambush. However, overanxious warriors sprung the trap prematurely allowing the majority of the soldiers to escape. The soldiers and civilians then took refuge in the fort and watched helplessly as the Indians plundered and burned the settlement. Mitchell gathered a column of soldiers together and conducted a fruitless pursuit. Meanwhile, the loose coalition of hostiles raided up and down the Platte River Valley, contemptuously avoiding all efforts by the Army to stop them. On 2 February, the Indians returned and pillaged Julesburg again. By midsummer, federal authorities had failed to end hostilities despite the commitment of 8,000 troops and the expenditure of $40 million. Therefore, the government focused on a negotiated settlement, and again Black Kettle was a significant participant in determining the outcome. Black Kettle survived Sand Creek, but he had lost considerable influence as a council chief. Nevertheless, he remained a staunch peace advocate and was able to convince many of his people to avoid hostilities. Early in 1865, 80 lodges of Southern Cheyenne followed him south of the Arkansas River. Then, in October, Black Kettle along with several other chiefs gathered on the Little Arkansas River for new treaty negotiations. The peace commission apologized for the many wrongs against the Cheyenne, repudiated Chivington's actions, offered reparations, and pushed for a new treaty. Black Kettle and other chiefs expressed a desire for peace. The chiefs tried to emphasize, however, that they only represented a small portion of the Cheyenne tribe; they wanted to delay the talks until more chiefs could be present. Still the government commissioners failed to understand that the few council chiefs present did not represent all 10 Cheyenne bands or that the participants could only speak for their own bands. In reality, within the Cheyenne culture a chief's authority did not bind any member of his band to the treaty. Many of the young men, in particular, continued to conduct raids whether their chief supported peace or not.

Because they did not understand the Cheyenne culture, the commissioners naively believed they had secured peace and a binding treaty with all the Cheyenne. The treaty established a new reservation that straddled the boundary of southern Kansas and the Indian Territory in present-day Oklahoma. It also required the Cheyenne to cede all their old lands in Colorado and Kansas. A confusing clause within the treaty allowed the Cheyenne to continue to roam and follow the buffalo until white settlement assumed control of the land. The treaty chiefs did not understand they had surrendered control of their land. They believed they were free to roam and follow the buffalo in Colorado and the western portions of Kansas. Their understanding was that they could not encamp within 10 miles of towns or traveled roads. Sadly, the great majority of the Cheyenne bands not present at the council did not even know a treaty had been agreed upon. Therefore, the treaty had little lasting value.

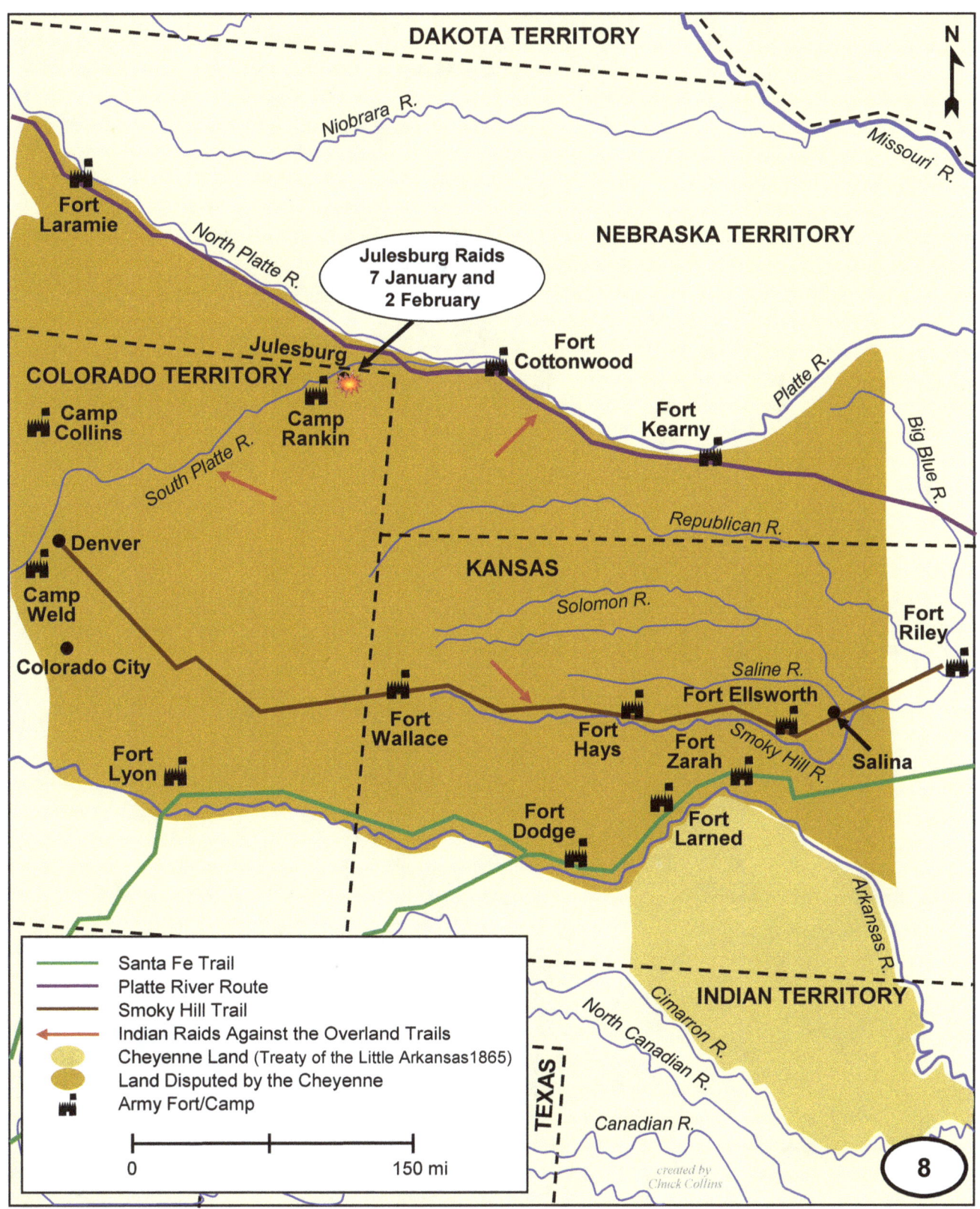

II. Hancock's War

9. An Unsteady Peace

"[The Cheyenne, Arapahos, and Kiowas] have assembled at or near our posts on the Smoky Hill, and on the Arkansas in numbers and strength manifestly beyond the control of their agents, and have in manner and word threatened to interrupt the use by our people of those roads. This cannot be tolerated for a moment. If not a state of war, it is the next thing to it, and will result in war unless checked. I therefore authorize you to instruct your commanding officers of post on a recurrence of the same or similar cases, to punish on the spot; and I authorized you to organize, out of your present command, a sufficient force to go among the Cheyenne, Arapahos, Kiowas, or similar bands of Indians, and notify them that if they want war they can have it now; but if they decline the offer, then impress on them that they must stop their insolence and threats, and make their conduct conform more nearly to what we deem right."[10]
— Lieutenant General William Tecumseh Sherman

The remainder of 1865 and 1866 saw comparative peace on the Southern Plains. Ironically, the decrease in hostility was not so much due to the Treaty of the Little Arkansas, but because the Cheyenne's thirst for revenge had cooled, and the warriors returned to the everyday matters of survival on the Southern Plains. Unfortunately, the peace was unsteady and fragile. Many of the Cheyenne bands disavowed the treaty and asserted they would never surrender the land between the Platte and Arkansas Rivers. For the most part, traffic flowed unmolested along the Platte River Road and the Santa Fe Trail. However, the Cheyenne harassed traffic on the Smoky Hill route to Denver. Most troubling for the Cheyenne was the constant westward creeping of Kansas settlements into the valleys of the Republican, Saline, and Solomon Rivers in north-central Kansas. Those Cheyenne who had been party to the treaty negotiations and agreements saw the white encroachment as a violation of the treaty. They did not understand that their signing of the treaty actually ceded their control of the land, nor did they realize that their right to roam the land was merely temporary and would last only until white settlements assumed control of the region. The Cheyenne Dog Soldiers band had shunned the Little Arkansas meetings and refused to make any concessions. They rejected all efforts to force them into surrendering their hunting grounds along the Smoky Hill Trail. Wynkoop, special Indian agent to the Cheyenne, met with the Dog Soldiers and attempted to avert another war. Wynkoop had some success, but again there were significant cultural misunderstandings. Wynkoop mistakenly believed he had secured peace and convinced the Dog Soldiers to stop their attacks along the Smoky Hill route. The Dog Soldiers had agreed to stop their attacks along the Platte River Route, but they mistakenly believed the government had granted and would protect their rights to the Smoky Hill valley and halt white intrusion onto their land.

Another threat to peace on the Southern Plains was the deteriorating situation on the Northern Plains. Red Cloud, an influential Oglala Sioux chief, was strongly opposed to the opening of the Bozeman Trail that cut through the heart of the non-reservation Sioux hunting grounds in Wyoming Territory. In mid-1866, after the US Army built three forts to protect commerce along the Bozeman Trail, Red Cloud influenced a large coalition of Sioux to go to war. However, the Sioux culture was much like the Cheyenne's, and Red Cloud did not have absolute authority over all the Oglala Sioux. Many of them chose not to participate in Red Cloud's War. One band of the southern Oglalas had close ties to the Cheyenne and normally roamed along the Platte and Republican Rivers. For some reason, this band took its migration much further south that year than was typical. Perhaps it was to avoid Red Cloud's conflict along the Bozeman Trail, or, more likely, they were just following the nomadic movement of the buffalo. Regardless of why, their arrival on the Southern Plains triggered fears that the Sioux were trying to orchestrate a partnership with the southern tribes to instigate a general Indian uprising on both the Northern and the Southern Plains. Then in December, Red Cloud's Indian coalition destroyed an Army detachment of 80 men commanded by Captain William J. Fetterman in a well-orchestrated ambush. The disastrous defeat on the Northern Plains shocked the Army and further heightened the fear on the Southern Plains that a major Indian uprising was imminent.[1]

---

1. Note: See Combat Studies Institute's *Atlas of the Sioux War, Second Edition* – Part II, The Sioux War of 1866-68 for details.

In the midst of all these troubles, a new commander assumed responsibility for the Kansas and Colorado territory, Lieutenant General William Tecumseh Sherman, commander of the Military Division of the Missouri which, in the post Civil War Army, comprised most of the Great American Plains. Sherman recognized the need for an exceptional officer to overcome the challenges on the Southern Plains. He asked for and eventually received General Winfield Scott Hancock, an officer of superb competence and vast experience in commanding large Army formations in the American Civil War. He was the hero of Gettysburg but had little experience in dealing with the Plains Indians. The climate that Hancock found himself in was one greatly influenced by the Fetterman disaster. His subordinates and the frontier settlers within his area of responsibility feared a similar catastrophe. The western newspapers fueled these fears by scorning the Army for timidity and calling for retaliation against the Indians. Sherman, as senior Army commander, wanted retribution against the Sioux in the North and freedom to force the Cheyenne onto reservations in the South. President Ulysses S. Grant overruled Sherman's plans for revenge in the Northern Plains and decided to pursue a policy of negotiation and peace with the Sioux. On the Southern Plains, the president empowered Sherman with the responsibility to maintain the peace. Sherman delegated the burdensome responsibility of maintaining peace onto Hancock's shoulders. The general anti-Indian mood on the frontier magnified the burden. Every incident, no matter how minor, was blown out of proportion. Hancock was beset with reports that indicated a general Indian uprising was imminent. Kansas Governor Samuel Crawford believed the Cheyenne and other tribes were concentrating in preparation for an all-out attack on the Kansas settlements. He feared the Indians would halt construction of the Pacific Railroad and demanded Hancock provide more troops to protect both the railroad and the settlements. In reality, the Southern Plains Indians were trying hard to avoid conflict, and the reports to Hancock contained more rumor and fearful supposition than credible intelligence. Nevertheless, Sherman and Hancock both believed they faced a serious Indian outbreak in the upcoming spring. Therefore, Sherman directed Hancock to mount an expedition to display the might of the US Army to intimidate the Indians into remaining peaceful. Sherman wanted a strong message sent to the Southern Plains tribes. However, the specter of the Chivington's Massacre at Sand Creek haunted Sherman and, in a communiqué to Hancock, he stated, *"I have no fear that you, or any other officer under you, will kill or injure unresisting people of any race or kind, and I will not suppose the case."*[11]

Hancock eventually raised a force of about 1,400 cavalry, infantry, and artillery from his department. He departed Fort Riley on 27 March 1867 having designated Fort Harker on the Smoky Hill River as the concentration point. Most of the units assigned to the expedition arrived at Fort Harker by 1 April. Hancock's column included seven companies of the 37th Infantry commanded by Captain John Rziha (brevet major), eight companies of the newly formed 7th Cavalry under Colonel (brevet major general) A. J. Smith, a battery of the 4th Artillery commanded by Captain Charles Parsons (brevet lieutenant colonel), and some Delaware Indian scouts. A few white scouts, the most notable being "Wild Bill" Hickock, accompanied the expedition. Hancock also asked Leavenworth (Indian agent of the Kiowas and Comanches) and Wynkoop (Indian agent of the Cheyenne and Arapaho) to participate in the expedition. Hancock planned to visit the tribes that Leavenworth and Wynkoop were responsible for and asked the Indian agents to inform their wards he wanted to talk with them. At Fort Harker, Hancock issued General Order 1 which stated,

> *"It is uncertain whether war will be the result of the expedition or not; it will depend upon the temper and behavior of the Indians with whom we may come in contact. We go prepared for war, and will make it if a proper occasion presents. We shall have war if the Indians are not well disposed towards us. If they are for peace, and no sufficient ground is presented for chastisement, we are restricted from punishing them for past grievances which are recorded against them; these matters have been left to the Indian department for adjustment. No insolence will be tolerated from any bands of Indians whom we may encounter. We wish to show them that the government is ready and able to punish them if they are hostile, although it may not be disposed to invite war."*[12]

Hancock's column departed Fort Harker on 3 April 1867. Marching with the column was Lieutenant Colonel George Armstrong Custer. Even though the aging Smith commanded the 7th Cavalry, he delegated most of the responsibility in the field to Custer, his second in command. For Hancock, hero of Gettysburg, and Custer, boy general of the Civil War, it was their first campaign against the Plains Indians. The command arrived at Fort Larned on 7 April.

> *"I was authorized to go among the Cheyennes, Arapahoes, Kiowas, Apaches, and Comanches, within the limits of this department, to make a display of force to them, to notify them that if they wished for war they could have it, and to explain to them fully that hereafter they must keep off the routes of travel – railroads and other roads; and that all depredations and molestation of travelers must cease forthwith. I was also empowered to arrest any offenders of the tribes above named who should be designated by their agents as being guilty of offenses against the laws; and to explain to the Indians and impress upon their minds the fact that all threatening of our military posts by them, verbally or by messengers or otherwise, must cease at once or war would ensue."[13]*

— Major General Winfield Scott Hancock

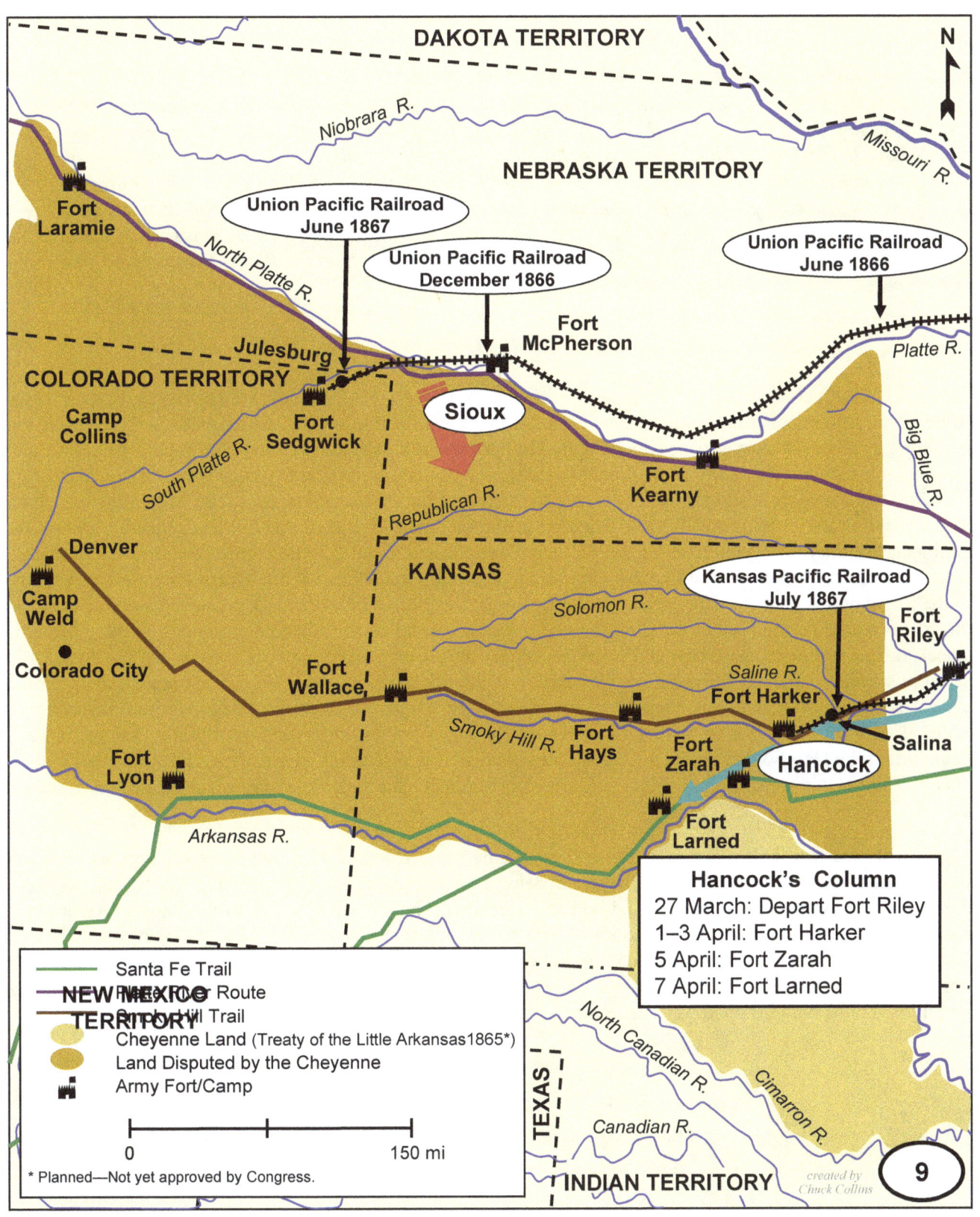

10. A Failure in Cultural Awareness

"Now the Indian is a man in every sense of the word; and like most other men, he has his share of reason, pride and ambition. And how galling it must have been to those Indian warriors—whose fearless hearts had braved a thousand dangers—to be talked to as if they were children. The "musts" and "wills" and "shalls" were more wounding to them than steel-pointed arrows. General Hancock talked to those Indian warriors and orators as a cross schoolmaster would to his refractory scholars. I do not find fault, in saying this, with the General. He is a soldier, and a soldier's tongue is not given to soft phrases, and then he was sent on the Plains to intimidate and, if necessary, make war on the Indians."[14]

— Army Surgeon Isaac Coates

Hancock's competence and experience were evident in the successful 150-mile march across the Kansas frontier. Now he would host negotiations with the Cheyenne Nation. It was a culture vastly different from his own and there was nothing in his previous experience that prepared him for the task. Wynkoop joined with Hancock at Fort Larned and assured the General that many of the Southern Cheyenne chiefs would meet for talks. A snowstorm and then the opportunity to participate in a buffalo hunt delayed the arrival of the chiefs by five days. The tardy Indian delegation finally arrived on the evening of 12 April. The delegation included several prominent Cheyenne and Sioux from a combined Southern Cheyenne and Oglala Sioux village located about 35 miles upstream from the fort on the Pawnee Fork River. Among them were Cheyenne council chiefs, Tall Bull and White Horse. Impatient and annoyed with the five-day delay and having expected a larger assemblage of chiefs, Hancock convened a council that very night. It was a confusing signal to the Cheyenne whose customs called for this type of council in the light of day. Hancock further confused the Cheyenne when he asked why Roman Nose was not present for the council. The General mistakenly believed Roman Nose was the head chief of the Cheyenne. He did not realize the prominent warrior was not a council chief and therefore not authorized by his people to conduct negotiations. Hancock's lack of cultural awareness led him to believe that because Roman Nose was missing from the discussions, it was an indication that the Dog Soldiers were hostile and not interested in discussing peace. The reality was that both Tall Bull and White Horse were council chiefs with the Dog Soldiers, and both were very much interested in securing peace.

An openly frustrated Hancock spoke to the proud chiefs and warriors as if they were children and delivered a stern peace-or-war ultimatum. The Cheyenne delegation accepted the demands and conditions for peace. Unfortunately, Hancock did not understand he had succeeded. The Cheyenne band on the Pawnee River wanted peace, but they could not speak for other bands of the Cheyenne. His lack of knowledge of the Cheyenne culture and refusal to accept advice from Wynkoop led him to believe that he needed to move the Army column to the village and arrange another meeting with more chiefs. Tall Bull urged Wynkoop to convince Hancock that neither the move nor additional talks with his band were necessary.

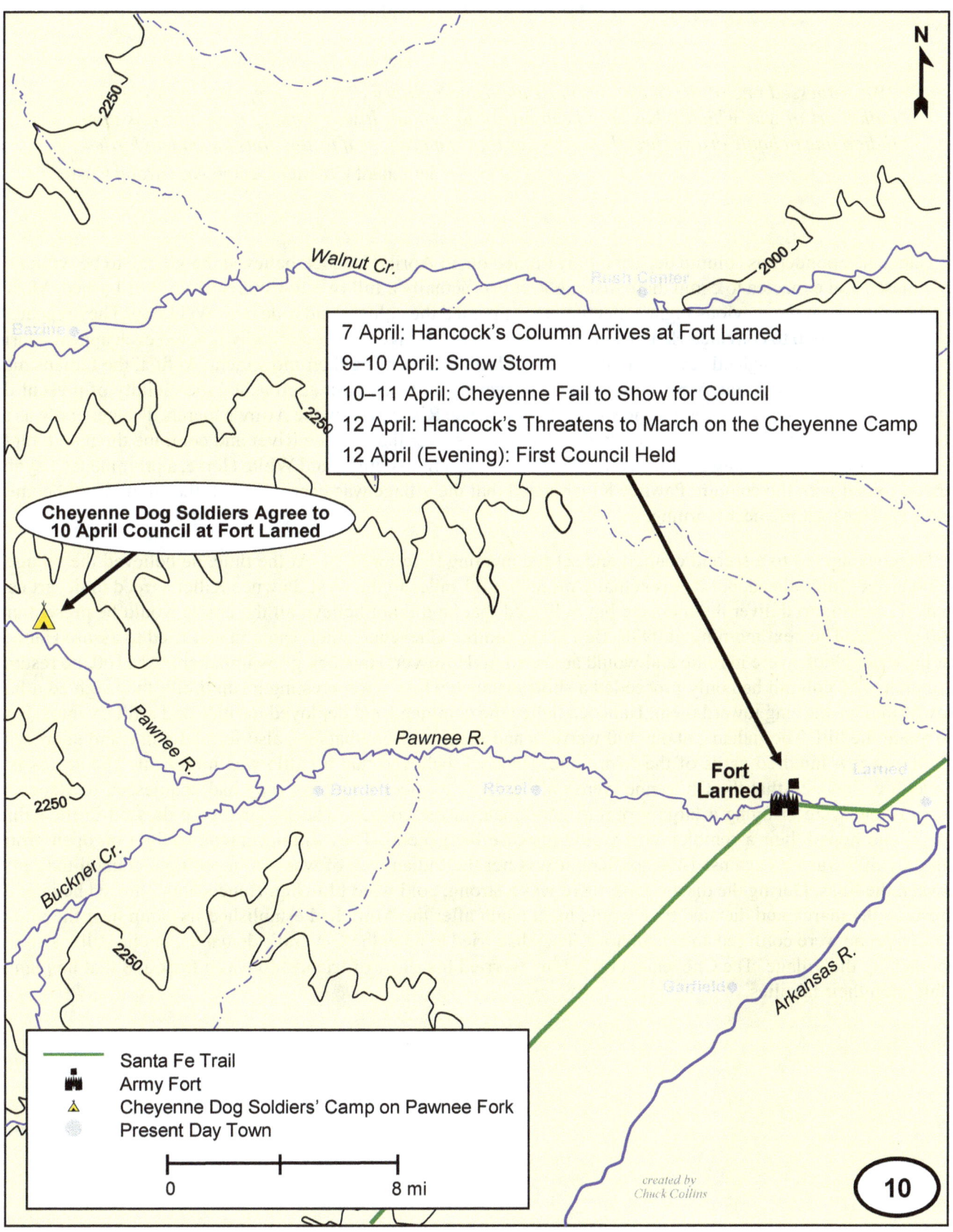

11. Confrontation Hill

"We witnessed one of the finest and most imposing military displays, prepared according to the Indian art of war, which it has ever been my lot to behold. It was nothing more nor less than an Indian line of battle drawn directly across our line of march; as if to say; thus far and no farther."[15]
— Lieutenant Colonel George Armstrong Custer

Hancock's ponderous column departed Fort Larned on 13 April. Hancock believed the village to be within one day's march and expected to camp there that night. It was actually a full two-day march from Fort Larned. Most of the Cheyenne from the previous night's meeting accompanied the column and rode near Wynkoop. They repeatedly beseeched Wynkoop to convince Hancock not to approach the village. Hancock rigidly ignored each appeal. During the march, the column sighted several small parties of Indians observing their movement. At first, the Indians made no effort to interfere with the Army's movement. However, as the column approached the vicinity of present-day Burdett, the Indians set fire to the prairie south of the Pawnee River to slow the Army's march. The general was not deterred by the Indians' actions. He simply decided to cross over the Pawnee River and continue the march on the other side. Soon after crossing over the river, Pawnee Killer, a Sioux chief, and White Horse, a prominent Cheyenne warrior, joined with the column. Pawnee Killer stated that the village was nearby and all the chiefs would come to meet with Hancock the next morning.

Hancock agreed to a second council and set the meeting time for 0900. At the time, he believed the village to be about five-miles ahead, but it was actually more than 11 miles to the west. Pawnee Killer agreed to depart early the next morning to deliver the message but indicated that he did not believe all the chiefs would be present until 1000 or 1100. The next morning at 0930, Bull Bear, another Cheyenne chief, came in and tried to assure Hancock that the other chiefs were in route and would arrive soon. However, Hancock grew impatient. At 1100, he resumed his march. The column had only proceeded a short distance when, upon cresting a small hill, they sighted a large body of Indians moving toward them. Hancock halted the command and deployed his men and artillery into a battle line along the hill. The Indians, about 300 warriors and many non-combatants, also formed a line and approached to within a few hundred yards of the Army line. Hancock believed that a battle was imminent. The scouts tried to reassure Hancock that the Cheyenne were only coming to meet with him; they had acquiesced to Hancock's demands and were bringing a large group to participate in the council. The Indians were dressed in their finest apparel and hoped their assembled host would appease the general. They did not intend to fight on open ground with only 300 warriors against 1400 soldiers; it was not the Indian way of war. An impromptu council took place between the lines. During the discussions, there was a strong, cold wind blowing. Hancock announced he intended to resume the march and dictated they would meet again after the Army had established its camp near the village. The Cheyenne were confused and suspicious. They had tried to meet the General's demands, but he still insisted on approaching the village. The Cheyenne chiefs now worried his show of friendship was a trick and that he planned to fall upon their families.

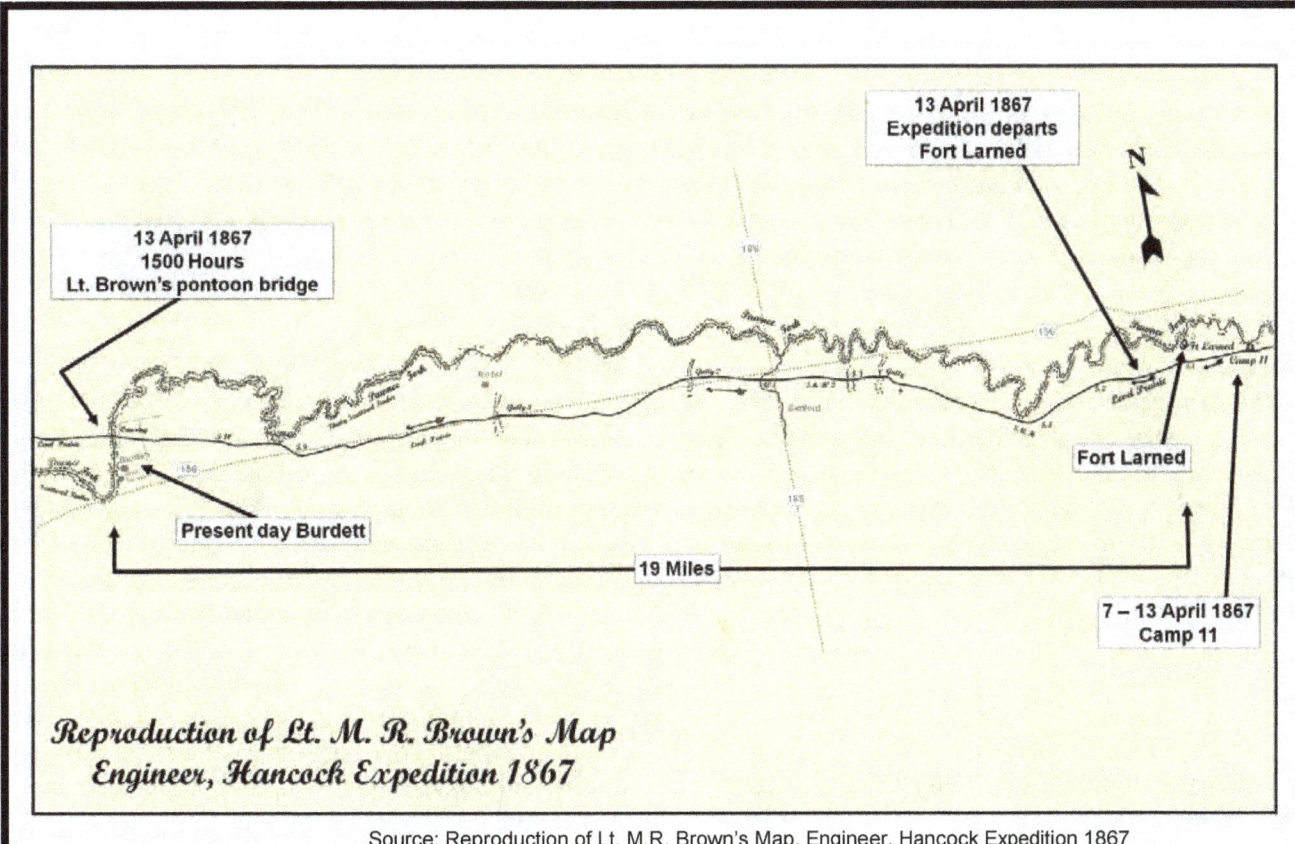

Source: Reproduction of Lt. M.R. Brown's Map, Engineer, Hancock Expedition 1867

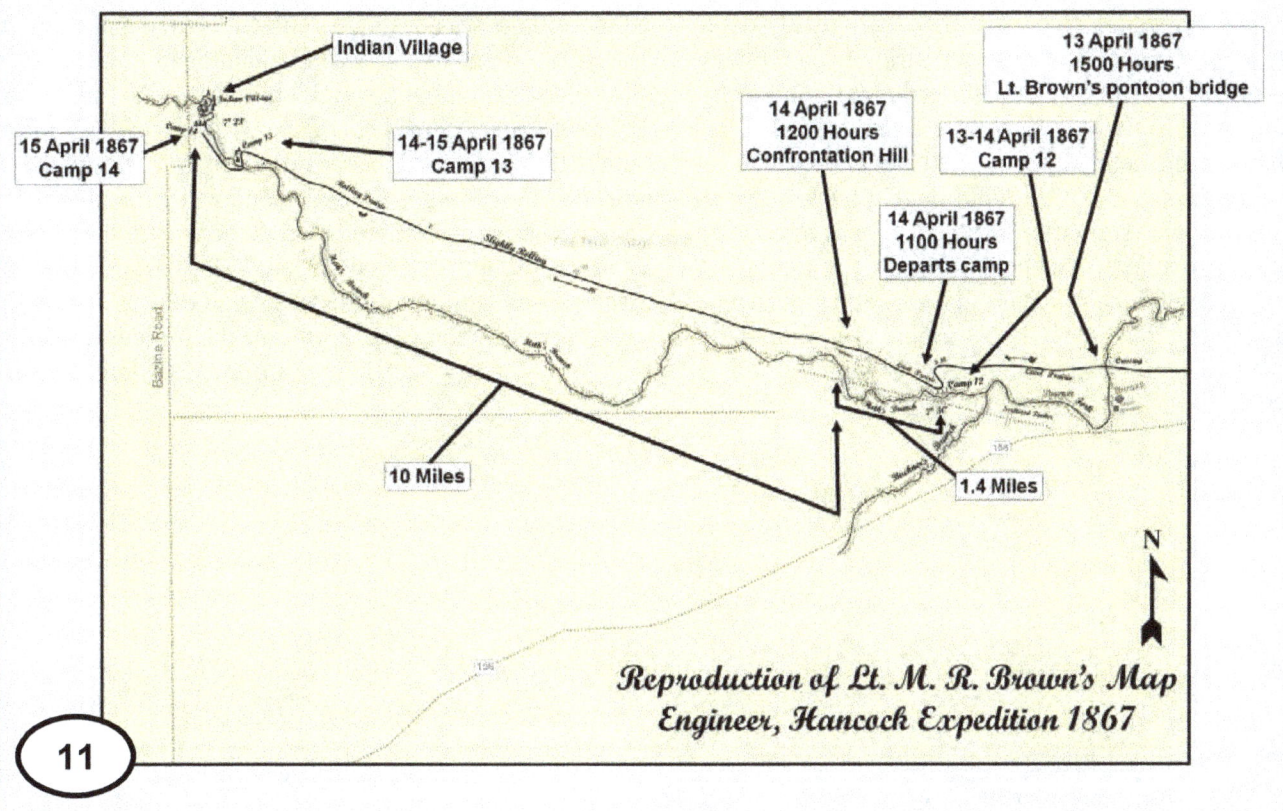

12. The Village at Pawnee Fork

"In the middle of the night, the 7th Cavalry had orders to saddle up very quietly. We immediately did so and started out in the darkness. This Indian camp was a very large one and we surrounded it by forming a circle around it in single file. Custer and some of our officers with scouts and interpreters entered the camp only to find that the birds had flown, the camp was empty. The Indians had left all their goods and fled in the night."[16]

— Trooper John Ryan

The Army column proceeded up the Pawnee River to within a half mile of the village and established a camp. Hancock, Custer, and the other key Army leaders failed to comprehend the impact of the Sand Creek Massacre on the Cheyenne psyche. The approach of an Army column so close to the village panicked the women and children, and the warriors were unwilling to subject their families to the possibility of another wanton slaughter. Unbeknownst to Hancock, most of the Sioux and Cheyenne women and children had already abandoned the camp as the ominous column approached. Soon after camping, Roman Nose, Bull Bear, Grey Beard, and Medicine Wolf (all prominent Cheyenne) came to the Army camp and informed Hancock that the women and children had fled the village. The increasingly frustrated Hancock demanded of the chiefs that they force their people back to the village. The chiefs seemed agreeable to persuading the people to return but wanted fresh Army horses to overtake them. Hancock agreed but was suspicious of their sincerity. He sent the half-Cheyenne interpreter, Ed Guerrier, to watch the village and instructed him to report every two hours. At about 2100, the scout reported the warriors were leaving the village. Soon after the column set up camp, the two chiefs who had borrowed horses returned saying they were unable to persuade the people to come back. Hancock ordered Custer to take the cavalry and surround the village to prevent the warriors from escaping. Custer moved out about 2200. After completing the encirclement of the village, Custer conducted a leader reconnaissance and quickly determined the village was deserted. The Cheyenne and Sioux had left in great haste. They had cut strips from teepees for use as temporary shelters and abandoned almost all their possessions. In the shelters, the soldiers found only one old Sioux woman and a sick child. Surgeon Isaac Coates thought her to be 8 to 10 years old, and stated, *"Her person had been brutally outraged."*[17] Hancock believed the Indians committed the crime and said it contributed to his later decision to punish the Indians by burning the village. Wynkoop was more of the opinion that the soldiers had committed the outrage. Several abandoned ponies, weak and on the verge of starvation, were also discovered in the village. Their condition indicated that one of the reasons the Indians had abandon their possessions was their ponies lacked the strength to carry the load. The situation presented Hancock with a significant dilemma. Having marched across Kansas with an impressive force of artillery, cavalry, and infantry, this great Civil War hero had wanted to talk. However, his attempt to intimidate the Indians into talking peace had been frustrated. Instead, he had intimidated them to flee. He now faced the troubling decision of what his next course of action should be.

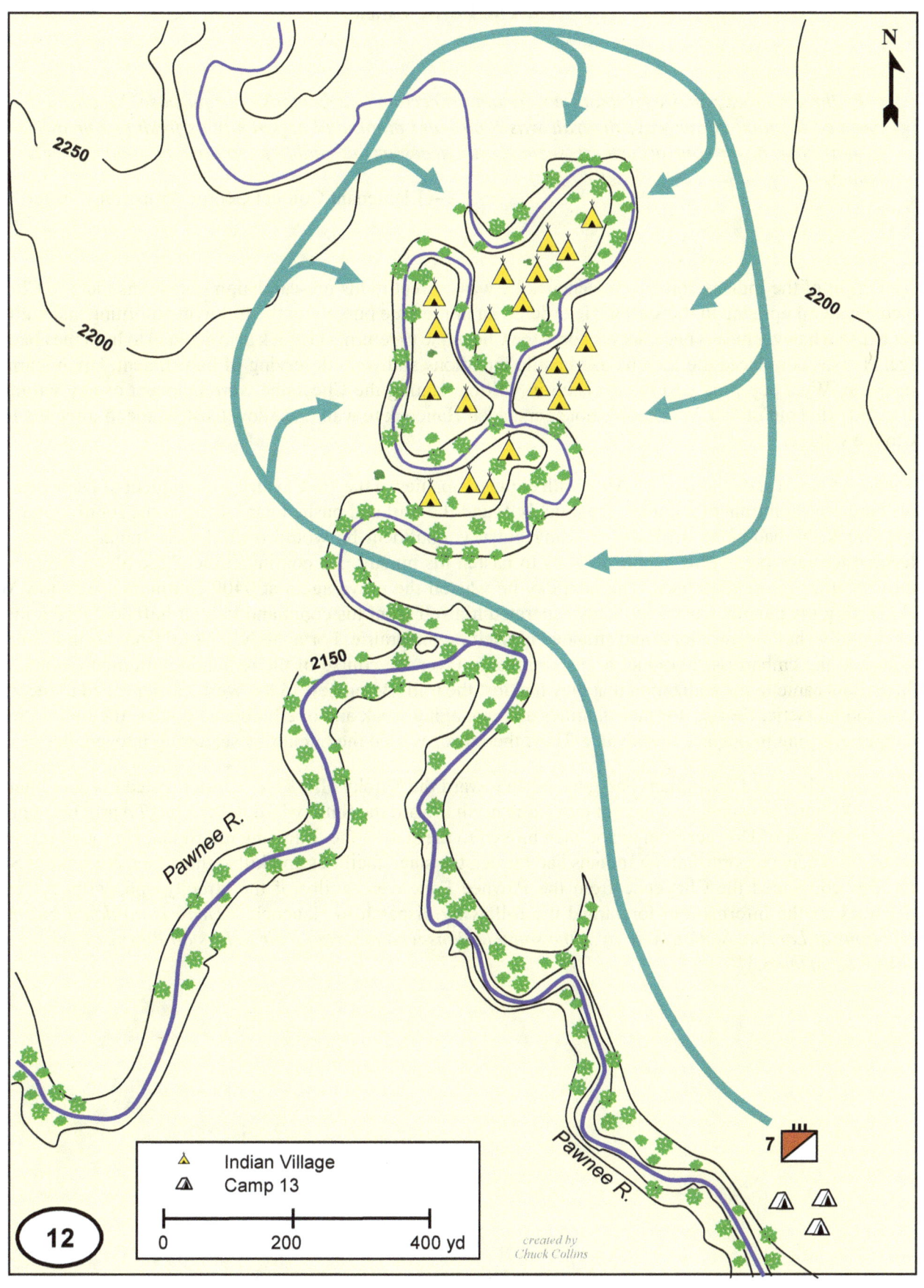

13. The Futile Chase

"By three o'clock p.m. we felt that we were almost certain to accomplish our purpose. No obstacle seemed to stand in our way; the trail was broad and plain, and apparently as fresh as our own. A half hour, or an hour at furthest, seemed only necessary to enable us to dash in upon our wily enemy."[18]

— Lieutenant Colonel George Armstrong Custer

The flight of the Indians convinced Hancock he was correct in his pre-campaign suspicions that the Cheyenne planned a general uprising in the spring. He ordered an immediate pursuit on the following morning and authorized Custer to use whatever means necessary to force the Cheyenne to return. Hancock also decided to burn the abandoned village. He was convinced the Indians had hostile intentions and were deserving of punishment. Upon learning of the decision, Wynkoop protested the decision in writing, stating the Cheyenne were innocent of any wrongdoing and had only fled out of fear. Wynkoop's note persuaded Hancock to wait and allow Custer time to force the Indians back to the village.

Custer departed at daylight on 15 April with eight companies of the 7th Cavalry, a contingent of Delaware Indian Scouts, and a wagon train of supplies. He quickly found the trail and pushed hard to catch the fugitive Indians. At Walnut Creek, he had some difficulty crossing but was confident he would overtake the Indians. At the creek, he decided to leave behind his supply wagons to hasten his pursuit. He continued the chase along Walnut Creek another 14 miles to the northwest. The next day he was on the move again at 0400 continuing to follow Walnut Creek. During the pursuit, Custer foolishly separated himself from his command to hunt buffalo. During his hunt, he accidentally shot his own horse and stranded himself on the prairie. Fortunately, a patrol from his unit found him and returned the embarrassed colonel to his command. Over the course of the remaining afternoon hours, Custer and his scouts came to the realization that they had lost the trail. Being new to the West, Custer failed to recognize a familiar Indian tactic. Fearing for their families and managing weak and overburdened ponies, the Indians realized the danger of trying to outpace the cavalry. They, therefore, evaded the pursuit by scattering into smaller groups.

The scouts believed the Indians had gone north toward the Smoky Hill River. Custer rested his command from 1400 to 1900, and then conducted a night move due north toward the Smoky Hill River. On 17 April, he camped his column to the west of Downer Station and then moved to the station the following afternoon. He found no warriors there but did receive reports that the Indians had burned the stage facilities and killed three men at Lookout Station. Custer was convinced the Cheyenne from the Pawnee Fork were guilty of the atrocity and, without verifying the accuracy of the information, forwarded the following dispatch to Hancock, *"There is no doubt but that the depredations at Lookout Station were by... the same Indians who deserted their lodges on Pawnee Forks... I shall treat them as enemies."*[19]

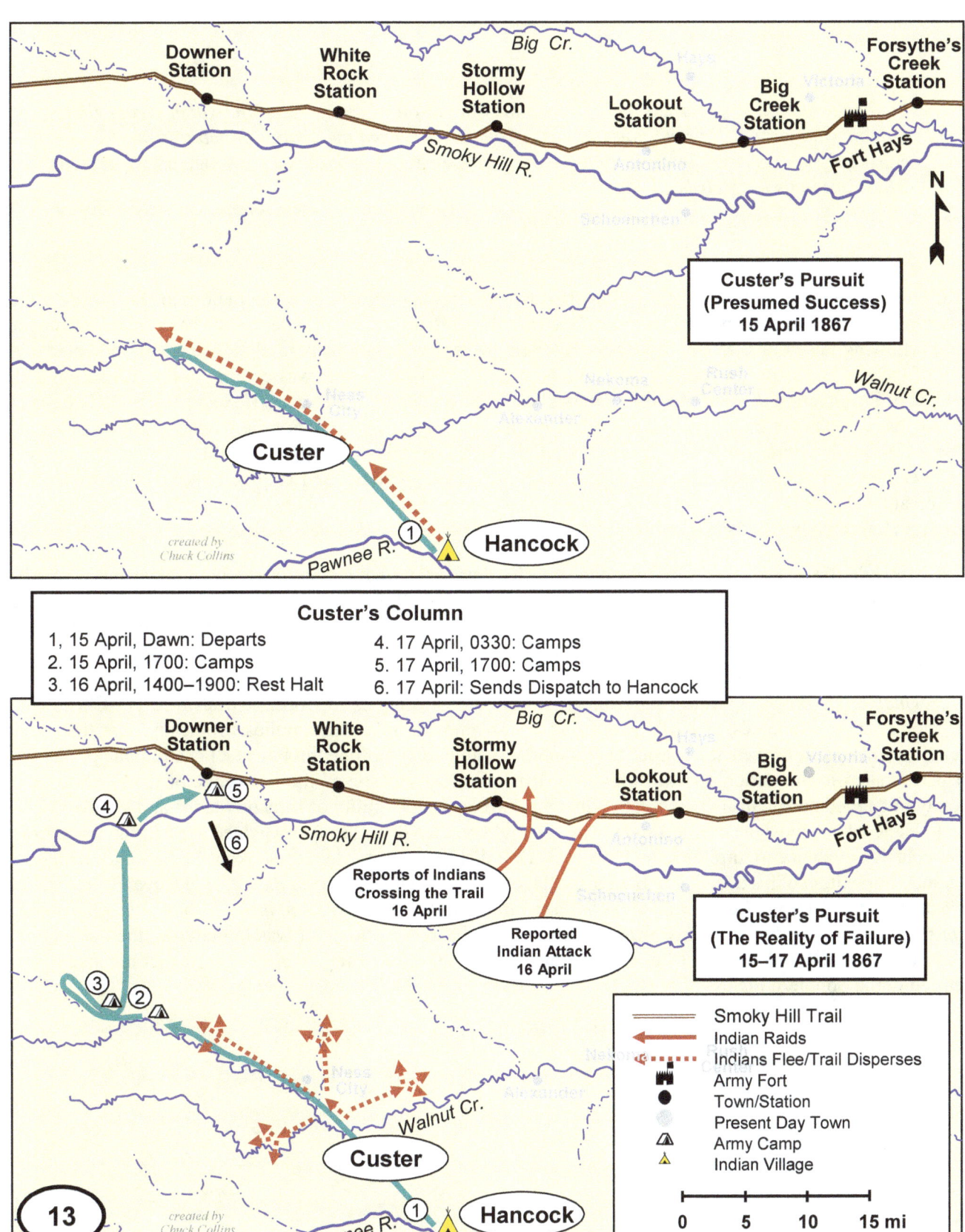

14. Lookout Station

"Lookout Station was burned and the men massacred on Monday the 15th, which clears those Indians who were at Pawnee Fork the day of our arrival from the charge of being present at the murder. I am confident, however, that the act was committed with their knowledge and approval, which accounts for their hasty flight."[20]

— Lieutenant Colonel George Armstrong Custer

Custer continued his pursuit the next day. It was a miserable day with cold sleet and rain. Each mile traveled eastward must have been a painful reminder to Custer of the fruitless westward miles he had been duped into covering while following false trails. At Stormy Hollow Station, he received significant intelligence which indicated a large body of Indians had crossed over the trail moving north on 15 April. Custer was coming to the realization that his estimate of the situation in the 17 April dispatch to Hancock was no longer correct. He had previously believed that the Indians crossed over the stage road beginning on the morning of 16 April. For the Pawnee Fork Indians to have made a 50-mile movement over a period of two nights and one day was a very plausible trek for Plains Indians. However, new information revealed they had actually crossed the road on the 15 April, 12 hours earlier. That would have meant covering 50 miles in less than 24 hours. This seemed much less likely to Custer considering the Indians were traveling with hundreds of women and children on weak and overburden ponies.

Meanwhile, far to the south, Hancock agonized for days over what action to take with the abandoned village. Wynkoop continued to insist that the Cheyenne were guilty of no offense arguing that their village should be spared. Nevertheless, on 18 April, having Custer's 17 April dispatch in-hand, Hancock made the decision to confiscate all Indian property and burn the combined villages. He believed the Cheyenne were guilty of *"bad faith"* and informed Sherman, *"I think we have provocation sufficient to destroy the camp... and by burning it we will certainly inaugurate a war which might otherwise have been avoided."* [21] On the morning of 19 April, he destroyed 111 Cheyenne and 140 Sioux lodges, hundreds of buffalo robes, and vast amounts of other supplies. Ironically, just the previous afternoon Custer had arrived at Lookout Station and was able to determine the Pawnee Fork Indians probably had not participated in the station attack. In his next dispatch, Custer absolved the Cheyenne of the Lookout Station atrocity but added the qualifying assumption that they were possibly guilty of foreknowledge and sympathy for the attack. Hancock received the new information at midnight on 20 April. He acknowledged to Sherman that there was no conclusive evidence to implicate the Pawnee Fork Indians in the murders at Lookout Station. Nevertheless, he remained impenitent of his decision to burn the village – *"it is possible that even the latest to leave the village might have been of the party who were at Lookout Station, although it does not seem to me to be of much importance, for I am satisfied that the Indian village was a nest of conspirators."*[22] The point was immaterial; the burning of the village could not be undone. The Cheyenne were enraged and, once again, determined to exact revenge; war had returned to the Southern Plains.

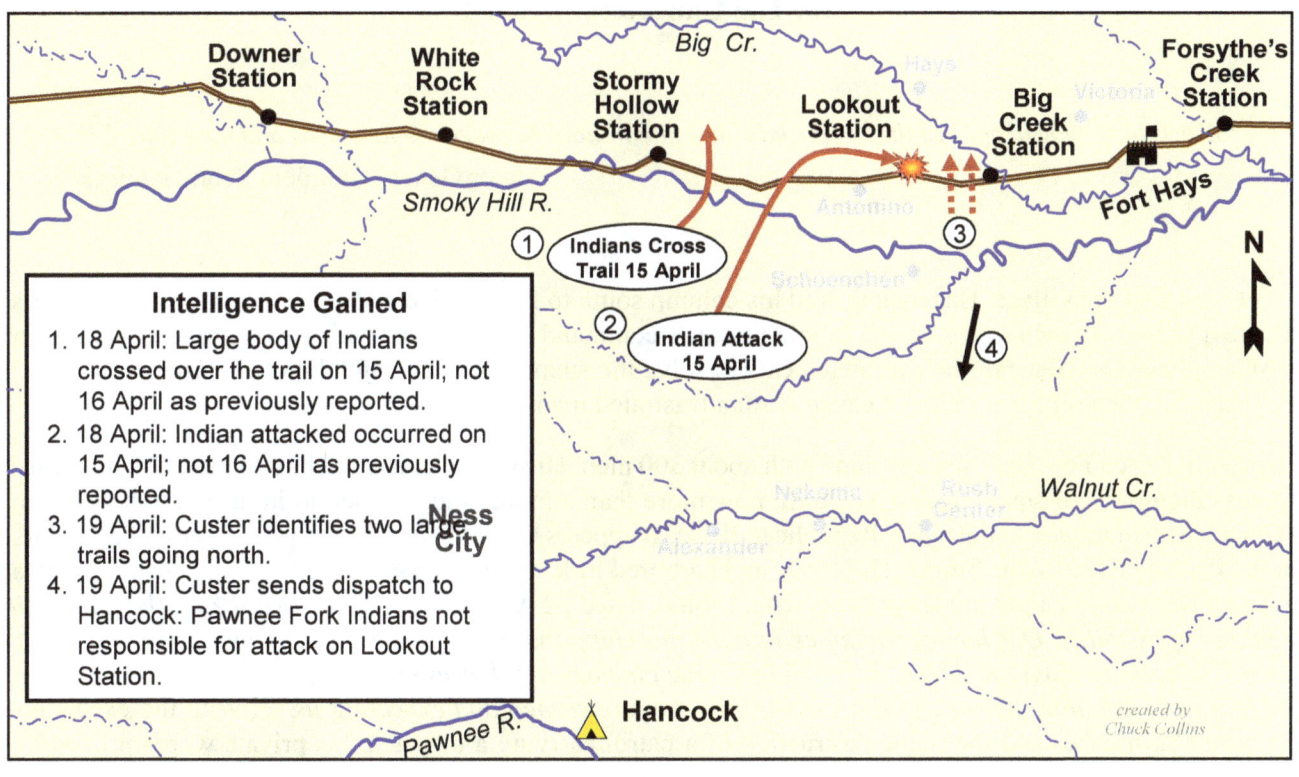
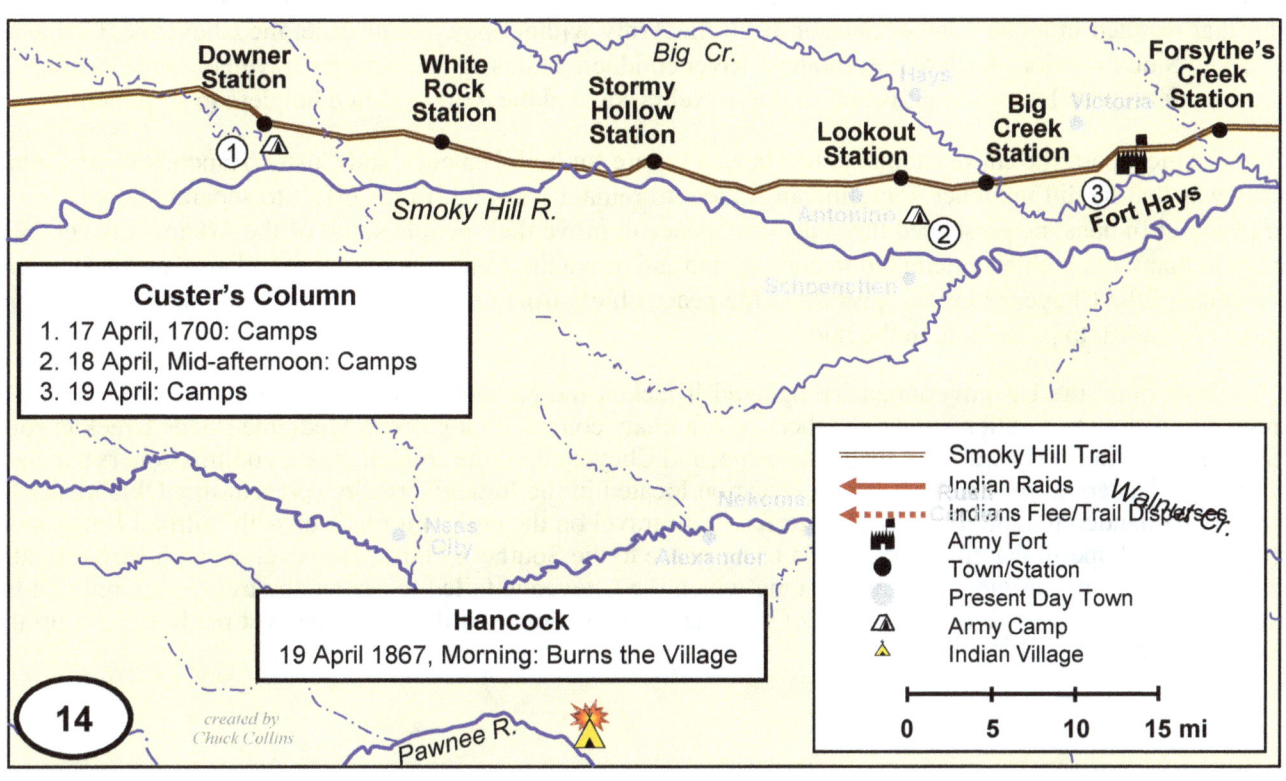

15. The Unnecessary War

"War is to be waged against the Sioux and Cheyenne Indians between the Arkansas and the Platte." [23]
— Major General Winfield Scott Hancock

After burning the village, Hancock moved his column south to Fort Dodge and continued his clumsy efforts to negotiate a peace. He then moved north to join Custer's command at Fort Hays which was stranded because of a lack of supplies. The General made arrangements to solve the supply problems and directed Custer to resume the chase. Hancock then returned to Fort Leavenworth a frustrated man.

Custer departed Fort Hays in early June with about 300 men. His mission required him to hunt down an elusive foe across thousands of square miles. The trail, now more than a month old, seemed to indicate the hostile Sioux and Cheyenne had moved to the upper Republican River. It appears Custer had reflected upon his first failed pursuit from the Pawnee River to the Smoky Hill River and harbored little confidence he could catch the hostile Sioux and Cheyenne. He stated in a private letter to his wife, Libbie, dated 22 April 1867, *"As for overtaking the Indians it is almost an impossibility. Our horses cannot endure the marching that their ponies can, fed on nothing but prairie-grass."* [24] In another letter, on 2 May, he confided, *"The chances are, however, that I shall not see any of them, it being next to impossible to overtake them when they are forewarned and expecting us."* [25] With the exception of a few minor skirmishes and the tragic destruction of a patrol carrying a dispatch, his private words proved to be very prophetic concerning the outcome of the chase.[26] From 1 June to 13 July 1867, Custer drove his men and their horses relentlessly in the fruitless chase accomplishing little more than exhausting his command. He battled desertion among his own men and, after settling the column in at Fort Wallace, abandoned his command under the pretense of going for supplies. A more likely motive was his desire to see his wife. It was a costly decision for Custer that resulted in a one-year suspension from the Army without pay. Meanwhile, the Cheyenne, Comanche, Kiowa, and Sioux warriors north of the Arkansas River conducted raids against unwary travelers, stage stations, and railroad work crews all across Kansas and southern Nebraska, and the Army seemed helpless to stop them.

For the most part, the entire campaign had been a failure for both Hancock and Custer. Hancock's only notable success was that he did influence some Indian leaders to remain peaceful. In his effort to separate hostile Indians from peaceful Indians, he persuaded those desiring peace to move their people south of the Arkansas River. Black Kettle and many other chiefs attempted to comply and did move their villages south out of harm's way. But again, the realities of the Cheyenne culture prevented the peace chiefs from enforcing their will, and many of the young warriors rode north to participate in the raids.

Over time, the US government recognized it lacked the resources to compel peace, so once again they attempted to negotiate a settlement. In October 1867, a treaty council took place at Medicine Lodge Creek in south-central Kansas with the Kiowa, Comanche, Arapaho, and Cheyenne. At the council, peace commissioners persuaded 14 Cheyenne leaders to relocate to a new reservation located in the Indian Territory (present-day Oklahoma). The new treaty demanded that the Indians not interfere with travel on the emigrant roads or with railroad construction. Both sides were hopeful that the treaty would bring peace to the Southern Plains. However, as with earlier treaties, there were significant misunderstandings among which the Cheyenne failed to realize the treaty required that they surrender all rights to any territory outside of their new reservation, and they were not yet ready to give up their nomadic way of life.

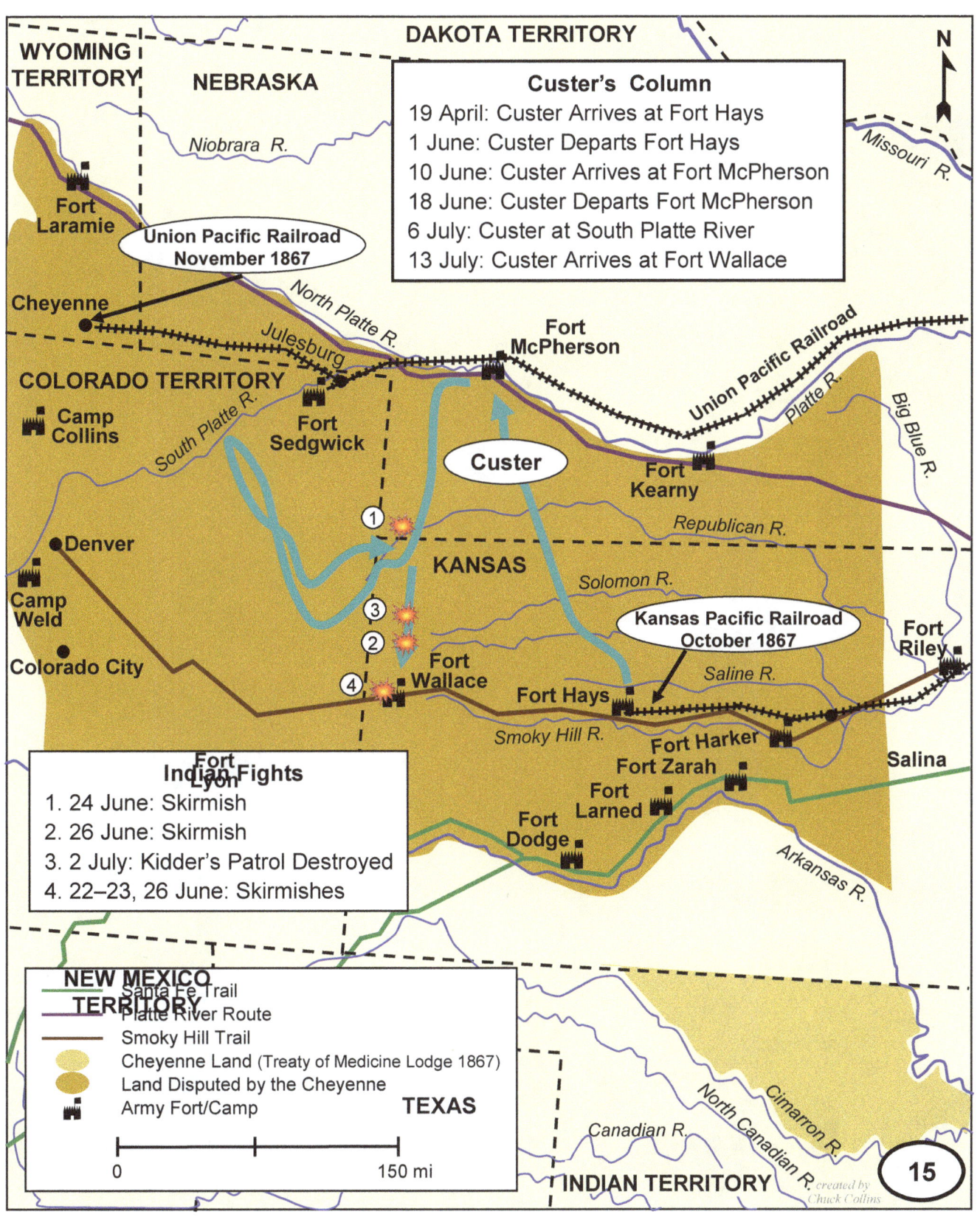

III. Sheridan's Summer War

16. Sheridan Takes Command

"At the outbreak of hostilities I had in all.., a force of regulars numbering about 2,600 men – 1,200 mounted and 1,400 foot troops... With these few troops all the posts along the Smoky Hill and Arkansas had to be garrisoned, emigrant trains escorted, and the settlements and routes of travel and the construction parties on the Kansas-Pacific railway protected. Then, too, this same force had to furnish for the field small movable columns, that were always on the go, so it will be rightly inferred that every available man was kept busy from the middle of August till November; especially as during this period the hostiles attacked over 40 widely dispersed places, in nearly all cases stealing horses, burning houses, and killing settlers."[27]

— Major General Phillip H. Sheridan

Unfortunately, the Medicine Lodge Treaty did not bring peace to the Southern Plains. The intent of the treaty was to convert the Cheyenne and other nomadic tribes into sedentary farmers. However, these proud people were unwilling to give up their land or their way of life without a fight. Many Cheyenne leaders refused to sign the treaty and continued to roam within their traditional lands between the Platte and Arkansas Rivers. Even those leaders who recognized the futility of resisting the US Government lacked the authority to compel their people to submit. Black Kettle and other peace advocates moved their bands to the south of the Arkansas River. However, many of their young men were strongly opposed to reservation life and frequently joined with their brethren to the north to raid the white settlements in Kansas. The raids complicated relationships between the cultures and made it difficult to distinguish between the Cheyenne bands that wanted peace and those that sanctioned the raids. In the months of August and October, warriors from bands both north and south of the Arkansas River raided repeatedly into central and western Kansas. They hit isolated farms and ranches, stage stations, and travelers on the emigrant trails. The marauders stole hundreds of cattle and mules and killed 79 settlers.

Major General Philip H. Sheridan replaced Hancock as the new commander of the Department of the Missouri. His friends referred to the 5-foot 5-inch General as "Little Phil." However, there was nothing little about his reputation. Like Hancock, he was a hero of the American Civil War with the reputation as a brilliant leader and a determined fighter. He reacted quickly to the new raids into Kansas and adopted the policy of punishment must follow the crime. However, with Hancock's and Custer's 1867 failure on his mind, he was reluctant to mount another large-scale expedition against the fast-moving and elusive Plains warriors. He also lacked the resources to mount a major campaign against the Indians. Nevertheless, it was his responsibility to protect the Smoky Hill Road and the Santa Fe Trail, ensure the safety of the Kansas Pacific Railroad work crews, and protect the Kansas settlements. Furthermore, it was against his nature to remain passively on the defense without responding to what he saw as *"the devilish work"* of *"red fiends."*[28]

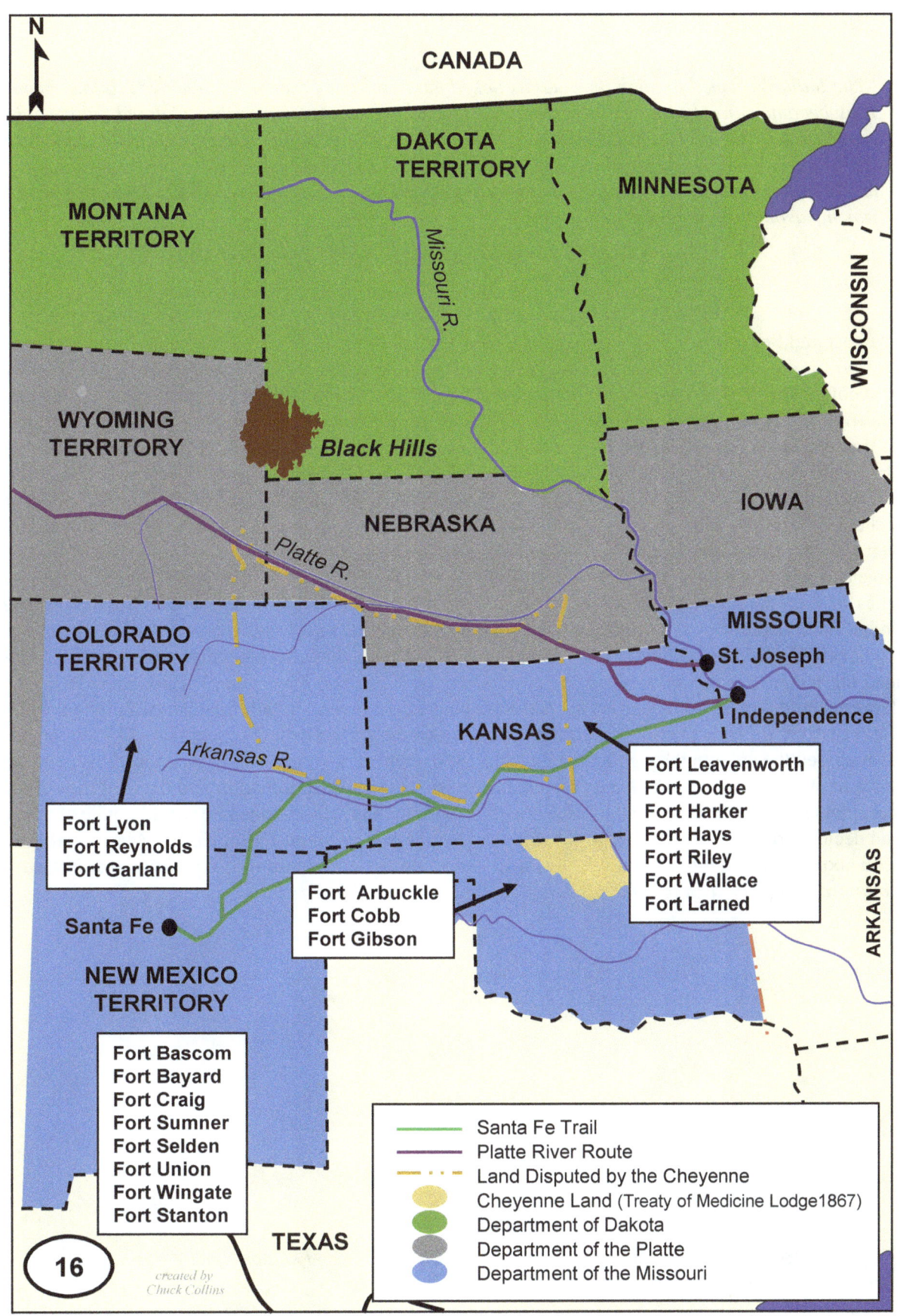

17. The Sully Expedition

"The Indians seemed to think they had us licked, and every day they would receive reinforcement. They became more daring, and when they became too numerous and daring, Colonel Sully would craw [crawl] out of his ambulance, have his orderly help him on his horse, then look things over and perhaps order a charge made. This state of affairs continued from day to day for some time, and finally the Indians commenced disappearing. Don't know why, unless they thought we were not worth wasting any more ammunition on."[29]

— Trooper Anthony C. Rallya, soldier with I Company, 7th U.S. Cavalry

In August and September 1868, Sheridan executed several limited offensive actions to provide some measure of protection for the emigrant trails, railroads, and Kansas settlements. Brevet Brigadier General Alfred Sully, the lieutenant colonel of the 3d Infantry and commander of the District of the Upper Arkansas, was first into the field.[30] Sully gathered about 500 men for the operation. The objective of his expedition was the Cheyenne and Arapaho villages thought to be camped along the Cimarron River. Sheridan believed an Army movement into the Indian Territory would pull the raiding Indians away from the Kansas settlements to protect their own people. Sully had a well-deserved reputation as a good soldier and experienced Indian fighter. He had led a highly successful campaign against the Sioux in 1863 and decisively punished the Santee Sioux at the Battle of Killdeer Mountain in 1864.[2] However, the 48-year-old Sully led the 1867 campaign from an ambulance. He exhibited none of his trade-mark aggressiveness and never managed to seriously threaten the hostile camps on the North Canadian River. His nine companies of the 7th Cavalry, one company of 3d Infantry, one mountain howitzer, and 30 supply wagons left Fort Dodge on 7 September. The first day the column marched 30 miles and camped that night on a branch of Crooked Creek. The command marched south the next day and late that afternoon discovered an Indian trail. They continued the pursuit for the next two days and reached the Cimarron River on 10 September. That day and the next Cheyenne and Arapaho war parties harassed the soldiers in several small skirmishes. Sully's column moved to the Beaver River on 12 September and fought a major skirmish there with the Indians. On 13 September, hostile warriors harassed the column throughout the day. On 14 September, a weary Sully bivouacked his command at the confluence of Wolf Creek and the Beaver River. There, he reassessed his situation and decided the Cheyenne and Arapaho villages were, without a doubt, forewarned of his approach. He reasoned he would not be able to overtake them and decided to return to Fort Dodge to resupply. He marched north on 15 September. Major Joel Elliott wrote to a friend about the expedition, *"I had the honor to command the cavalry on that expedition and if it was fighting, then Indian wars must be a huge joke."*[31]

---

2. Note: See Combat Studies Institute's *Atlas of the Sioux War, Second Edition* – Part I/Map 4. The Sioux Campaigns of 1863 and 1864 for details.

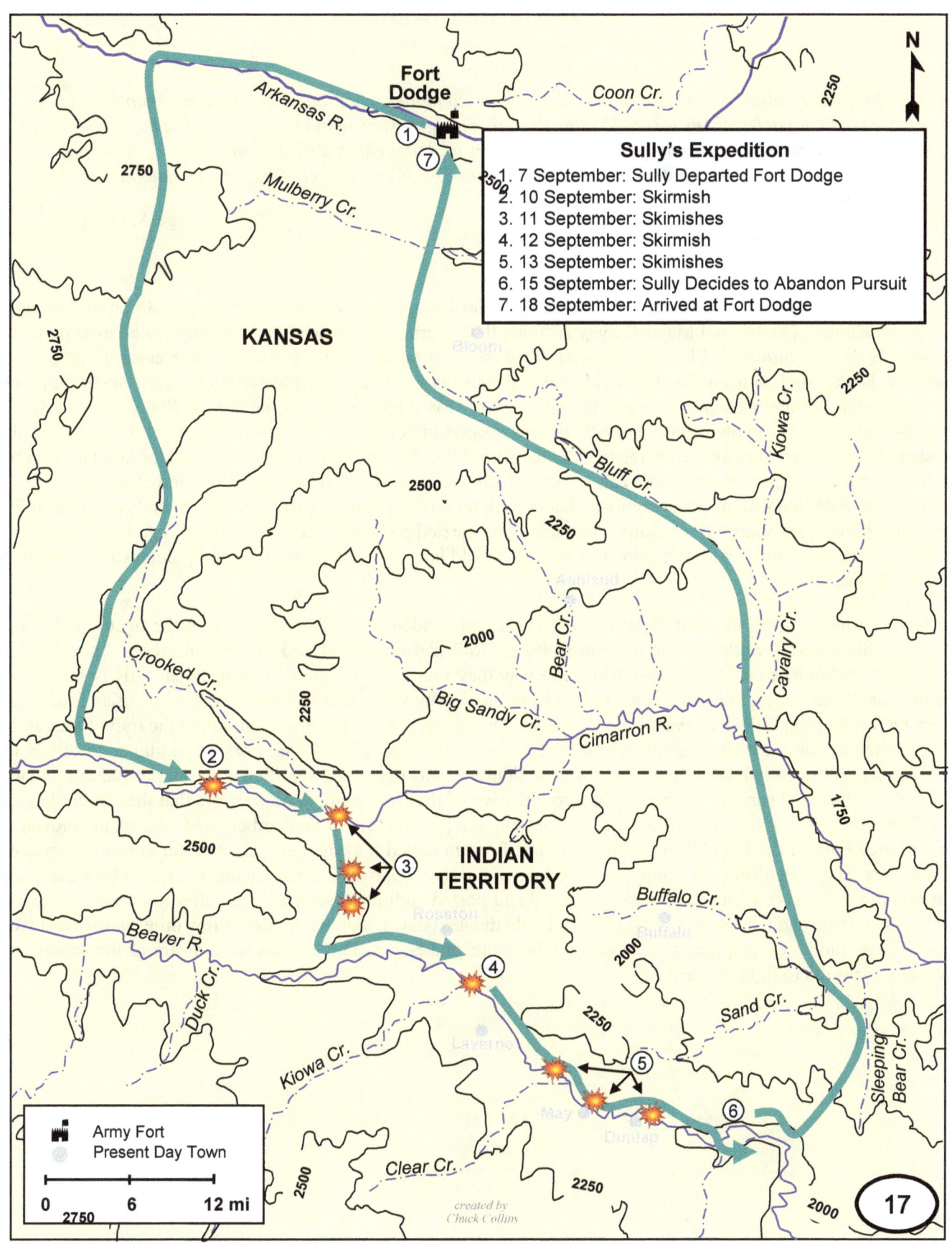

18. Forsyth's Scouts

"I had determined to find and attack the Indians, no matter what the odds might be against us. If we could not defeat them, we could show them that the government did not propose that they should escape unpunished for want of energy in their pursuit. I thought that with 51 men, even if could not defeat them, they could not annihilate us. Furthermore, it was expected that the command would fight the Indians, and I meant it should do so. [32]*"*

— Major George A. Forsyth

At the same time Sully was campaigning south of Fort Dodge, Sheridan had another expedition campaigning in western Kansas. He directed Major George A. Forsyth to recruit an independent company *"to be used as scouts against the hostile Indians.*[33]*"* Forsyth enlisted *"50 first-class hardy frontiersmen"* at the Kansas forts, 30 men from Fort Harker and 20 from Fort Hays. Officially, the scouts were quartermaster employees. As such, they were paid one dollar per day plus an additional 35 cents per day for supplying their own horses. Many were Civil War veterans and experienced plainsmen. Forsyth and his second in command, Lieutenant Frederick H. Beecher, also insisted that each man have above average marksmanship skills. The unit was lightly equipped for rapid movement. Each man had a Spencer repeating rifle and an Army Colt revolver with 140 rounds of rifle and 30 rounds of pistol ammunition. Additionally, the scout company had a pack train of four mules carrying 4,000 rounds of ammunition, medical supplies, and some extra rations. The mules also carried picks and shovels for digging to find water in the dry water courses common to the region. The shovels would later prove valuable in digging defensive positions at Beecher Island.

On 29 August 1868, the unit departed Fort Hays and headed west. Their target was the hostile tribes that frequently harassed the work crews of the Kansas Pacific Railroad and raided the Kansas homesteads. The command arrived at Fort Wallace on 5 September. Along the way they found many signs of recent Indian activity but did not see Indians. Within days, Forsyth received word from the nearby settlement of Sheridan, Kansas, of an Indian raid against a freight train killing several of the teamsters. The scouts marched to Sheridan, found the trail of the raiders and commenced an immediate pursuit. The trail led toward the Republican River. Forsyth continued to follow the trail which grew steadily broader until there was no doubt he was tracking a significant number of Indians. He was short of supplies, and some of his men were apprehensive of the large number of warriors that they might have to face. Nevertheless, Forsyth was determined to continue the pursuit. On 16 September 1868, the scouts moved up the Arikaree Fork of the Republican River. That day, Forsyth halted his command about noon to rest the men and their horses. They establish their camp near the banks of the river opposite a small island. The major took extra care that night to make sure all his horses were secured and posted additional sentries. He believed he was closing on the hostile village and expected to bring them to battle the next day. Unknown to him, a few miles to the west were several large Indian encampments of Arapaho, Cheyenne, and Sioux. The Indians were aware of the scouts, and they, too, expected to fight the next day.

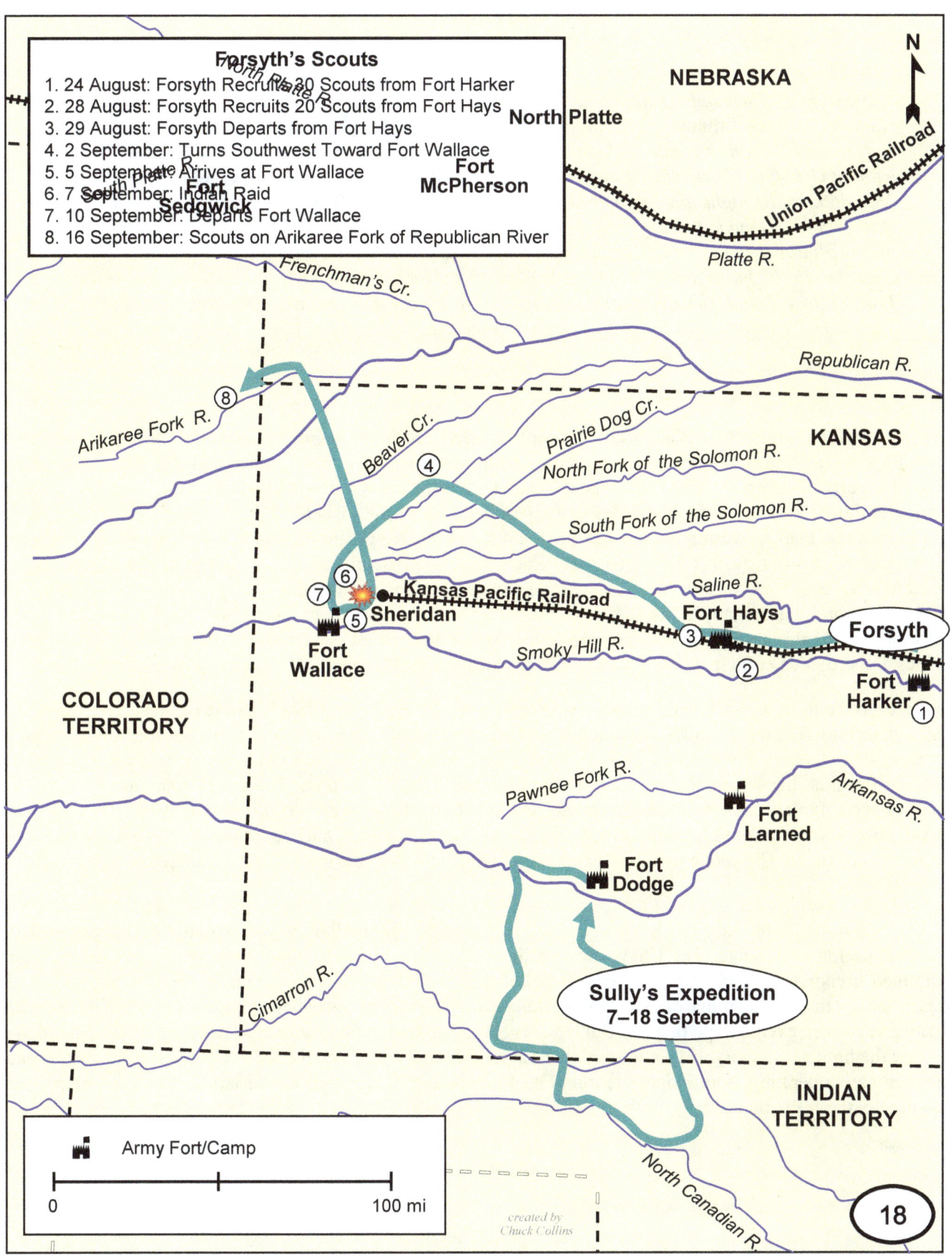

19. The Battle of Beecher Island

"Thursday 17 [September] About 12 Indians carched [caught] on us stampeedet [stampeded] 7 Horses 10 Minuts [minutes] after about 600 Indians attacktet [attacked] us Killt [killed] Beecher, Culver, and Wilson. Woundet [Wounded] 19 Man [men] & Killt [killed] all the Horses We was without Grubb & Water all Day dug Holes in the sand whith [with] our Hands. Friday, September 18, 1868. in the night dug my hole deeper cut of meat oof [off] of the Horses & hung it up on Bushes, Indians made a charge on us at Day brake [break], but retreatet [retreated] Kept Shooting nearly all day they Put up a White Flag, left us at 9 o clock in the evening Raind [rained] all night Saturday 19 the Indians came back again Kept sharp shooting all day 2 Boys startet [started] For Fort Wallace Raind [rained] all nigh Sunday 20 Dr. Moore died last night Raining part of the day snow about 1 inches thick Indians Kept sharp shooting."[34]

— Diary of Scout Sigmund Shlesinger

Mindful of the massacre of Black Kettle's people at Sand Creek in 1864 and Hancock's burning of the Pawnee Fork village in 1867, the Cheyenne were unwilling to allow soldiers near their women and children. They gathered a large war party of several hundred Cheyenne, Sioux, and Arapahoe warriors and attacked the scout camp the next morning at dawn. The scouts formed a defensive perimeter on a small island in the riverbed. The scouts worked in pairs with one man protecting the other as he dug out a defensive position. That first day, the warriors executed several massed charges against Forsyth's men. Each time, the disciplined volley fire from the scouts' Spencer repeating rifles beat back the attackers. The second day, the Indians attempted a few half-hearted assaults but then relied mainly on long-range rifle fire to harass and hold the dug-in scouts in their positions. The Indians gave up their objective of destroying the soldiers and departed the area on 21 September having already shielded their families and provided sufficient time for their safe departure from the area.

Early in the fight, Forsyth had solicited volunteers to go for help. Fortunately, some of those volunteers made it through to Fort Wallace, 85 miles to the south, and on 25 September, a relief force from the 10th Cavalry rescued the desperate defenders. Forsyth and 15 of his scouts were wounded in the fighting, and six of his men were killed including Beecher, his second in command, and the surgeon, John H. Moore. The entire command's horses were killed, as well. Indian casualty counts were not certain. Forsyth estimated 35 killed and 100 wounded. Indian sources later acknowledged only nine killed: six Cheyenne, two Sioux, and one Arapaho.[35] Their casualties did include the prominent Cheyenne warrior Roman Nose, who was killed during one of the massed charges on the first day of fighting.

The Indians had achieved a costly victory. It had been a relatively small fight, yet the battle significantly affected future Plains Indian warfare. The Cheyenne and their allies would rarely again attempt direct assaults against disciplined firepower. It reinforced the Army's belief that, in Indian warfare, numbers were not significant. The Army reasoned that small groups of disciplined soldiers could hold their own against large numbers of undisciplined warriors. However, even though they were able to repel the massive Indian assaults at Beecher Island, Sheridan did not view the fight as a victory. He recognized that his scouts barely survived the fight. He deemed the experimental scout company operating as an independent unit as a failure and made plans to use larger forces to compel peace upon the Southern Plains.

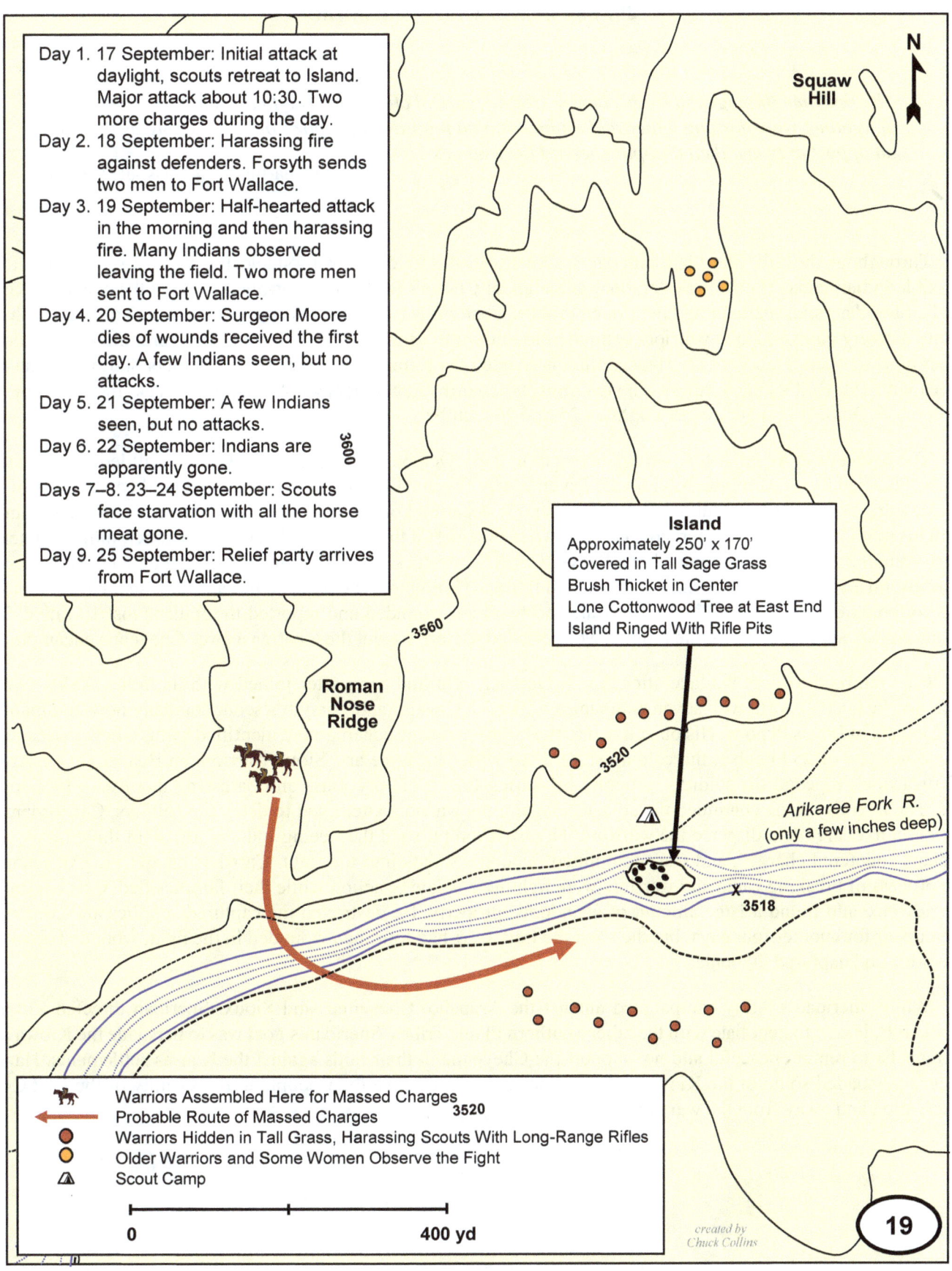

20. The Beaver Creek Skirmishes

"By this time the engagement became of a more general character. The Indians in their open order of fighting, were dashing hither and thither without regard to discipline order, shooting as they got an opportunity and then dropping behind their horses."[36]

— Department of Missouri Report

Throughout the fall, Sheridan kept units actively in the field trying to shield the Kansas settlements from possible Indian raids. The 7th Cavalry, once again under Custer's leadership, patrolled south of the Arkansas River. Sully, Sheridan, and Sherman had petitioned to have Custer released from his one year suspension. Even with the Army actively patrolling, the warriors continued to raid north of the Arkansas River. Therefore, Sheridan directed other units to operate north of the river. Columns scouted the Republican River and in October skirmished several times with Tall Bull's Dog Soldiers. The two most noteworthy encounters were at Beaver Creek: the 10th Cavalry fight on 18 October and 5th Cavalry fight on 25 and 26 October.

The events leading up to the two fights began in early October when Major William Royall led a large patrol of the 5th Cavalry to patrol the Republican River. Major Eugene Carr, the newly assigned field commander of the 5th Cavalry, arrived at Fort Wallace on 12 October. He departed Fort Wallace two days later to look for and join up with his new command. His escort consisted of two companies of the 10th Cavalry. On 18 October, Indians attacked Carr's small command as it moved down Beaver Creek. The attacking Indians greatly outnumbered the soldiers, so Carr established a defensive perimeter on a small hilltop. Throughout the day, the Indians harassed the soldiers and did not break off the fight until evening. Carr had two men wounded and reported the Indians lost 10 killed. The soldiers also captured one wounded Indian who revealed to Carr's scout the location a large Cheyenne encampment.

Carr returned to Fort Wallace after the 18 October fight and soon after joined with the 5th Cavalry. On 23 October, he headed north with seven companies of the 5th Cavalry and Forsyth's scout company now commanded by Lieutenant Lewis Pepoon. His objective was the large Cheyenne encampment identified by his Cheyenne captive. The afternoon of 25 October, the column skirmished with Cheyenne and Sioux warriors on Beaver Creek. About 200 warriors impeded the soldiers' progress by setting fire to the dry grass and harassing them with long-range fire. The next day, Carr continued the advance. Again, the warriors attempted to delay the soldiers. Carr ordered a battalion to charge and disperse the warriors. The battalion pursued the fleeing Indians for about three miles. The Indians countered charged, and Carr committed Pepoon's scouts into the fight. Carr had caught the Cheyenne in the process of breaking camp and warriors were fighting a delaying action while their families fled. Carr continued the advance and found a large amount of abandoned property. He destroyed the captured supplies and continued the pursuit for another four days, but then lost the trail. Carr had four men wounded in the fight, wounded about 10 warriors, and captured 70 ponies.

While Sheridan's Army campaigned against the Arapaho, Cheyenne, and Sioux, Sheridan directed Colonel William B. Hazen to negotiate with the other Southern Plains Tribes. Sheridan's goal was to persuade the Kiowa and Comanche to remain peaceful and not support the Cheyenne in their raids against the Kansas settlements. Hazen, in turn persuaded some of the Kiowa and Comanche chiefs to move their people to the vicinity of the Fort Cobb reservation and away from the war zone.[37]

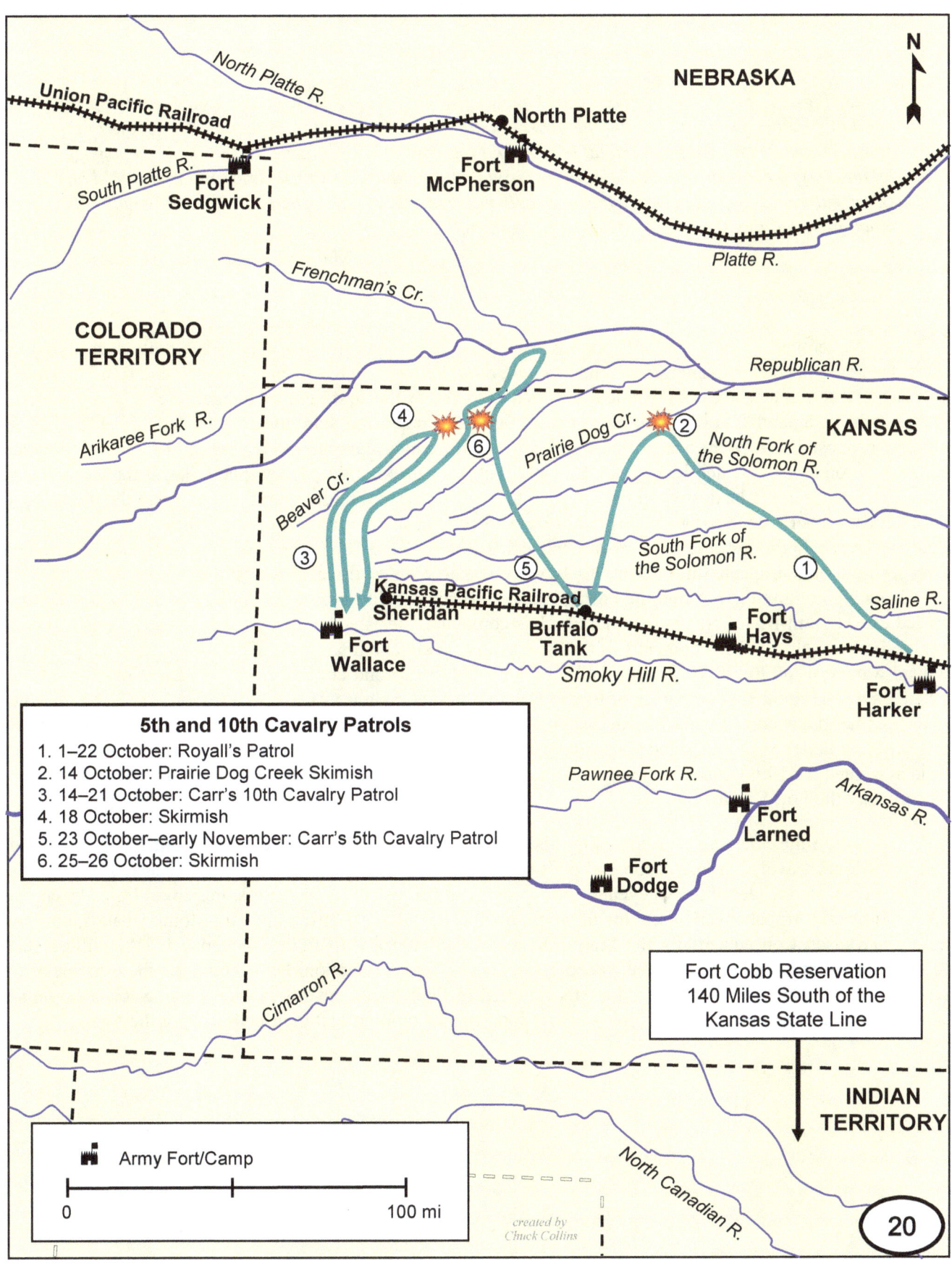

21. Sheridan's Winter Campaign Plan

"Realizing that their [the Indians] thorough subjugation would be difficult task, I made up my mind to confine operations during the grazing and hunting seasons to protecting the people of the new settlements and on the overland routes, and then, when winter came, to fall upon the savages relentlessly, for in that season their ponies would be thin, and weak from food, and in the cold and snow, without strong ponies to transport their villages and plunder, their movements would be so much impeded that the troops could overtake them."[38]

— Major General Phillip H. Sheridan

Before November, all of Sheridan's actions were little more than holding actions attempting to contain the raiders. He recognized the advantages the Indians held over the Army in the spring, summer, and fall. The warriors could strike when and where they wanted and then disperse at the first sign of danger. He believed the Army columns, which depended upon grain-fed horses, could not match the stamina of grass-fed Indian ponies. He, therefore, proposed to take the war to the Indians in a bold winter campaign. He planned to put into practice a technique of total war in which he targeted Indian villages for destruction. He reasoned that, if the Indians' food, ponies, and shelter could be destroyed or captured, they would be at the mercy of the Army and the elements and would have no other recourse than to surrender. He wanted to strike the Indians camps believed to be south of the Canadian River. He did not intend to repeat Hancock's errors of the 1867 war where the Indians easily avoided Custer's single pursuing column. Instead, his strategy was to employ three converging columns. Therefore, even if an advancing column did not find the hostile Indians, it would help to drive the Indians into the other columns. Carr led one column from Fort Lyon, Colorado. His command consisted of his own 5th Cavalry, four companies from the 10th Cavalry, and one company of the 7th Cavalry; in all, about 650 men. His mission was to move toward the head waters of the Red River. Major Andrew Evans led the second column from Fort Bascom, New Mexico. He had about 563 men: six companies of the 3d Cavalry, two companies of the 37th Infantry, and four mountain howitzers. Sheridan wanted Evans to push east along the South Canadian River. The third and strongest was the Fort Dodge column under Sully. His force consisted of 11 companies of the 7th Cavalry and five companies of Infantry. Sheridan wanted the 19th Kansas Volunteer Cavalry to join with the column in the campaign area. Sheridan planned to accompany the Fort Dodge column.

At the same time Sheridan was launching his columns against the Cheyenne, Black Kettle and the Arapaho Chief Big Mouth traveled to Fort Cobb and petitioned Hazen for peace and protection. Hazen recognized Black Kettle as a respected leader of the Cheyenne and a proponent for peace. Nevertheless, there was little Hazen could do. Cheyenne and Arapaho warriors, some of whom belonged to Black Kettle's and Big Mouth's bands, continued to raid into Kansas. Consequentially, the Army considered itself at war with all the Cheyenne and their allies. Hazen told the chiefs they could not bring their people to Fort Cobb for protection. He encouraged them to speak with Sheridan about peace. The disappointed chiefs returned to their encampments on the Washita River hoping the vastness of the Southern Plains and winter weather conditions would protect their people from the Army.

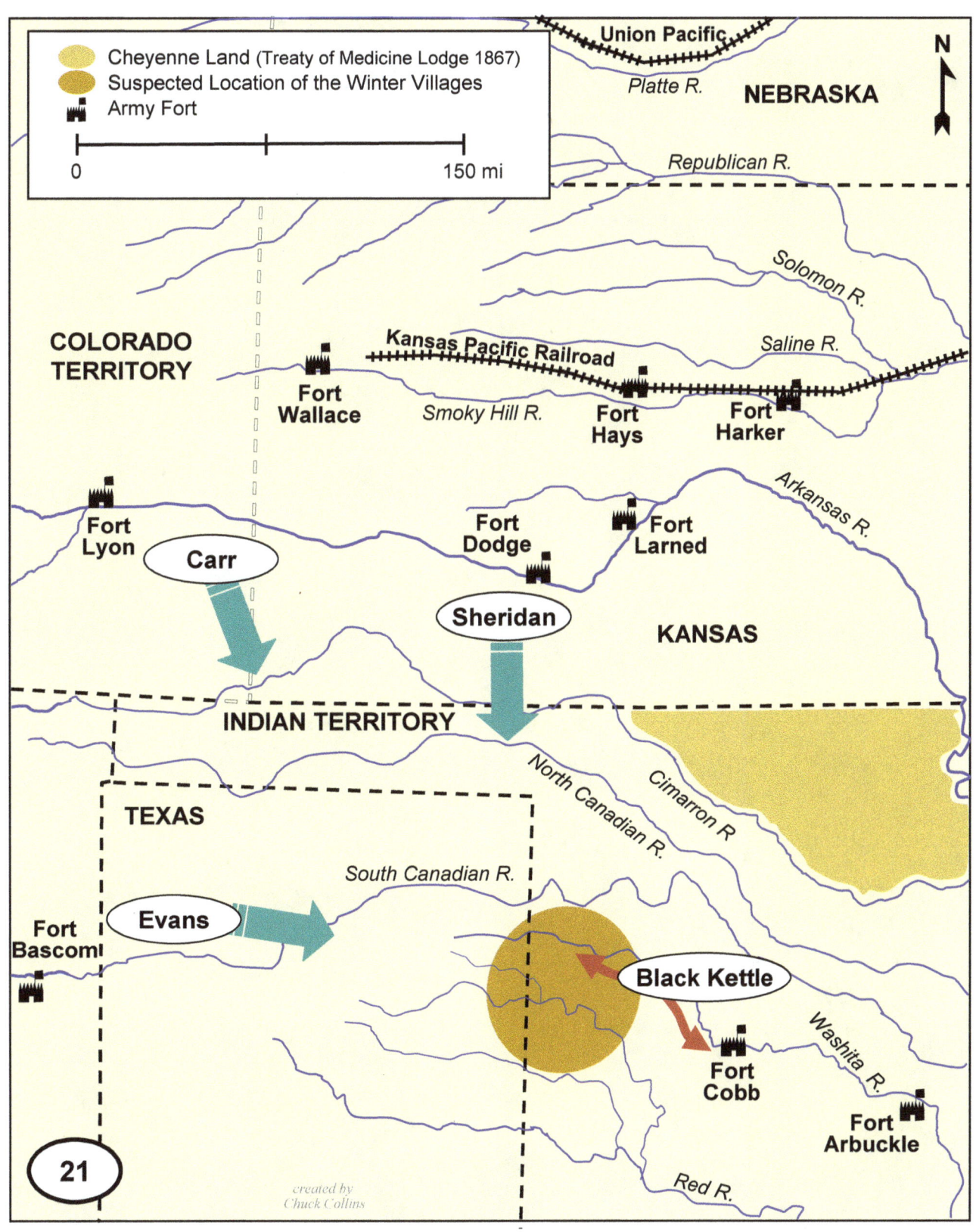

IV. The Fight at the Washita

22. The March to Camp Supply

"Nothing occurred giving us any clue to the whereabouts of [the] Indians until we had been marching several days and were moving down the valley of Beaver Creek [River], when our Indian guides discovered the trail of an Indian war party, numbering, according to their estimate, from 100 to 150 warriors, mounted and moving in a northeasterly direction. The trail was not over 24 hours old, and by following it to the point where it crossed Beaver Creek [River] almost the exact numbers and character of the party could be determined from the fresh signs at the crossing. Everything indicated that it was a war party sent from the very tribes we were in search of..." [39]

— Lieutenant Colonel George Armstrong Custer

The Fort Dodge column got under way on 12 November 1868 with Sully commanding. His command consisted of Custer's 7th US Cavalry, Captain John Page's five companies of the 3d US Infantry, a large wagon train, and an accompanying herd of cattle. The plan called for the 19th Kansas Volunteer Cavalry to link up with Sully's force on the Beaver River. Over the next several days, the column pushed south. They camped the first night along Mulberry Creek and pushed further south the next day to the headwaters of Bluff Creek. The third day, Sully halted the column on Bear Creek just to the north of present-day Ashland, Kansas, and continued the march to the Cimarron River on 15 November. Great effort was required to get the heavily loaded wagons over the creeks, streams, and rivers, while snow, ice, and high winds presented further complications with each crossing. On 16 November, the command moved into the Indian territories and, after marching 25 miles, bivouacked on the Beaver River not far from present-day Laverne, Oklahoma. That night Custer and his scouts boosted morale with a feast of meat from the buffalo and pronghorn sheep shot during the day. It is not clear whether they shared their bounty with the hard-marching infantry. On 17 November, Sully continued the march down the valley of the Beaver River. All along the trek, the column marched prepared for trouble placing two cavalry companies forward as an advance guard with additional companies on the flanks and two companies acting as rearguard. The wagons and the cattle herd lumbered along inside the cavalry perimeter closely guarded by the infantry. Nevertheless, to date, there had been no signs of the anticipated hostile Indians. As the movement continued on 18 November, they crossed over a fresh trail left by what was believed to have been a war party presumably headed north to attack Kaw or Osage villages. Custer requested permission to take his cavalry down the Indian back-trail to attack the war party's home village. However, Sully was reluctant to release Custer on his own accord with the majority of the column's combat power. He justified his decision stating he believed the Indian camp would be alert and ready, and might easily ambush Custer's cavalry. A disappointed Custer believed a *"fine opportunity"* [40] had been neglected. That same afternoon, after marching about 110 miles from Fort Dodge, the column camped near the confluence of Wolf Creek and the Beaver River.

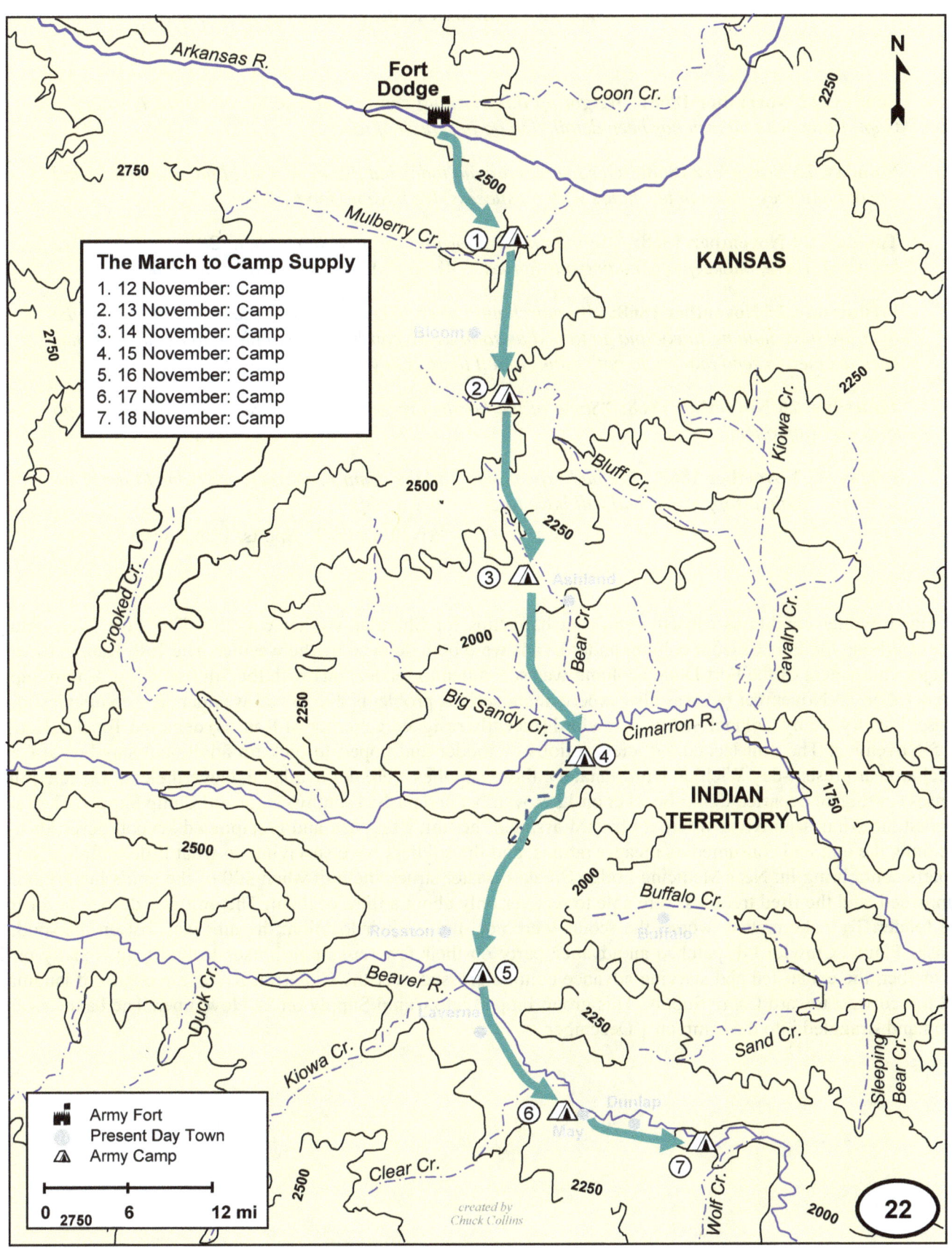

23. 19th Kansas Cavalry

Sunday, 22 November 1868: *"We got up this morning covered with snow several inches deep... Capt. Pliley with 60 men has been detailed to go in search of food..."*

Monday, 23 November 1868: *"Our hunters are out today but the snow is so blinding and the wind so cold that they return in few hours with no success. We have no food..."*

Tuesday, 24 November 1868: *"We march this morning through snow about 20 inches deep, we know not where, but keep on, leading our horses... We can eat almost anything just now."*

Wednesday, 25 November 1868: *"We march until after 10 o'clock, leading our horses most of the time. We have nothing to eat and go to bed as soon as we can find a good place to lie down. It has been decided to send hunters to both flanks and if there is any game to bring it in at once."*

Thursday, 26 November 1868: *"Some of the horses are getting pretty weak and we have to go slow and stop often."*

Friday, 27 November 1868: *"We had expected to find the camp near where we came to the river, so we are again disappointed and will have to go hungry a while longer."*[41]

— Private David L. Spotts, 19th Kansas Cavalry

Harsh winter conditions caused significant hardships for Sheridan's other columns. The Fort Lyon column under Carr and the Fort Bascom column under Evans were both delayed by the weather. The 19th Kansas Cavalry, a major component of the Fort Dodge column was scheduled to rendezvous with the 7th Cavalry at Camp Supply no later than 24 November but was also experiencing serious problems due to bad weather. Ten companies of the Kansas cavalry led by Colonel Samuel Crawford (recently resigned governor of Kansas) departed Topeka, Kansas, on 5 November. The unit lacked sufficient rations or fodder and hoped to pick up additional supplies at Camp Beecher near present-day Wichita. Unfortunately, those supplies were not available. Nevertheless, the determined Kansas contingent departed Camp Beecher on 12 November and pushed southwest toward Camp Supply. They soon reached the Ninnescah River where a blizzard assailed the unit's bivouac and precipitated several desertions. By this time, the unit had consumed its meager rations, and the soldiers were surviving on what little buffalo meat the hunters could bring in. Near Medicine Lodge Creek, disaster struck the unit when 300 of the unit's hungry horses stampeded, and the tired troopers were able to recover only about a third of them. The unit was desperate for food and fodder. To make matters worse, the scouts were not sure of their location; the unit was lost on the southern Kansas Plains. Crawford dispatched an advance party on their few remaining horses to find help. Finally on 26 November, the exhausted and starving advance column crossed over the Cimarron River, a recognized landmark, and turned west toward Camp Supply. This group limped into Camp Supply on 28 November. The balance of the command straggled into the camp on 1 December.

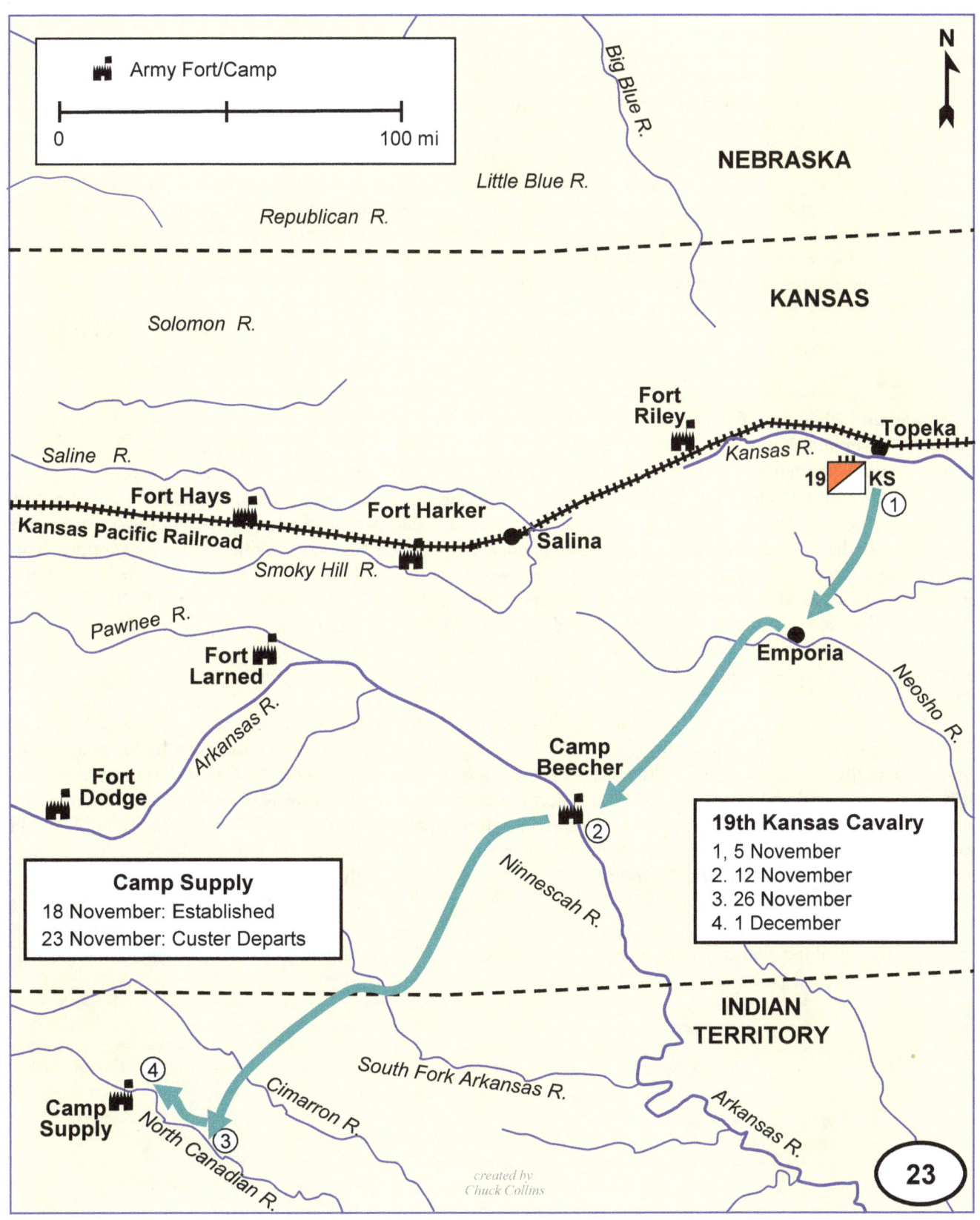

24. Camp Supply

"Here, as General Sully announces... a camp of supply for the troops operating south of the Arkansas is to be located, and until further orders it is to be designated 'Camp Supply.' A log structure is to be erected here for the protection of the Infantry about 150 men, who are to remain here, and as a magazine for supplies, while two columns of Cavalry, one (comprising 11 companies of the 7th Cavalry) under Genl. Custer, and the other (comprising 10 companies of the 19th Kansas Vol. Cav.) under Col (Governor) Crawford are to march southward, with 25 or 30 days supplies, to punish the Indians... The prospects are that we will be obliged to stay here for a couple of weeks, before we will be allowed to go, for the Infantry have no idea of being left 'unprotected' before the new Post is completed."[42]

— Captain Albert Barnitz, 7th Cavalry

While the 19th Kansas Cavalry struggled to survive the Kansas winter, the troops waiting at the confluence of the Beaver River and Wolf Creek constructed a supply base. The unit orders designated the base as "Camp Supply." The same orders directed the cantonment was to be a temporary work built of logs. The plan called for the infantry to occupy the stockade and guard the supplies while the cavalry moved south against the Indians. Work commenced on 19 November and progressed quickly. The hastily built stockade had two blockhouses, one at the northwest corner and another at the southeast corner. Storehouses lined the south and east walls with additional supplies housed in tents. The infantry living quarters served as protective lunettes outside the fort walls. Custer's cavalry camped northwest of the stockade along the Beaver River. It appears Lieutenant F. M. Gibson, A Company, 7th Cavalry, was not overly impressed with Camp Supply; he stated, *"Camp Supply now became, as its name would indicate, a base of supplies. In many respects this turned out to be a misnomer, for while there was a partial supply of everything, there was not an adequate supply of anything, at least for such a prolonged and far reaching campaign."*[43]

The mutual animosity between Sully and Custer intensified during the time spent at Camp Supply. Both were lieutenant colonels in the Regular Army. Sully was the senior colonel both by date of rank and by his assignment as commander of the Upper Arkansas District. Custer served only as commander of the 7th Cavalry Regiment. However, the rival colonels realized Colonel Crawford, incoming commander of the 19th Kansas Cavalry, outranked them both; they feared he might assert his right to command all the troops. The Articles of War further complicated the situation with the convoluted system of brevet, or honorary rank, applied when volunteer officers such as Crawford served with Regular Army officers. Therefore, to assure his command, Sully warned he would exercise his authority based upon his Regular-Army brevet rank of brigadier general. Custer, in turn, claimed the right to command based upon his Regular-Army brevet rank of major general. Nevertheless, none of the positioning for command would come into play until the Kansas troops arrived, so Sully continued to command as the senior lieutenant colonel.

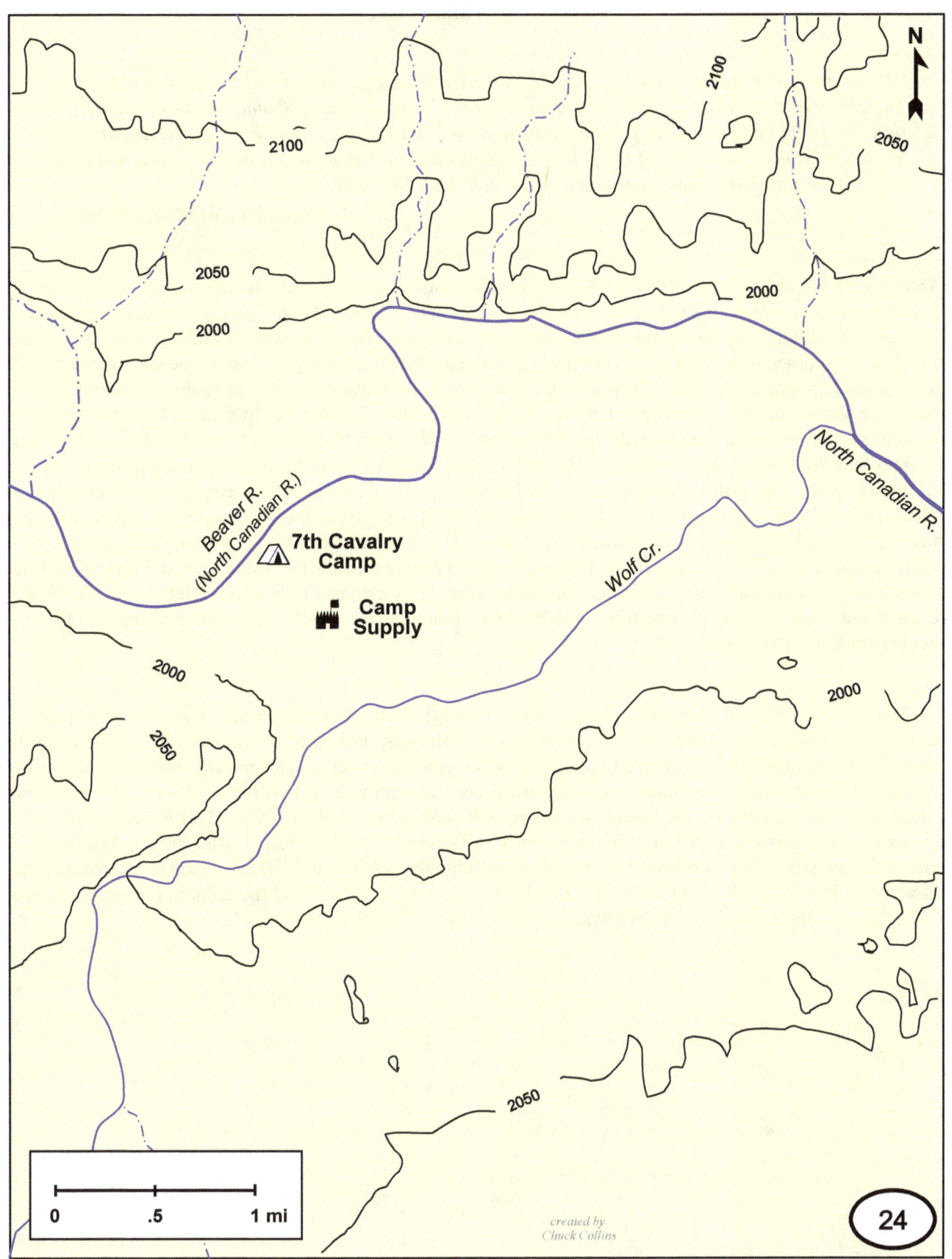

25. General Sheridan's Decision

"These directions are only general and may be varied by circumstances or by your own judgment. The object of this movement is to operate against the hostile Indians. Should any be encountered, they are to be attacked, their villages destroyed and stock killed. Should any surrender, it must be unconditional, and some of the principal chiefs and head men should be hung; you will then conduct the remainder, with women and children to Fort Cobb."[44]

— Department of Missouri Orders

Sheridan arrived at Camp Supply on 21 November. The winter campaign was his experiment, so he believed his presence was necessary to evaluate the conduct of the operations. In route to Camp Supply, his party spotted several small groups of Indians and, during one night's bivouac, exchanged fire with several Indians. Most significantly, Sheridan's party crossed over a war party trail leading to the northeast, probably the same one discovered by Custer and Sully a few days earlier. Sheridan agreed with Custer that Sully showed unjustified caution in not following the back trail. He settled the issue of command by ordering Sully back to Fort Harker to resume his responsibilities as district commander. Sheridan then placed Custer in command of the Fort Dodge column. Sheridan wrote in a letter to Sherman that Sully was *"incompetent."*[45] He shared his opinion that had Sully permitted Custer to follow the trail of the war party, it probably would have resulted in the capture of a large village encamped somewhere on the Canadian River. Also troubling Sheridan was the whereabouts of the 19th Kansas Volunteer Cavalry. In his letter to Sherman, he correctly surmised their situation when he wrote, *"The Kansas troops have not yet arrived. I fear the snow has set them astray."*[46] Nevertheless, Sheridan decided not to wait for the volunteers and directed Custer to strike south toward the suspected location of the Indian villages. Sheridan's orders to Custer stated that he was to move south toward Fort Cobb then west into the Wichita Mountains toward the headwaters of the Red River, and then return north to Camp Supply.

By late November 1868, Sheridan's campaign of converging columns was clearly not coming to pass as he envisioned. The 19th Kansas Volunteer Cavalry was lost to the east, near starvation, and still a week away from reaching Camp Supply. Carr's Fort Lyon column was delayed by winter conditions 200 miles to the northwest and would not march until 2 December. Evans' Fort Bascom column was 200 miles to the west. Having departed Fort Bascom on 18 November, they were struggling eastward along the North Canadian River in blizzard-like conditions and would not enter the objective area until 15 December. Nonetheless, Custer prepared his troops and equipment for the strike. On 23 November 1868, the unit sounded reveille at 0300 and made final preparations for the movement. Then, at 0600, the trumpeters sounded *"Boots and Saddles,"* and the column mounted and moved out as the 7th Cavalry band played a Civil War favorite, *"The Girl I Left behind Me."*

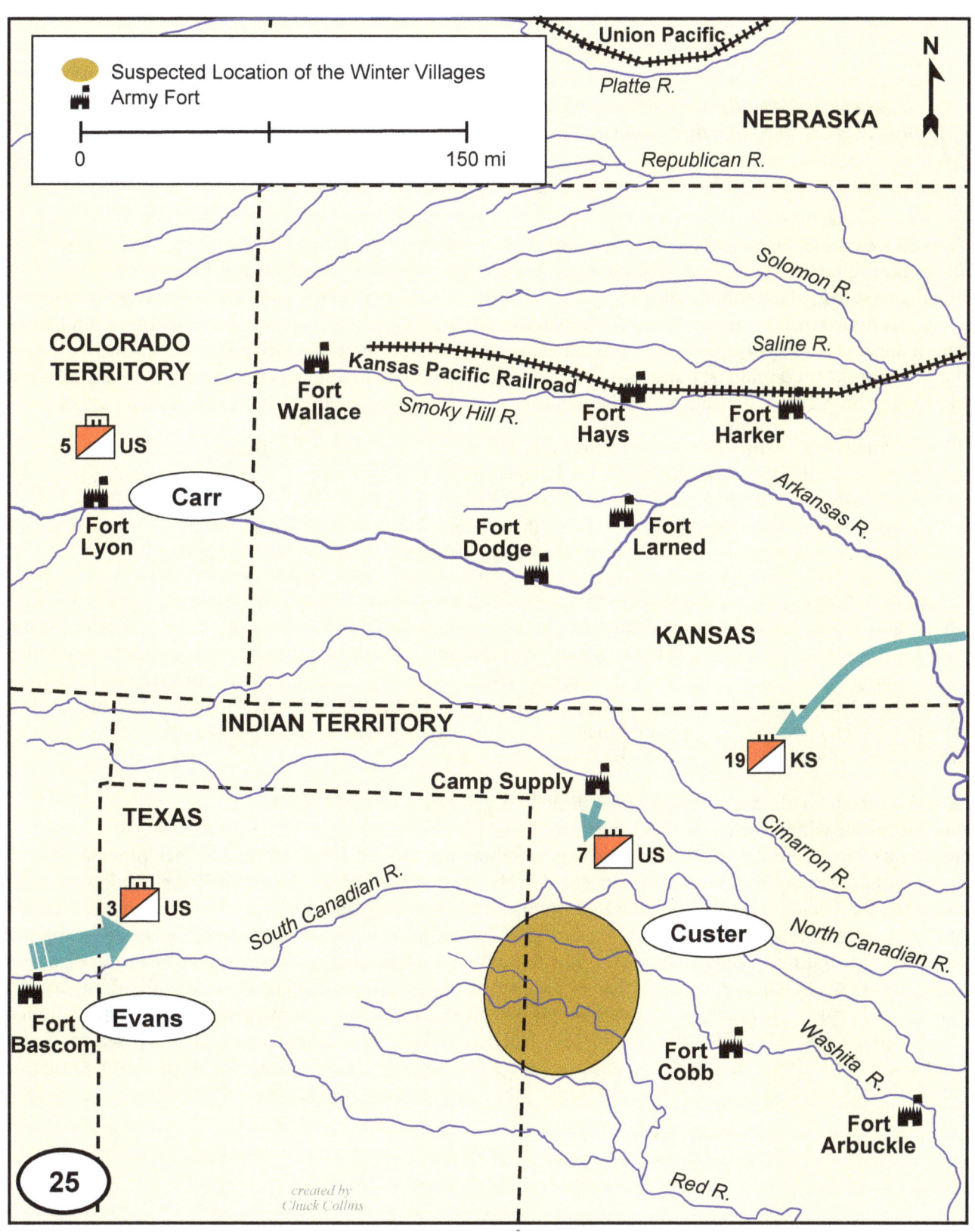

26. The March to the Canadian River

"I remember we had quite a time drying ourselves before fires made of dry rushes, weeds and wild prairie grass- anything that would make a blaze."[47]

— Trooper John Ryan, 7th Cavalry

Custer's command marched on 23 November through about a foot of snow in a blinding snowstorm. A literal whiteout prevented the scouts from spotting distant landmarks, and they quickly lost the way. At that point, Custer personally took lead of the column and, using a hand-held compass, guided the unit to the southwest. At about 1400, the column crossed over to the west side of Wolf Creek with the wagons trailing far to the rear. The storm had abated earlier in the day, but the 14-mile march through heavy snow was extremely wearing on the men and their animals. Fortunately for the tired soldiers, timber for fires and rabbits for supplementing their rations were plentiful along the creek. Even with the fires, it was a miserable night for most as they contended with wet or frozen clothes.

The command sounded reveille early the next morning. They awoke confronted with an overnight snow accumulation of 18 inches. Custer wanted a quick departure, so the soldiers hastily ate their breakfast and prepared for the march. However, several of the teamsters did not move with what Custer deemed sufficient haste. Because they delayed the command's departure, Custer had them arrested and, as punishment, directed they walk beside the wagons through the heavy snow as the command resumed its march not long after daylight.

The column made another difficult 16-mile march on 24 November. During the march the column forded Wolf Creek several times. The creek was frozen over, but the ice was not thick enough to hold the weight of the horses. The ice broke each time the lead company crossed over the creek, and the soldiers had to continue with icy wet feet and legs. Camp that night was again a trying ordeal. The next morning, Custer decided to strike due south for the Washita River. He based his decision upon the general plan of operation and his belief that he would find the Indians somewhere on the upper Washita River drainage. Soon after daylight, the column resumed its march with the scouts steering the command due south toward the South Canadian River.

On the march south, the column passed through a game-rich environment where wildlife had sought shelter during the storm within the timber and brush near the various water courses along the way. When the column spotted a number of buffalo, the almost holiday atmosphere that ensued demonstrated the lack of respect the Army held for its adversary. No one seemed concerned with small bodies of soldiers or officers leaving the column. Custer permitted small groups of soldiers to drop out of the march to shoot and butcher the large beasts thereby supplementing the expedition's rations. Even Custer and other officers took advantage of the sporting opportunity to chase and kill buffalo. About nine miles into the march they spotted the Antelope Hills in the distance and anticipated finding conclusive evidence that would lead to the Indian's whereabouts. It was the third day of hard marching, and some of the mules and horses showed signs of exhaustion. The wagon train was especially having trouble keeping up with the column. At times, they had to double up their mule teams to get the wagons over small streams and other difficult terrain. Although they were still about one mile short the Canadian River, Custer called a halt for the day after roughly 18 miles and allowed the troops to establish a snowy bivouac.

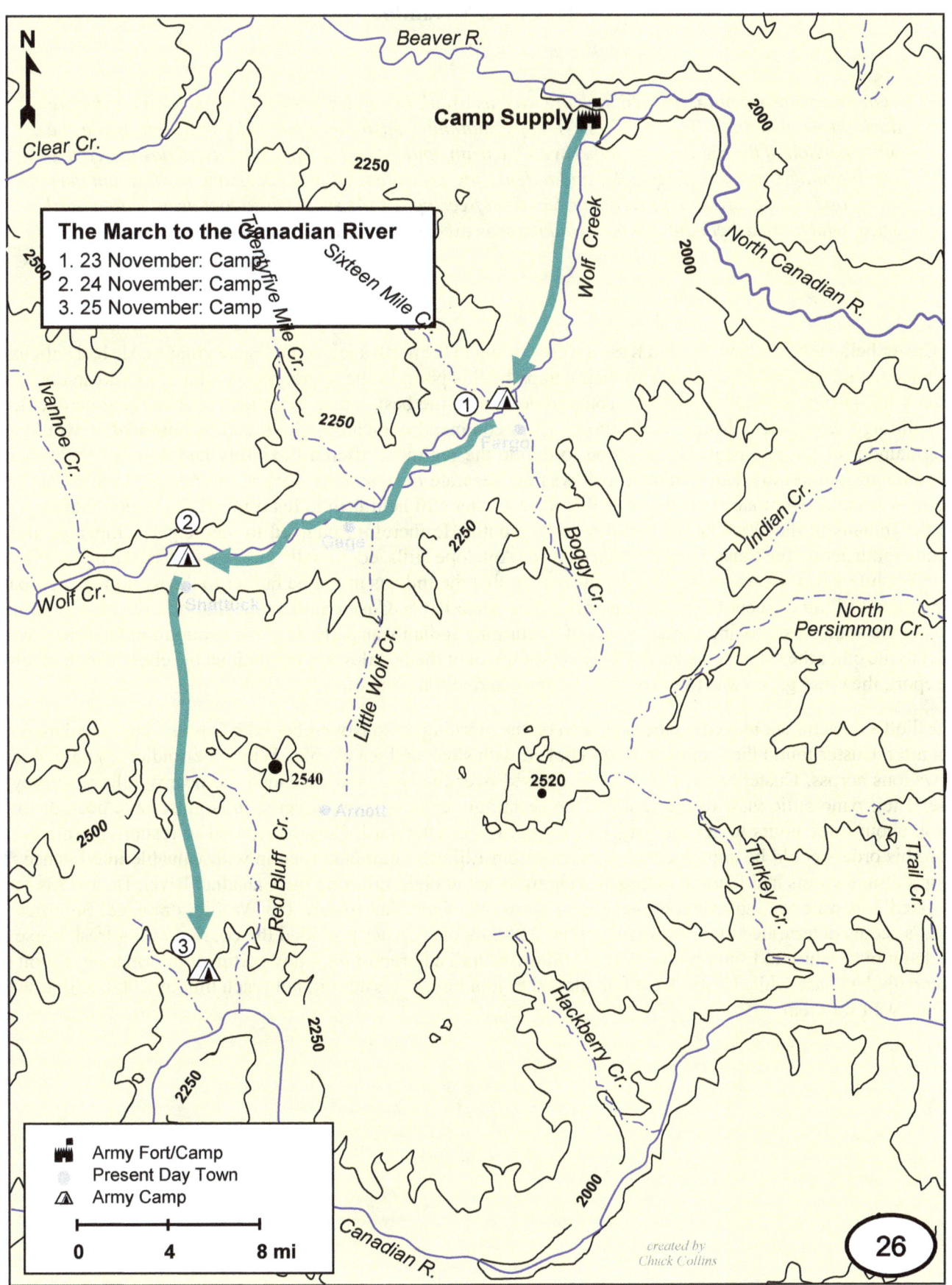

27. Custer's Gamble

"On Thursday morning, Nov. 26, reveille was, as usual, two hours before daylight, and just before daylight we marched, 'G', 'M' & 'H' Troops, marching upstream under Major Elliott, while the other portion of the regiment, together with the train, under Genl. Custer proceeded downstream… The morning was excessively cold, and a dense fog prevailed…It was necessary to dismount very often, and walk in order to prevent our feet from freezing. As the snow was a foot deep, with a hard crust, which broke beneath our feet, walking was exceedingly difficult and tiresome."[48]

— Captain Albert Barnitz, 7th Cavalry

Custer believed the Cheyenne and Kiowa were raiding in the north against the Osage villages. He had anticipated finding signs of war parties returning to their camps by this point in the operation. The failure to do so concerned Custer who, in turn, consulted with his scouts to determine the best course of action. That evening he decided to risk splitting the regiment. Major Joel Elliott was to command companies G, H, and M, and Custer would keep the remainder of the regiment. His decision to divide the regiment offered flexibility and doubled their chances of finding an Indian trail. The imminent risk was the separate detachments were more vulnerable to defeat if the Indians were to concentrate against one or the other. Custer still held firm to his original estimation that he would find the Indians in the Washita River valley to the south. He therefore planned to take eight companies and the wagons south across the Canadian River and over the Antelope Hills, continually pushing toward the upper tributary of the Washita River. However, to mitigate the danger that the Indians might be farther to the west than anticipated, he instructed Elliott to scout the north bank of the Canadian River. Custer authorized Elliott to proceed as far as 15 miles to the southwest looking for any signs of a returning Indian war party. If either group found a trail, it was to report to the other the estimated size and direction of travel of the hostiles and to continue the chase. Upon receiving the report, the other group was to move cross country and join the pursuit.

Elliott's detachment moved out before dawn on the morning of 26 November with Custer's command marching soon after. Custer found the Canadian River choked with slush and ice chunks. While the soldiers struggled to get the wagons across, Custer and a few officers crossed over the river and ascended the nearby hills to survey the route. Their panoramic view to the south of the seemingly endless snow-covered hills must have been daunting. It took about three hours to get the wagons over the river. Afterward, Custer prepared to resume the march, but before his orders could be implemented, a courier from Elliott's command rode in with valuable intelligence. The major's Osage scouts had found two large Indian trails about eight miles up the Canadian River. He and his scouts estimated 150 warriors moving south-southeast across the Canadian toward the Washita drainage. Significantly, Elliott's scouts determined the trail was less than 24 hours old. Custer provided the courier with a fresh horse and directed him to return to Elliott with orders to follow the trail and report back any pertinent information. Elliott was to keep up the chase while Custer's column moved to join him. If Custer did not reach him by 2000, Elliott was to halt and wait for them.

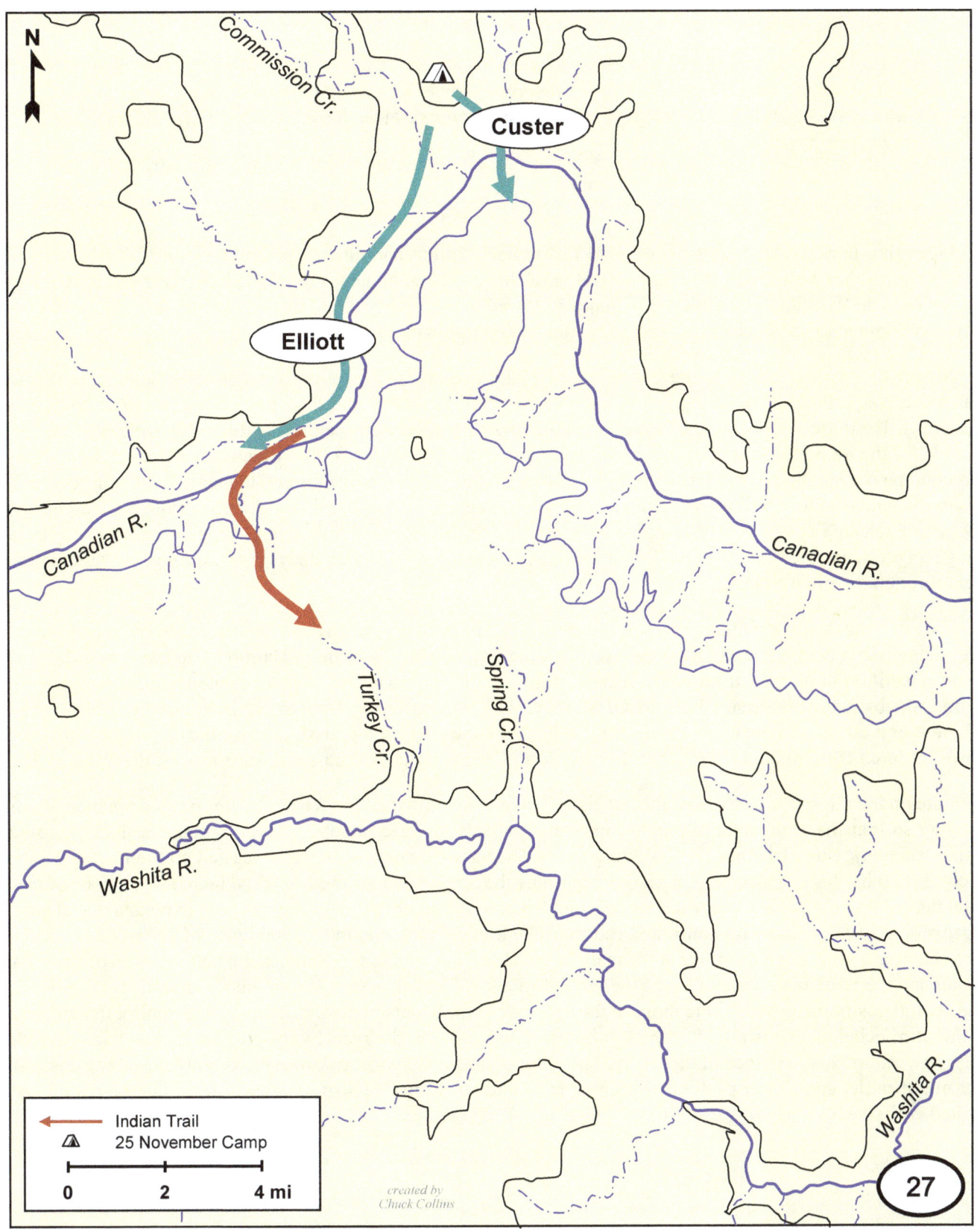

28. Movement to Contact

"I acquainted them with the intelligence received from Elliott, and at the same time informed them that we would at once set out to join in the pursuit, a pursuit which could and would only end when we overtook our enemies."[49]

— Lieutenant Colonel George Armstrong Custer

Operating in accordance with his original instructions, Elliott had already resumed the pursuit when Custer's messenger reached him late in the afternoon. He took his detachment across the Canadian River and over the high ground into the Washita River valley. The major followed the war party's trail throughout the day without stopping until sometime after 1500 when Custer's messenger caught up with him.

Meanwhile, Custer analyzed the information he had received and formulated a course of action. He reasoned that speed was critical because they now had a known trail to follow and the deteriorating weather could easily obscure it. He therefore decided to leave the cumbersome wagon train behind to follow as well as it could. To provide for the immediate logistical needs of the strike column, he directed First Lieutenant James Bell to organize and command a small, detached, combat train of two supply wagons and four ambulances. Believing it would be two to three days before he linked up with his main trains again, Custer distributed supplies from the wagons to the troopers. Each soldier carried 100 rounds of ammunition for his Spencer carbine and enough hardtack, coffee, and forage to get by for a couple of days. Both officers and men donned additional layers of clothing, as well, to protect them through the night from the cold.

To insure the security of the trailing wagons, Custer had his officers form a detachment of about 80 men from those with the weakest horses. He assigned the officer of the day, Captain Alexander Hamilton, to command the wagon escort. Hamilton implored Custer not to separate him from his company, so Custer relented and allowed Hamilton to find a substitute. Lieutenant Edward G. Mathey, who was suffering from snow blindness, agreed to remain behind as the escort's commander. Confident that he had done everything possible to set the conditions for success, Custer ordered the column to move out. For the rest of the day, he pushed southward toward the Washita River.

Late on the afternoon of 25 November, Custer's scouts identified Elliott's trail. Custer pushed his men 30 miles that day so that the main column finally joined the major's bivouac about 2100. That night as many across the nation were enjoying elaborate Thanksgiving feasts, Custer's exhausted command feasted on their meager rations of coffee and hardtack. Custer was anxious to continue the pursuit and allowed his tired men only an hour of rest; at 2200 the column moved out following the Washita River to the southeast. Despite his haste to resume the chase, his organization of the column demonstrated caution. The first echelon, the most experienced Osage scouts, marched far to the front, away from the noise of the main body. This allowed them to watch and listen for signs of the village. Custer and the remaining scouts formed the second echelon. They marched several hundred yards behind the lead. The central position allowed him to monitor the progress of the scouts in the first echelon and control the movement of the third echelon, or main body, which followed a half mile to the rear. Every precaution was taken to reduce noise and minimize the chance of discovery. The non-commissioned officers supervised tying down any equipment that might rattle, and Custer prohibited trumpet calls and smoking. He also directed that all talk be conducted in limited whispers.

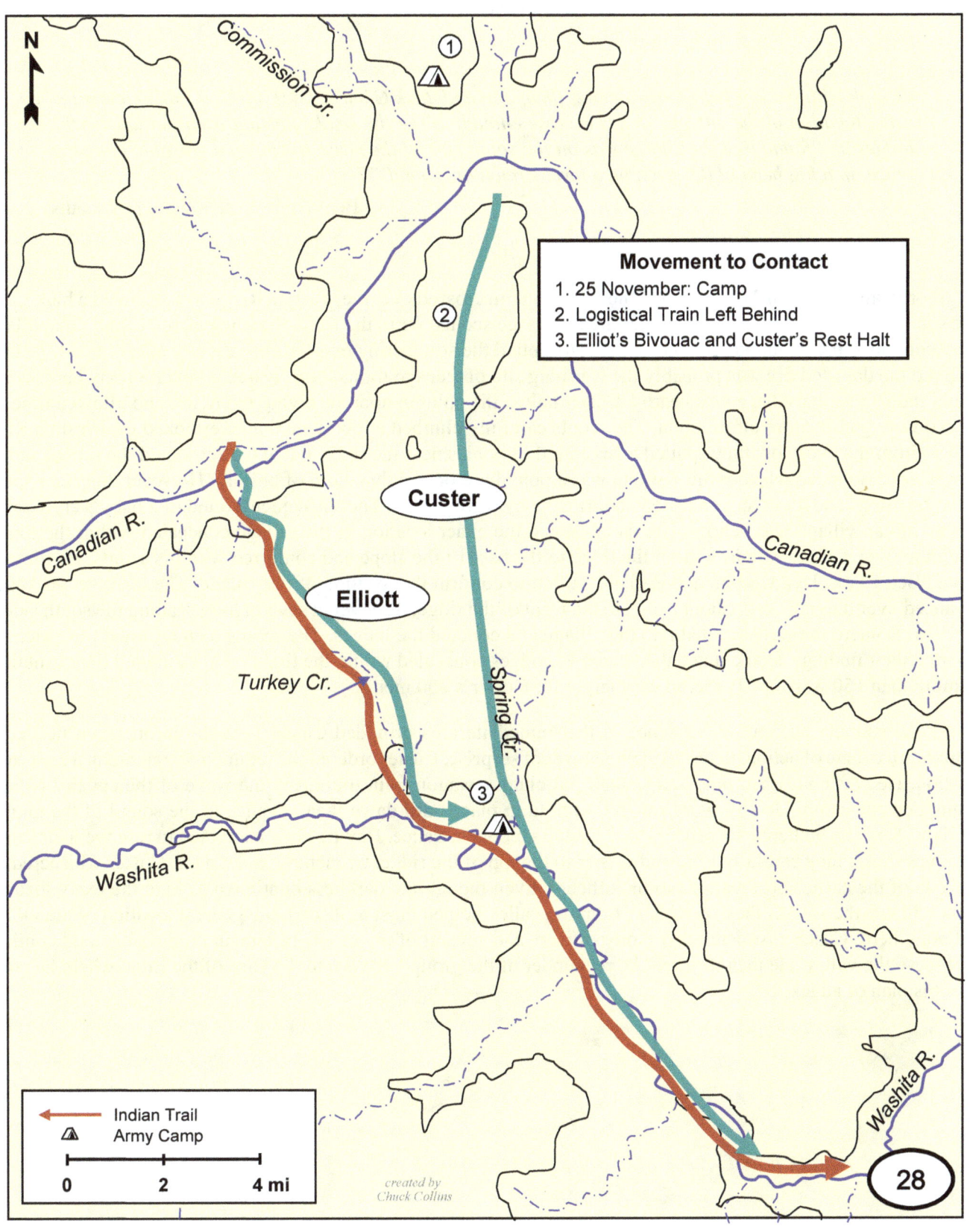

29. Tactical Pause

"I took with me several scouts, among them Joe and Jack Corwin [sic], and set out to learn the exact location of the village. We drew close enough to see the smoke curling from the tops of the lodges and found that the village was on the south side of the river. It was an admirable camping place, in a big bend of the river, on a level stretch of ground."[50]

— Ben Clark, Custer's chief of scouts

Shortly after 0200 on 27 November 1868, the column crossed over the Washita River and ascended a high ridge. The smell of smoke was the first sign alerting the Osage scouts, far to the front, that they were closing on a village. They continued their cautious advance and soon spotted the smoldering embers of a recently abandoned fire. They believed the deserted fire was probably the warming site of teenage Indian boys watching over a pony herd, which would indicate that a village was nearby. Custer halted the column upon receiving the news, and allowed time for the scouts to gather more information. The scouts carefully climbed a low ridge that overlooked the Washita River valley. From the overlook, they spotted a large herd of ponies near the river. When Custer joined the scouts, at first he was not convinced whether the sighting was a pony herd or merely a herd of buffalo. However, the clear sound of barking dogs and a tinkling bell soon confirmed they were ponies. The subsequent sound of a baby's cry verified that an Indian village was nearby. The darkness hid the exact location of the village concealed within the timber along the river. Custer withdrew from the ridge to the base of the slope and conferred with his scouts. He directed Scouts Ben Clark, Jack Corbin, and Rafael Romero to confirm the location of the village. The three scouts warily advanced over the ridge and, about a mile to the front of the ridge, discovered several lodges along the south side of the river. Romero daringly scouted into the village and counted the lodges. The scouts then returned to Custer and reported their findings. Clark stated there were 51 lodges concealed within the timber and estimated they contained no more than 150 warriors. It was an easy target for Custer's 800 men.

The amazingly accurate intelligence of the immediate area provided Custer with the information needed to formulate a course of action. Insuring their element of surprise, Custer ordered the regiment to remain in a concealed location. He was concerned that Bell's small but clumsy wagon train trailing in the wake of the cavalry column might alert the camp. He sent word for Bell to hold in place until dawn then advance to the sound of the guns at daylight. Next, he gathered his officers for a leader's reconnaissance. Having been instructed to remove their sabers to reduce noise, they carefully followed Custer to the top of the ridge. Crouching in the dark, Custer whispered his analysis of the earlier observations to his officers. Even though the darkness continued to hide the exact location of the village, the sounds they could hear from the valley helped most to discern the general location of the village and pony herd. Custer instructed two junior officers and several of the scouts to remain on the ridge and continue to observe the valley. He then directed the remainder of the group to return to the base of the ridge where he could brief his plan of attack.

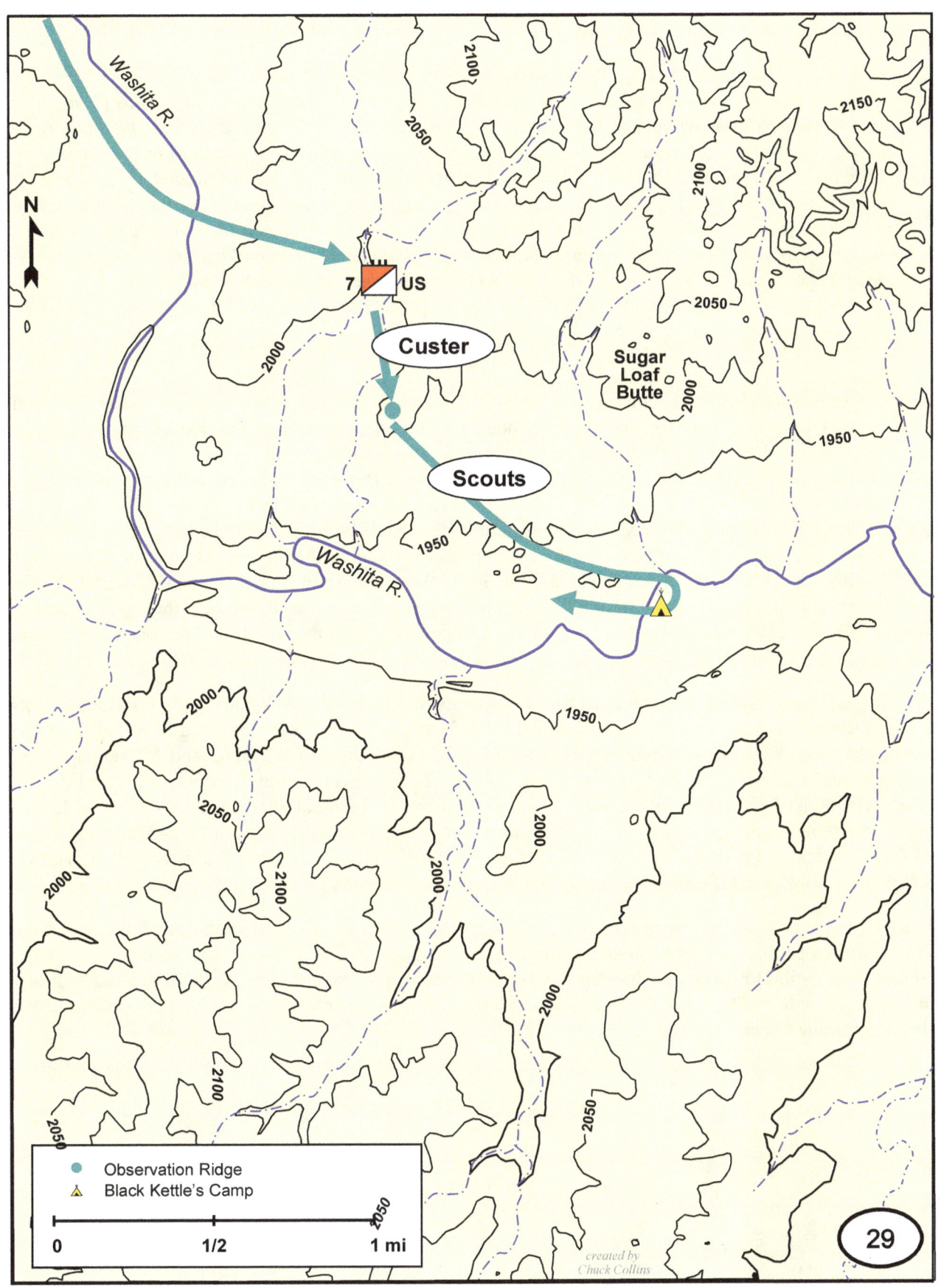

30. Plan of Attack

"The attack was to be made at day break, and in the meantime each column was to get as close as possible to the village without giving any alarm. If however, in spite of all precautions, the Indians should discover our advance, and endeavor to escape, or fire upon any portion of the command, the attack was to be made at once; otherwise, the signal of attack was to be sounded, at daybreak by the band, which was to play on the summit of the ridge from which Genl. Custer's column was to advance, and instantly, at the appointed signal, or at the firing of a gun, the advance was to be made from all directions – all were to go in with a rush and this was particularly enjoined upon all the officers, by Genl. Custer, as he fully realized the importance of concentration."[51]

— Captain Albert Barnitz, 7th Cavalry

Custer assembled the officers behind Observation Ridge and formulated a general plan of attack. He assigned three companies to Elliott: Captain Frederick Benteen's battalion of H and M companies and Captain Albert Barnitz's G Company. He instructed Elliott to pass around the Red Hills and position his command to the east of the village. Elliott moved out about 0300 with only Barnitz's company. Benteen's battalion was far to the rear guarding Bell's combat trains and had to be called forward by messenger. Custer assigned companies B and F to Captain William B. Thompson. His mission was to countermarch along the back trail, cross over the river, then circle east through the hills and position his unit south of the encampment. He was further instructed to cooperate with Elliott's command to his east and prevent the escape of any Indians to the south. Thompson also moved out at 0300. Captain Edward Myers' command consisted of E and I companies. Myers' mission was to move to the south and cross over the Washita River. Custer wanted Myers to deploy his companies in both the woods and the open ground south of the river to prevent escape to the west.

Custer positioned himself with the units that would conduct the main attack. He divided those units into two battalions. Captain Louis M. Hamilton commanded the left wing; his command consisted of A and D companies. Captain Robert M. West commanded the right wing; his command consisted of C and K companies. Custer retained personal control of his staff, the band, and the scouts. He also positioned a company of 40 dismounted sharpshooters, under Lieutenant William W. Cooke, to the front of the main attack. Custer instructed his column to occupy positions northwest of the village. The plan called for all units to be in position and attack at dawn. The signal for the attack was to be the band blaring out the regimental song, *"Gary Owen."* Custer further instructed all units to attack immediately if they were discovered before the signal was given.

Custer's intent was to *"prevent the escape of every inmate of the village."*[52] Nevertheless, it was a complicated plan that required precise coordination and timing. Up to this point in the operation, his famous *"Custer's Luck"* had served him well. However, considering the difficult terrain, the limited time available for the four separate columns to move into position, and the failure to scout the surrounding area, it appears he was continuing to count on his good fortune to carry the day.

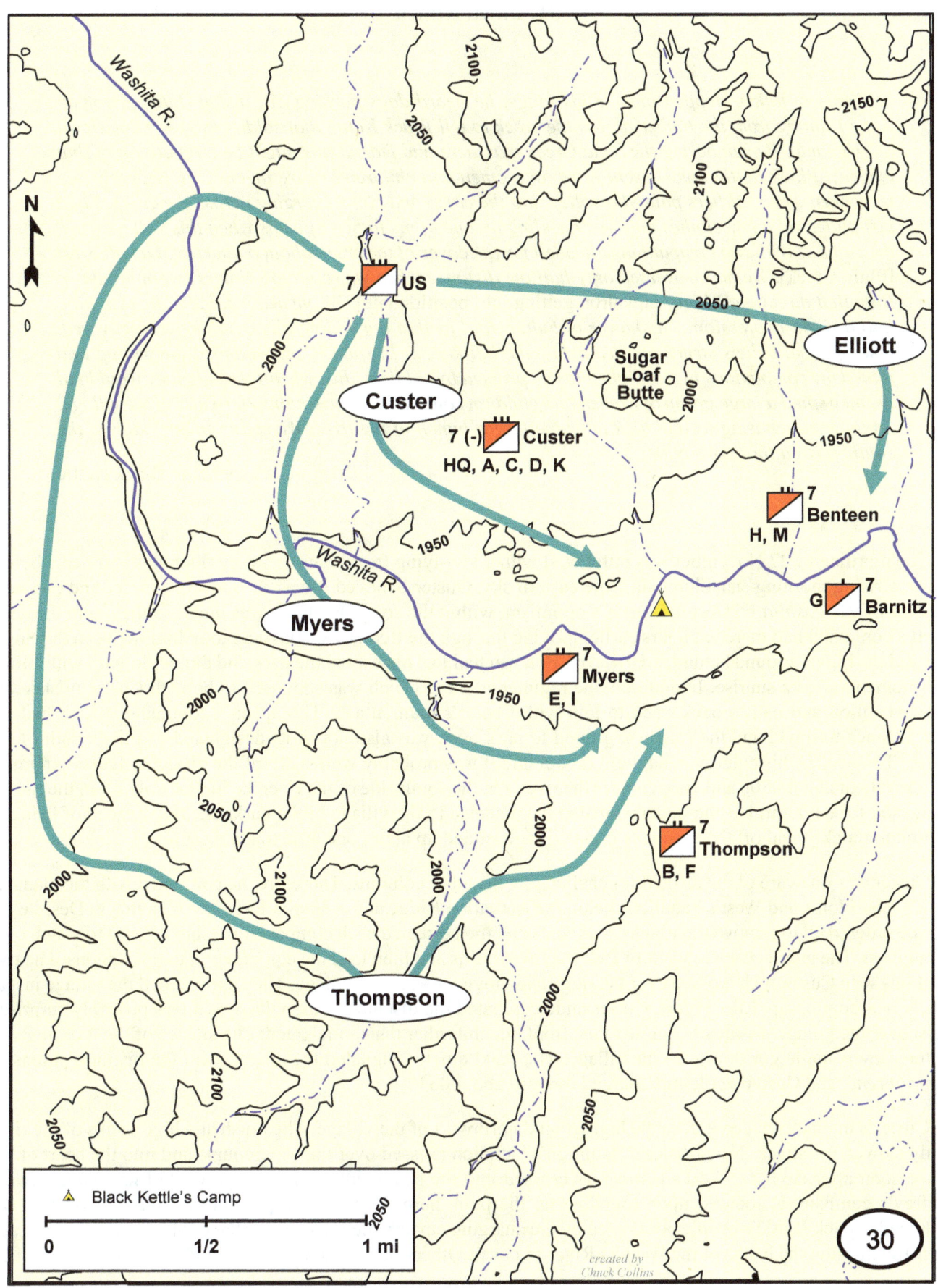

31. Dawn Attack

"When my father stepped outside his lodge, he heard dogs barking. An instant later a woman came running from the timber across the creek to tell Black Kettle that soldiers were riding down on the camp. Remembering the Sand Creek massacre and fearful this might be a repetition of that tragedy, Black Kettle quickly sent word for women and children to save themselves. Scarcely had he spoken when soldiers poured a volley into the camp and came charging across the creek. I had just pulled on a few clothes and was buckling on one of my father's pistols when this volley struck the camp... With two companions I headed for the cover of the creek about a quarter of a mile west [Plum Creek]. We had traversed only half the distance when we ran into soldiers swooping down from that direction [Myers' squadron getting into position late]. We turned south, finally dropping into a slight depression... A shower of bullets told us that our hiding place had been discovered. One of these bullets struck me just below the left knee... In spite of my wound, I jumped up and joined my companions in our flight, closely pressed by soldiers. Just when I thought they would kill us, they spied a large group of women and children coming from the southeastern end of the village. So they quit chasing us and took after the larger bunch of fugitives. We ran over the ridge to the south, passed those two buttes..."[53]

— Magpie, a nephew of Black Kettle

The morning of 27 November was bitter cold with a low-lying fog along the valley floor, and moments before sunrise a rising morning star illuminated the eastern sky. Custer believed it was an omen of victory and named it *"the Star of the Washita."*[54] Despite Custer's optimism, within the command there was much confusion in the dark. Elliott's command had marched hours earlier moving through the Red Hills. His route took him between the Sugar Loaf and the higher ground behind it. However, Benteen had lost his way in the dark and did not join up with Elliott until moments before sunrise. In addition, the regimental band which was supposed to be with Custer mistakenly followed Elliott and had to back track to join with Custer's main attack. Thompson's command, which had the most distance to travel and the roughest ground to pass over, was also not in its designated position south of the village. The head of his column at daylight (about 0600) was probably well south of the village. Myers' command had moved out about 0500 and crossed over the river. On the south side of the river, he hid his column in the timber and waited for daylight. He had underestimated the distance to the village in the darkness and, instead of being in position to quickly seal off the west side of the village, ended up about one mile to the west.

Custer was unaware of the difficulties challenging his other columns. Therefore, he continued with the plan. He formed Hamilton's and West's battalions behind Observation Ridge and prepared for a daylight attack. Despite the cold, he ordered all to remove their bulky overcoats and then directed each company to assign a guard to watch over the baggage. The guards were to wait for Bell's combat trains and then load the equipment into the wagons. The two battalions with Custer then crossed over the ridge and moved toward the village. They approached the village just as the sun was coming up. Like Myers, Custer underestimated the distance to the village and was probably surprised to discover the village was nearly a mile to the front, much farther than anticipated. The silence of the morning was shattered by a single gunshot from the village. The band quickly signaled the charge with the opening strains of *"Gary Owen,"* and Custer's columns charged forward about 0630.

Custer's main attack came from the high ground northwest of the village. The brush and high banks of the river briefly slowed the attack. Nevertheless, Hamilton's battalion crossed over the watercourse and into the heart of the village soon after daylight. West's companies crossed into the south side of the village while Lieutenant Edward Godfrey's company K focused upon rounding up the pony herd. Cooke's sharpshooter company stayed on the north bank. Black Kettle's people, awakened by the charging cavalry, fled from the village. Most made their escape downstream using the banks of the Washita River as cover. Others fled to the west toward Plum Creek or south into the hills. Although Black Kettle's people stood no chance against the overwhelming Army attack, the fight was not completely one-sided. One of the first Army casualties occurred along the brush line of the river just as the attack columns crossed over the river into the village. Hamilton, who had just hours before implored Custer to allow him to accompany the attack was killed in the first few moments of the battle. He was a popular officer and, unfortunately, much rumor surrounded his death. The medical report clearly stated that he died instantly from a gunshot wound near the heart. Even so, some believed he was accidentally shot by his own men because there was a bullet hole in the back of his jacket but none in the front. It is believed that perhaps the captain had his shell jacket unbuttoned giving reason for no bullet hole in the front.

There is great historical and emotional debate surrounding the events on the Washita River when considering whether those events should be deemed a battle or a massacre. Without question, the events associated with 27 November 1868 were a great tragedy in American history. The most heartbreaking character of the story was the Cheyenne Chief Black Kettle. The 67-year-old chief was a long-time advocate of peace. He recognized the futility of armed resistance to the white encroachment onto Indian lands and tried to promote a path of peaceful coexistence. Black Kettle had moved his people to the Washita River valley away from Kansas settlements and emigrant trails to avoid contentious contacts with the whites. Just days before the attack, he had returned from a 100-mile trip to Fort Cobb where he had negotiated unsuccessfully with Colonel William B. Hazen to obtain a promise of peace and the Army's protection. Hazen had lacked the authority to make peace with the Cheyenne considering that Sherman and Sheridan had decided that the Cheyenne's *"past acts"* must be *"both punished and avenged."*[55] Nevertheless, the old chief believed his people would be able to wait out the winter in the remote Washita River valley in peace. He was aware that Army units were maneuvering in the region seeking out Indians hostile to the American government. However, since he did not consider his band hostile, he did not believe the Army posed a major threat to his encampment. Ironically, the evening before the attack, Black Kettle's wife, Medicine Woman Later, had beseeched her husband to relocate the camp nearer to the larger Cheyenne, Arapaho, and Kiowa camps to the east. However, not knowing the close proximity of Custer's 7th Cavalry, Black Kettle reasoned there would be time the next day to make the move.

Unfortunately, Black Kettle and the other Southern Plains Indian elders had been unable to control the urges of their young men to raid into Kansas. Those same young men doomed the old chief and his people. Custer and his regiment had followed the war party's trail, which tragically led to Black Kettle's village. The old chief had survived the infamous Sand Creek Massacre in 1867 and immediately recognized the sounds of the cavalry charge. He could easily imagine what was held in store for himself and his people. His lodge was on the west end of the village. He knew that his people would scatter and that any expectation of a successful defense was hopeless. Black Kettle and his wife immediately mounted a single pony and made a dash for safety. The Army's main attack was driving into the west end of the village, so it appears the chief tried to escape to the east. Although the exact location of his death is unknown, in all probability, he attempted to cross over the Washita River or to use the banks as cover somewhere in the vicinity of where the river bends back to the east. It is known that they did make it into the water. It was there Cooke's sharpshooter company fired from the north bank, probably killing them. It is believed that, of the 200 to 300 inhabitants in the village, 40 men, 12 women and six children died in the fighting. Some of the accounts speak of mutilated dead, unborn babies cut from the womb, and scalping. According to the Scout Ben Clark, much of this was done by the Osage Scouts who Clark stated shot down women and then mutilated their bodies. However, not all of the atrocities may be attributed to the Osage Scouts; in his own account of the battle, Trooper John Ryan boasted of scalping a dead warrior.

Almost simultaneous with Custer's charge into the west side of the village, Elliott's command attacked the east side of the village. His units had moved down from the Red Hills about a half mile to the east of the village and then turned to the west toward the village. During Elliott's attack, Benteen's battalion conducted a mounted attack on the north side of the river while Barnitz's company dismounted and provided supporting fire from the south side. In all probability, the opening shot of the fight that prompted Custer's charge was probably fired from the east side of the village. It appears the advance of Elliott's command surprised several Indian boys caring for the pony herd on the village's eastern edge. Their warning then resulted in the first shot from the village. Many of the refugees fleeing from Custer's main attack into the west side of the village found their route of escape blocked by Elliott's command.

The story of a 14-year-old Cheyenne girl, Moving Behind Woman, portrays the terror of the early morning attack.

> *"We heard a woman saying in a low voice: 'Wake up! Wake up! White men! White men are here! The soldiers are approaching our camp.' We became frightened, and did not know what to do. We arose at once. At the instant, the soldiers let out terrible yells, and there was a burst of gunfire from them. My aunt called to me, but as I started to go out, the girl with whom I had stayed all night grabbed me by the arm and pulled me back saying, 'Don't go out, stay inside; the white men might see you outside and shoot you.' My aunt called me again, and told me to hurry up and come out. I became so frightened that I was trembling, but went outside... Many Indians were killed during the fight. The air was full of smoke from gunfire, and it was almost impossible to flee, because the bullets were flying everywhere. However, somehow we ran and kept running to find a place."*[56]

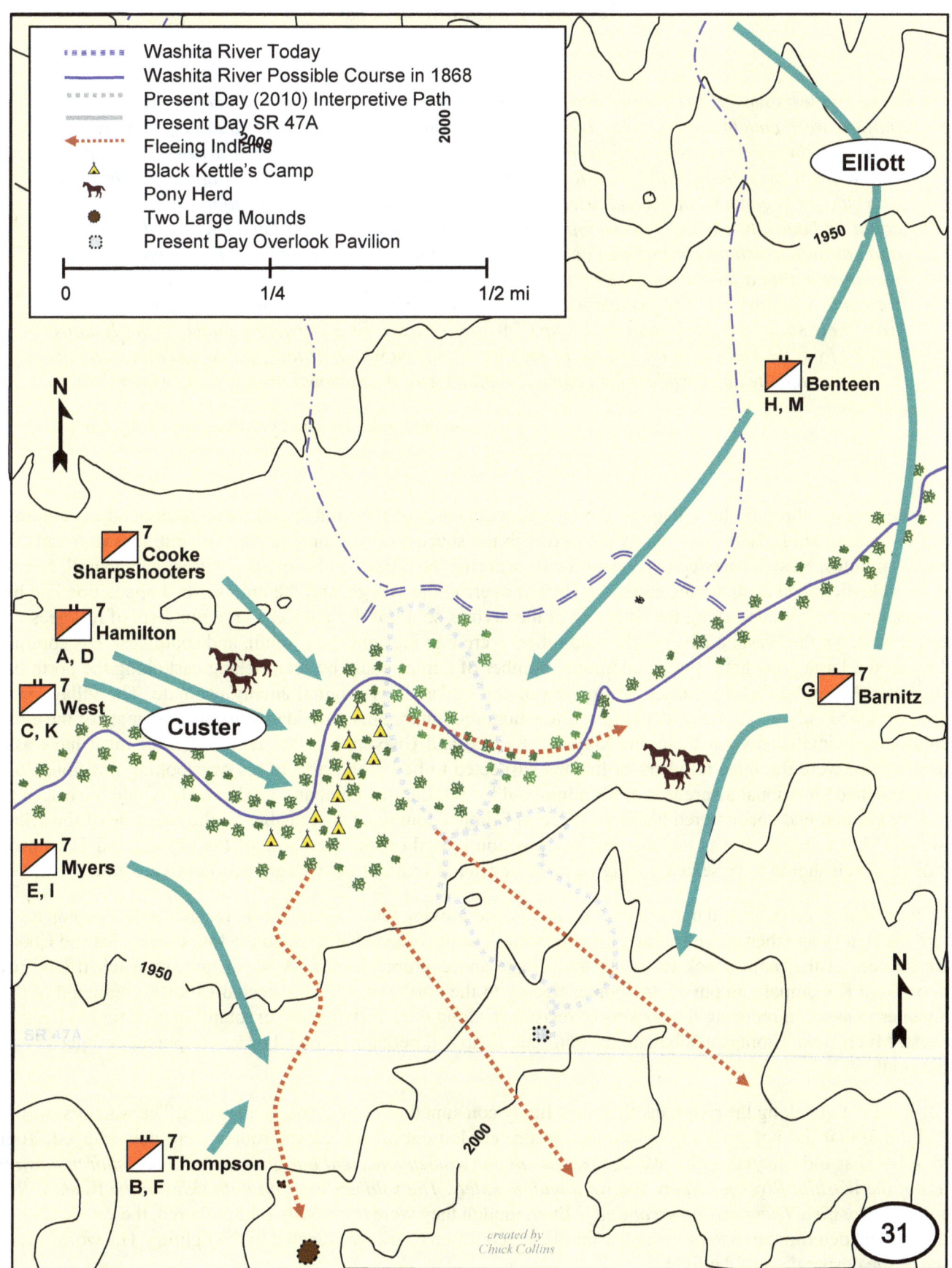

32. Custer's Command Post

"The bugles sounded the charge and the entire command dashed rapidly into the village. The Indians were caught napping; but realizing at once the dangers of their situation, they quickly overcame their first surprise and in an instant seized their rifles, bows, and arrows, and sprang behind the nearest trees, while some leaped into the stream, nearly waist deep, and using the bank as a rifle-pit began a vigorous and determined defense. Mingled with the exultant cheers of my men could be heard the defiant war-whoop of warriors, who from the first fought with a desperation and courage which no race of men could surpass. Actual possession of the village and its lodges was ours within a few moments after the charge was made, but this was an empty victory unless we could vanquish the late occupants, who were then pouring in a rapid and well-directed fire from their stations behind trees and banks. At first onset, a considerable number of the Indians rushed from the vicinity of the village in the direction from which Elliott's party had attack. Some broke through the lines, while others came in contact with the mounted troopers and were killed or captured."[57]

— Lieutenant Colonel George Armstrong Custer

Custer passed through the village to the terrace wall south of the village and there positioned his command group on a small knoll. He was probably pleased with the success of his main attack. The initial assault had taken about 30 minutes. Next, he needed to concentrate on securing the objective. From his position on the knoll, he could look over the field and evaluate the situation. He had overrun the village, and the only serious opposition had been a few pockets of resistance along the river and in the ravines south of the village. Large numbers of refugees were fleeing east down the Washita River valley and others were moving southeast, south, and southwest. His command had secured a large pony herd, but an additional number of ponies could be seen fleeing east along the north bank of the river. More than likely, Custer also reviewed and updated his original enemy estimate. The village in the valley contained only 51 lodges with at most, a few hundred inhabitants. Sheridan's original estimate of the enemy strength approximated several thousand Arapaho, Kiowa, and Cheyenne in the region. Custer must have asked himself where were the large numbers of Indians suspected to be in the area? In his overlooking position, Custer also established situational awareness of his command by sighting the company guidons. He would have seen that not every column had encountered his same success. Elliott's command was visible on the east side of the village. However, Myers' battalion was late moving into position to seal off the west side of the village, and Thompson's battalion, which should have seized the high terrace of ground south of the village, was not in position.

Custer almost certainly did not remain long on his overlooking knoll. He probably reached a decision on how to secure his victory and then moved among his companies issuing orders. He directed the four companies and Cooke's sharpshooters of the main attack to secure the village and captured ponies. West, in turn, dispatched Godfrey's platoon from K Company to pursue the ponies fleeing to the northeast. Custer directed Elliott's command of three companies to assist in reducing the pockets of resistance along the riverbank and in rounding up refugees fleeing to the east. Myers' and Thompson's battalions, both late to arrive, perhaps received orders to pursue refugees fleeing to the south.

It was the fight along the riverbank that most likely consumed most of Custer's attention. The warriors, women, and children that did not get away before the cavalry cordon cut off the escape routes were now trapped. Young Bird, a 14- year-old Cheyenne girl, stated, *"We ran all our women folks and our girls and all our children down the banks of the Washita River for safety, but we found no safety. The soldiers were on both sides of the Washita River shooting a crossfire. There was no escape..."*[58] Even though they were hopelessly outnumbered, the warriors fought with fanatical determination to protect their families. Scout Ben Clark participated in the fighting. His words vividly describe the desperation of the fight.

> *"I heard heavy firing down river in the direction of Cooke's sharpshooters. I rode rapidly in that direction and found a small party of warriors, with their women and children, at bay under the embankment... The Indians were firing at the sharpshooters on the other side of the river. The latter were unable to dislodge them, but poured a hail of bullets at them. The shots of the Indians gradually grew fewer until they ceased altogether. The warriors were dead. It was then that I saw a terrible example of a Cheyenne mother's despair. The squaw arose from behind the barricade, holding a baby at arm's length. In her other hand was a long knife. The sharpshooters mistook the child for a white captive and yelled, 'Kill that squaw. She's murdering a white child.' Before a gun could be fired the mother, with one stroke of the knife, disemboweled the child, [and] drove the knife to the hilt in her own breast and was dead."[59]*

In many cases, the soldiers attempted to spare the noncombatants. Benteen encountered a young Indian boy attempting to escape through the lines. The boy boldly charged the captain banishing a pistol. Benteen not wanting to harm the child tried to encourage the boy to surrender. Three times the lad fired at Benteen. Each time the captain tried unsuccessfully to get the *"dusky little chieftain"*[60] to put down the gun. Eventually, the boy got so close that Benteen recognized that the boy's next shot would probably strike home. When the young warrior leveled the pistol for the fourth shot, Benteen reluctantly shot down the boy.[61] Captain George Yates also tried to demonstrate compassion during the fighting along the riverbank. At one point, he was attracted by something glittering in the underbrush. As he approached the brush, he was fired upon. He and his men backed away from the brush then approached the hiding place from a different direction. Upon approaching the brush again he found an Indian woman standing in the stream, one leg broken, and holding a baby close to her. He stated that the *"malignant hate in her eyes was something a little worse than any venomous expression he had ever seen."*[62] The woman despite her broken leg fought fiercely and resisted all attempts at capture. Eventually the soldiers subdued her and turned her over to the surgeon to care for her broken leg, but it was not before, in one last act of defiance, she threw her pistol into the river rather than let it fall into her captor's hands.

While Custer focused on the fighting at the river, he lost control of other dispersed elements of his command. Some of his officers were caught up in leading squad level units instead of commanding their companies and battalions. Barnitz, Myers, and Elliott are the most prominent examples. In the attack, Barnitz spotted a group of refugees moving into the hills south of the village. About 0700, he detailed a sergeant and 10 soldiers to pursue the group. He then decided to follow the squad to determine the location of Thompson's absent battalion. In itself, a reasonable action, but the decision to leave his company and travel alone during the securing of the objective was questionable. Somewhere in the hills south of the current battlefield pavilion area, he traded fire with an Indian and received a severe gunshot wound. All alone and recognizing the severity of the wound, he attempted to return to the village, but his pain quickly forced him to dismount and take cover among some boulders. Other Indians soon appeared and would probably have killed the wounded captain had it not been for the timely arrival of Thompson's tardy battalion about 0800. Custer also failed to maintain positive control of Myers' battalion. The captain's mission was to attack along the south bank of the Washita River and prevent the Indians from escaping to the west. Having misjudged the distance to the village in the dark, Myers missed the initial assault on the village and, instead, veered to the south to pursue fleeing refugees. In his pursuit, he allowed his men to shoot down several of the fugitives instead of herding them back to the village. His failure to ensure discipline in his command necessitated that Custer take actions to regain control of the battalion.

Custer's most damaging failure in maintaining effective command and control of his regiment involves the actions of Elliott. Elliott had successfully led his command through the Red Hills north of the village in a difficult night march and then positioned his companies on the east side of the village in accordance with Custer's orders. Soon after the opening of the fight, Elliott positioned himself on a small hill just east of Custer Knoll. As it had been for Custer, it was an excellent position for overlooking and supervising the operations of his three companies on the east side of the village. Then around 0800, the major observed a group of refugees fleeing along the high ground toward present-day Cheyenne, Oklahoma. It was at this point that the major failed to act as the senior officer commanding a cavalry battalion. His rank and position called upon him to direct and coordinate the fight on the east side of the village and to organize the pursuit of the fleeing Indians. Instead, he abandoned his command responsibilities and personally led a poorly organized and uncoordinated pursuit. Along with his orderlies and regimental Sergeant Major Walter Kennedy, he rode down to Benteen's battalion and asked for volunteers. The makeup of Elliott's ad-hoc force (HQ staff 2; E Co. 3; H Co. 4; I Co. 2; and M Co. 7), which included soldiers from both Myers' and Benteen's battalions, shows that many of the battalion and company commanders had lost control of their units, an overall command failure for which the responsibility belongs to Custer. Elliott's poor decision and Custer's failure to restrain the rash major had dire consequences for the 18-man detachment. Elliott prophesied his own fate as he moved out when he called over to the commander of Company M, Lieutenant Owen Hale, *"Here goes for a brevet or a coffin."*[63] Elliott's detachment departed the village area and moved up onto the high ground south of the village then turned east in reckless pursuit of the fugitives.

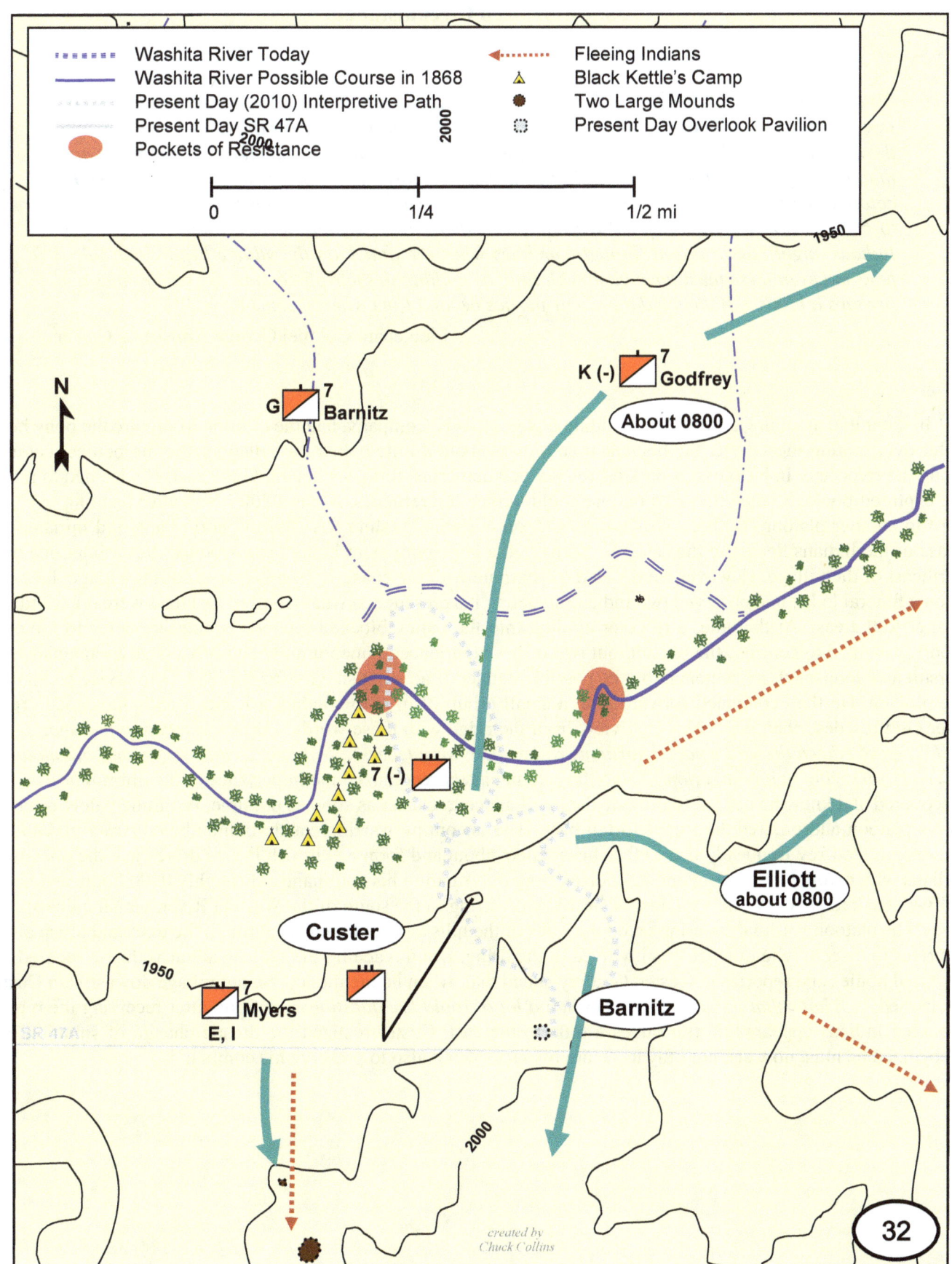

33. Unforeseen Circumstances

"It was perhaps 10 o'clock in the forenoon and the fight was still raging when to our surprise we saw a small party of Indians collected on a knoll a little over a mile below the village... Examining them through my field glass, I could plainly perceive that they were all mounted warriors; not only that, but they were armed and caparisoned in full war costume... , nearly all wearing the bright-colored war-bonnets and floating their lance pennants. Constant accessions to their numbers were to be seen arriving from beyond the hill which they stood. All this seemed inexplicable. A few Indians might have escaped through our lines when the attack on the village began, but only a few, and even these must have gone with little or nothing in their possession save their rifles and perhaps a blanket. Who could these new parties be, and from whence came they?"[64]

— Lieutenant Colonel George Armstrong Custer

In the initial assault, Godfrey, commanding a platoon of K Company, had the mission to capture the pony herd. After overrunning the village, the lieutenant continued about a mile below the village gathering ponies scattered along the river line. In his movement, Godfrey noticed numerous refugees fleeing to the east. He decided to return the captured ponies to the village so that he could pursue the refugees. About 0800 hours after handing over the herd to another platoon, Godfrey crossed his platoon over the Washita River to the north bank and initiated his chase of the Indians fleeing to the east. He discovered a large pony herd hidden in a wooded draw about one mile northeast of the village. However, he decided to continue with the chase. Two miles south of the village, he came upon a funeral lodge and observed two Indians signaling his presence to what Godfrey assumed were other Indians further to the east. At the time, a ridge protruding into the valley blocked his view along the valley to the east. Godfrey wanted to continue the pursuit, but two of his experienced noncommissioned officers advised against the pursuit and counseled the lieutenant on the possible danger of an ambush. Godfrey heeded their advice and halted the platoon. He then continued forward with a small group of men to conduct a leader's reconnaissance. Years later Godfrey described the unexpected view from the ridge with these words: *"I was amazed to find that as far as I could see down the well wooded, tortuous valley there were tepees... Not only could I see tepees, but mounted warriors scurrying in our direction."*[65] Godfrey immediately recognized the importance of the information he had discovered and knew he needed to provide the intelligence to Custer as soon as possible. He immediately returned to his platoon and ordered the troops to fall back. The oncoming warriors vastly outnumbered Army platoon. In the retreat, Godfrey frequently had to face his soldiers about and form a skirmish line to drive back the oncoming Indians with carbine fire, to prevent the Indians from overrunning his command. At roughly 0900 hours and about halfway back to Black Kettle's village, he heard heavy firing to the south of the Washita River, which quickly died away. His platoon was maneuvering up on the sides of the hills and could not see through the trees and brush along the river to discern who or what was involved in the firing. Upon reaching the village, about 1000, he secured the captured ponies and reported to Custer. Godfrey stated that, when he mentioned the big village downstream Custer exclaimed, *"'What's that?' - and put me through a lot of rapid fire questions."*[66] Soon after receiving the report, mounted Indians appeared on the ridges a mile to the east. Custer realized the drastic change of situation and recognized he must now act, not only to secure his victory, but also to preserve his command.

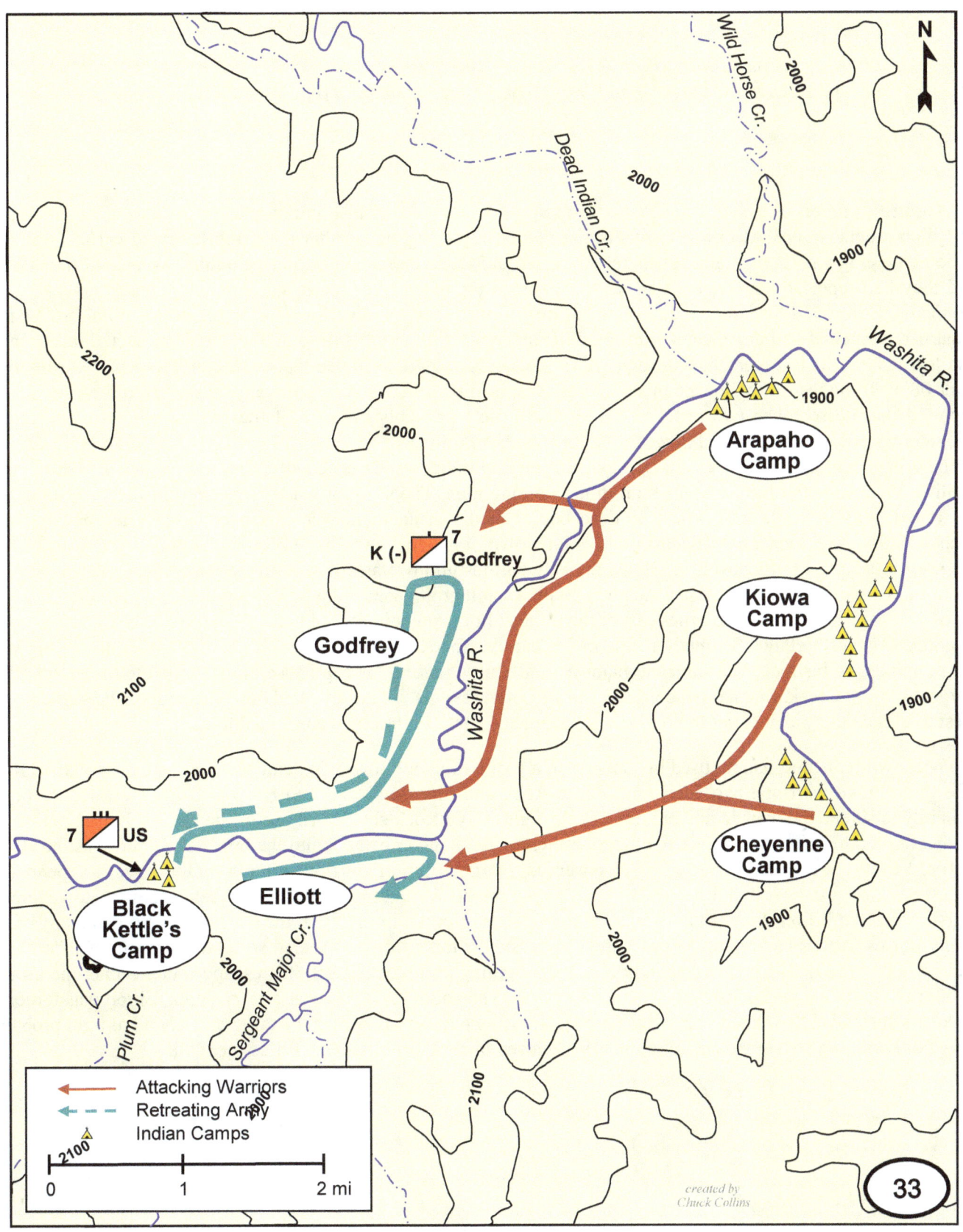

34. A Brevet or a Coffin

"The fight did not last longer than it would take a man to smoke a pipe four times."[67]

— Roman Nose Thunder

Godfrey's report of heavy firing to the south of the Washita River also initiated inquiries into the whereabouts of Elliott's detachment. At first, Custer dismissed Godfrey's suggestion that the firing he heard earlier might be Elliott engaging with the Indians downstream. Custer had several companies fighting on the east side of the village, and they had reported nothing unusual. Custer decided the mystery of the missing major required investigation. Ironically, Elliott and his men were more than likely already dead by the time Custer began the initial probes into what had happened to them. Custer confirmed Elliott was not among the dead and wounded collected in the camp and learned he was last seen chasing fugitives to the east. Custer determined that the major had departed sometime after 0800. In hopes of finding the missing men, Custer dispatched Myers' company to search to the east. Myers reported that he searched two miles to the east, but most probably because of the growing threat of an Indian counterattack, did not go beyond Sergeant Major Creek. Additionally, sometime after 1200, in an aggressive defense of the village perimeter, Benteen charged the surrounding Indians and pushed all the way to Sergeant Major Creek. Neither Myers nor Benteen saw any sign of the missing men. The story of what happened to Elliott would not be put together until weeks later when the dead bodies of the detachment were discover in early December 1868. Although the exact location of his last stand is unknown, it is believed to have been in the area just to the north of the present-day town of Cheyenne, Oklahoma.[68] Indian testimony states that Elliott's detachment pursued several groups of runaways to the east. They caught up with a small group consisting of seven women and children guarded by two teenage boys about two miles east of the village. In the pursuit, the soldiers killed the two boys and captured the others. Elliott detailed Kennedy to escort the captives back to the village and then continued the chase with the remainder of his men. The sergeant major had difficulty herding his captives along and, just to the west side of Sergeant Major Creek, four Arapaho warriors from Little Raven's village attacked him. Kennedy made a dash to the west to escape the warriors but to no avail; the Arapahos chased him down and killed him.

Meanwhile, Elliott had focused his pursuit on a group of about 20 women and children guarded by three men. The three brave warriors, two Cheyenne: Little Rock and She Wolf, and one Kiowa: Trails the Enemy, fought valiantly to screen the women and children. In the fight, Little Rock shot down one of the cavalry horses before the soldiers killed him. The remaining two warriors herded the noncombatants into the brush along the Washita River. Before Elliott could overrun the group, he observed a large group of warriors coming up the river. It appears that Elliott attempted to retreat and probably hoped to use the banks and brush along the creek as cover. However, the warriors pushed Elliott away from the creek onto the open ground. In the fight, the warriors shot down many of the Army horses further hampering Elliott's attempt to flee. Elliott's fate was sealed when the Arapaho warriors who had earlier killed Kennedy now moved toward the fighting and blocked Elliott's escape route. Sometime around 0900 (the same time that Godfrey heard the heavy firing) and about 200 yards east of the creek, Elliott was forced to make a last stand. The soldiers formed a loose circle with no cover other than the tall grass. The final fight probably lasted only minutes when the encircling warriors closed in on the soldiers and killed them all.

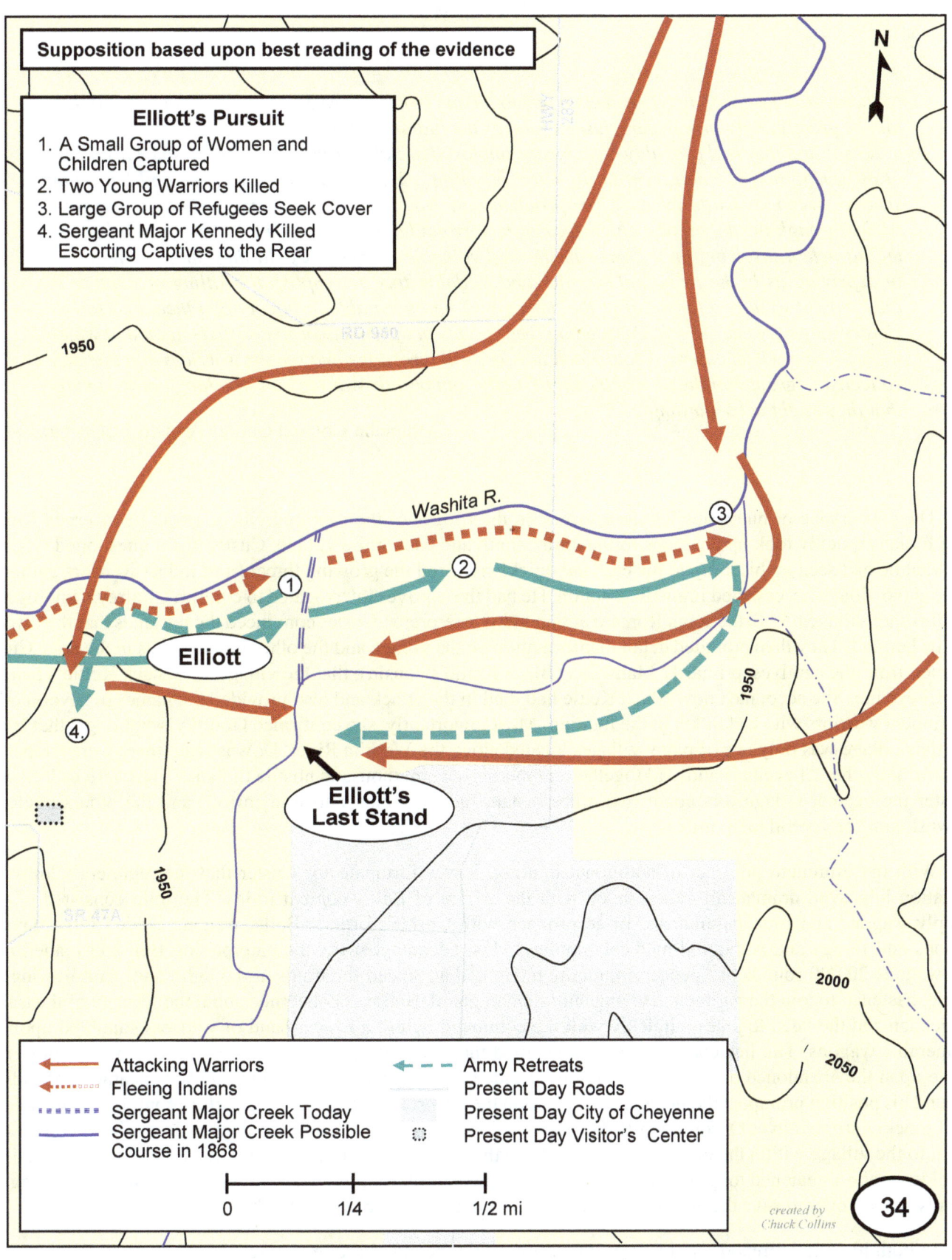

35. Total War

"What was to be done? For I needed no one to tell me that we were certain to be attacked and that, too, by greatly superior numbers, just as soon as the Indians below could make their arrangements to do so: and they had probably been busily employed at these arrangements ever since the sound of our firing had reached them in the early morning... We had achieved a great and important success over the hostile tribes... The problem now was how to retain our advantage and steer safely through the difficulties which seemed to surround our position. The Indians had suffered a telling defeat involving great losses in life and valuable property. Could they succeed, however, in depriving us of the train and supplies and in doing this accomplish the killing or capture of the escort it would go far to offset the damage we had been able to inflict upon them and render victory an empty one. As I deliberated on these points in the endeavor to conclude upon that which would be our wisest course, I could look in nearly all directions and see the warriors at a distance collected in groups on the tops of the highest hills, apparently waiting and watching our next move that they might act accordingly."[69]

— Lieutenant Colonel George Armstrong Custer

The appearance of numerous Indian warriors on the fringes of the captured village greatly concerned Custer. The Indians quickly took up positions to the north, south and east of the village. Custer again questioned Godfrey on what he had seen on his foray to the east and quickly realized the growing threat from Indian warriors gathering around the village necessitated immediate action. He had the captives interrogated to confirm Godfrey's intelligence on the other villages. With the scout Romero acting as his interpreter, Custer convinced the hostages that they would not be harmed. They then provided detailed information on the village and the other Indian bands in the area. Custer learned from the captives, primarily Mahwissa (Black Kettle's cousin), that the village was Black Kettle's band of the Cheyenne. She accounted how Black Kettle had died in the attack and also provided the names of several other prominent warriors who had fallen in the fighting. Most importantly, she confirmed Godfrey's sightings; that Black Kettle's village was only one of many villages located along the Washita River. Downstream there were Arapahoe, Kiowa, and other Cheyenne bands, all together numbering several thousand hostile Indians.. The captives informed Custer the nearest village was about two miles distant (actually closer to four miles), and the others stretched downstream for several more miles.

With the imminent prospect of additional fighting, it was fortunate for Custer that the regiment's logistical situation improved dramatically about noon with the arrival of Bell's combat trains. The train consisted of two supply wagons and four ambulances. In accordance with Custer's orders, Bell's wagons carried three days of rations and forage and additional medical supplies. Most advantageously, the enterprising Bell had loaded onto his wagons 20,000 rounds of Spencer ammunition. He had advanced the trains at daylight, and upon hearing the firing, hastened to join the regiment. Having only a small guard, Bell was concerned about the security of the trains; he recognized the need to join up quickly with the command before a roving band of warriors stumbled upon his vulnerable wagons. The lieutenant was also concerned that the regiment may need the reserve ammunition. Bell came upon the abandoned overcoats and initially decided to load them on the wagons. The appearance of Indians around his position prompted the lieutenant to abandon the undertaking and move out before completing the upload. Bell quickly crossed over Observation Ridge and raced into camp sometime before noon. In the headlong rush to get into the village within the protecting screen of cavalry companies, the grease on one of the wagon wheel axles smoldered and threatened to ignite into flames. The soldiers in the camp quickly improvised a solution tipping the supply wagon over to save the ammunition and then extinguishing the fire with snow.

In both his official report and other writings about this second phase of the fight at the Washita River, Custer implied that the regiment faced an overwhelming threat and that the situation was extremely desperate. The reality of the situation may not have been as dire as it appeared at first glance. The village was secured, and the surrounding terrain was defensible. The regiment had sustained relatively light casualties with two killed, 18 missing, and 15 wounded, only a few of which were serious. The immediate logistical situation was good because of the arrival of Bell's combat trains. Although numerous, the surrounding warriors probably did not significantly outnumber the regiment by much if at all. They seemed reluctant to threaten the defensive perimeter around the village in an aggressive manner. Therefore, Custer decided to deploy his regiment to defend the village and arranged to burn the village with all its accompanying personal property and to destroy the pony herd.

The destruction of the village and the large pony herd was a time consuming project that took several hours to complete. During that time, there was significant skirmishing around the village between the defending soldiers and the attacking Indians.. The warriors initially massed on the hills north and northeast of the village. They tested the strength of the defensive perimeter by looking for weaknesses in the soldiers' deployment. Before long, they had surrounded the entire village. Custer conducted an aggressive defense and initially directed Captain Thomas Weir's and West's battalions to conduct a local counterattack to push back the threat to the north (Weir had taken command of Hamilton's battalion). The primary Indian threat then moved to the east side of the village. At that point, Benteen took command of Myers' battalion (Myers was suffering from snow blindness), and he counterattacked against the threat on the east side. Ironically, Benteen's attack pushed to within a mile of where Elliott was later found but, unfortunately, he saw no sign of the missing detachment. The Indians then switched to long-range harassing fire from the north. Custer stopped the fire by placing the captured Indian women and children along the north side of the village in the line of Indian fire. This questionable and unacceptable tactic of using the women and children as human shields effectively ended most of the Indian fire. However, some of the snipers did shift to the west and south of the village.

Custer assigned the task of destroying the village to West, and, before long, West's men were piling the camp equipage into large bonfires. Godfrey recalled years later, *"As the fires made headway, all articles of personal property – buffalo robes, blankets, food, rifles, pistols, bows and arrows, lead and camps, bullet-molds etc. – were thrown in the fires and destroyed."* [70] They completed the burning of the village by about 1400. Custer recognized that destroying the village and denying the Cheyenne their ponies rendered the Indians destitute; the total war strategy would inevitably force the Cheyenne to accept the will of the government and submit to life on the reservation. Meanwhile, the issue of the pony herd was a demanding problem for Custer; he lacked the resources to drive the captured ponies successfully back to Camp Supply. He acknowledged that the ponies had to be destroyed. The dilemma was how to accomplish the task. Godfrey had accounted for two herds totaling about 400 ponies. Others, including the scouts, had brought in more than 400. An estimated total of 875 ponies and mules were turned over to West. His men corralled the animals along the terrace wall southeast of the village. The command selected out about 225 animals for use by the unit: Custer allowed each officer to select two each, the scouts received several ponies each, and troopers with unserviceable mounts were allowed to select a replacement. Lieutenant Bell also replaced many of the worn out mules hauling the supply and ambulance wagons.

Custer instructed West to kill the remaining ponies. The ever-active Godfrey participated in the destruction of the pony herd and later recalled, *"We tried to rope them and cut their throats, but the ponies were frantic at the approach of a white man and fought viciously."* [71] The process of killing the ponies proved to be very time consuming, and Custer grew impatient. The arrival of Bell's combat trains and the fortuitous supply of 20,000 .50-caliber rounds of Spencer ammunition provided Custer the option to shoot the ponies. West positioned one company above the ponies along the south terrace wall and then positioned another company and the regimental sharpshooters in a ring around the ponies. The two units on the low ground fired volley after volley into the corralled animals. Even so, the killing of 800 ponies took time and the executioners did not complete their task until about 1600. The destruction of the pony herd enraged the warriors surrounding the Army's defensive perimeter. They appeared to be preparing for an attack and stepped-up their harassing fire against the soldiers. However, whether it was the danger of harming the Indian women and children captives in the village or the lack of sufficient combat power to challenge the defending cavalry companies, they made no serious effort to stop the slaughter.

"Now commences the slaughter of the ponies. Volley on volley is poured into them by too hasty men, and they, limping, get away only to meet death from a surer hand. The work progresses! The plunder having been culled over, is hastily piled; the wigwams are pulled down and thrown on it, and soon the whole is one blazing mass. Occasionally a startling report is heard and a steam-like volume of smoke ascends as the fire reaches a powder bag, and thus the glorious deeds of valor done in the morning are celebrated by the flaming bonfire of the afternoon." [72]

— Captain Frederick Benteen

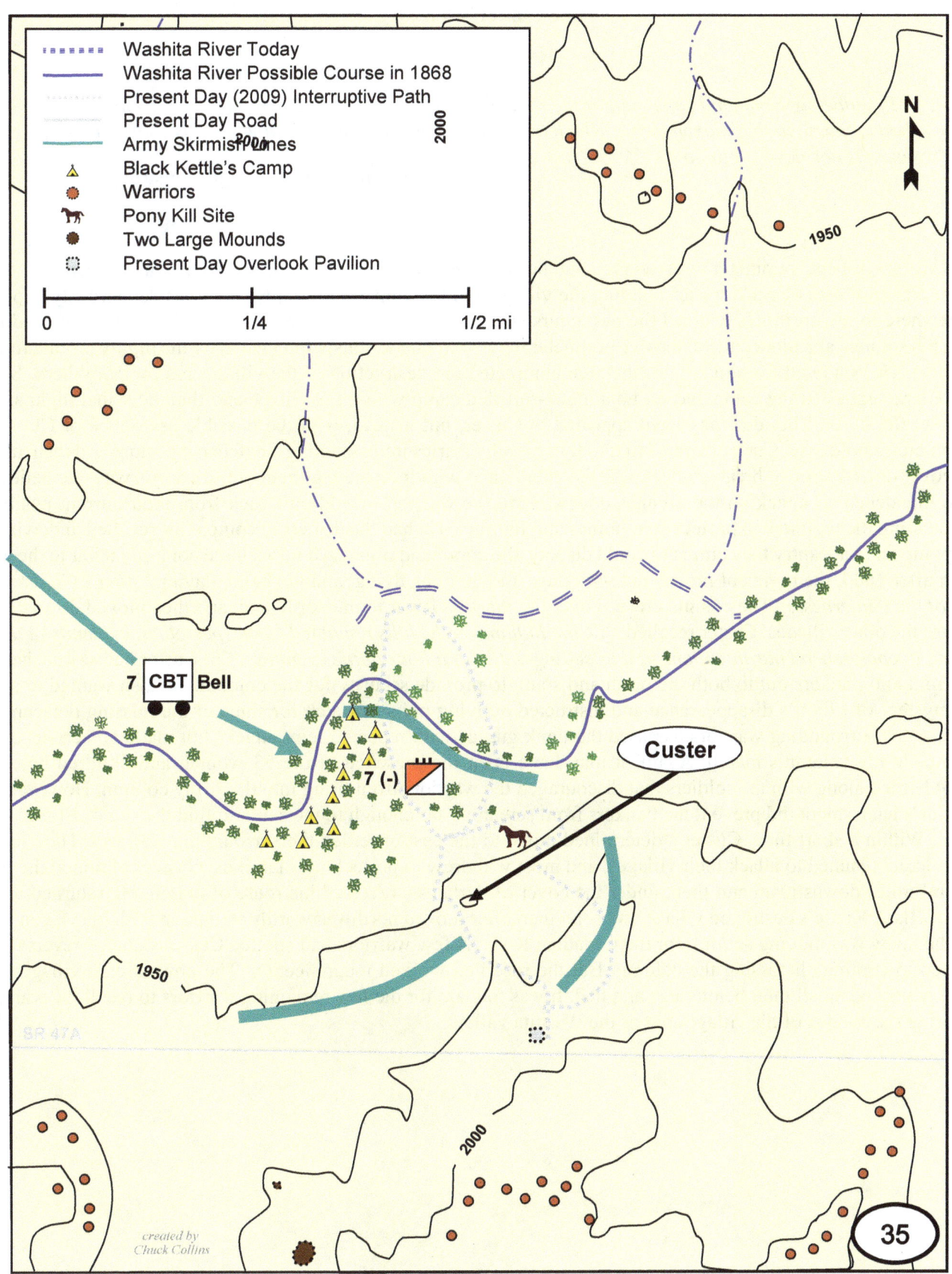

36. Custer's Victory

"To guide my command safely out of the difficulties which seemed just then to beset them I again had recourse to that maxim in war which teaches a commander to do that which his enemy neither expects nor desires him to do."[73]

— Lieutenant Colonel George Armstrong Custer

Custer's village perimeter was secure, but he also recognized his overall situation was vulnerable; there were large numbers of warriors surrounding the village and his vulnerable supply train was dangerously exposed somewhere to the north. He decided the best course of action was to withdraw. However, he also recognized that once his soldiers abandoned the defensive perimeter they would be seriously threatened by the highly mobile Indian warriors. He pondered the situation as the men completed the destruction of the village and the pony herd. Scout Ben Clark suggested the command set up a mock-fortified camp within the village and then later that night sneak away to the north. The idea may have appealed to Custer, but instead, with the possible assistance of Clark, he formulated a bold ruse. Custer planned first to fool his adversaries into assuming a defensive posture and then, under the cover of darkness, to break contact with the enemy and withdraw the regiment out of harm's way. He believed, if he threatened an attack on the villages downstream, the warriors would pull back from their current positions surrounding the regiment to protect their homes and families. He had the dispersed companies recalled and, with all the pomp and pageantry the command could display, the command organized into a large column facing to the east. Soon after 1600, the regiment moved out with flags and guidons flying, and the band playing *"Ain't I Glad to Get Out of the Wilderness."* The column crossed over the Washita River to the north bank and then moved downstream toward the other villages. Custer recalled, *"… the Indians on the hills remained silent spectators, evidently at a loss at first to comprehend our intentions in thus setting out at that hour of the evening..."*[74] Custer had skirmishers to the front and flankers out to both the north and south to provide security for the column. He also wanted to solve the mystery of Elliott's disappearance and instructed outlying units to watch for signs of the missing detachment. At first, the surrounding warriors harassed the flank guards with repeated feint attacks but made no serious effort to impede the column's march. Again, it may have been the presence of the 53 women and children hostages being herded along with the soldiers that discouraged the warriors from firing into the Army column. However, the warrior's harassment did prevent the flankers from screening far enough to the south to find the site of Elliott's last stand. Within a short time, Custer's determined move to the east unsettled the surrounding warriors. They feared the soldiers planned to attack their villages, and most withdrew to protect their families. Custer continued the feint several miles downstream and then, under the cover of darkness, reversed his route of march. He returned to the site of Black Kettle's destroyed village and soon thereafter moved northwestwardly to link up with his wagon train that he knew was moving south from the Canadian River. A few warriors had spotted Custer's course reversal and wanted to continue harassing the column. But the ruse had worked magnificently. The downstream villages had quickly packed up all their belongings and fled. It was too late for the few remaining warriors to recall the warriors covering the exodus of the villages out of the Washita valley.

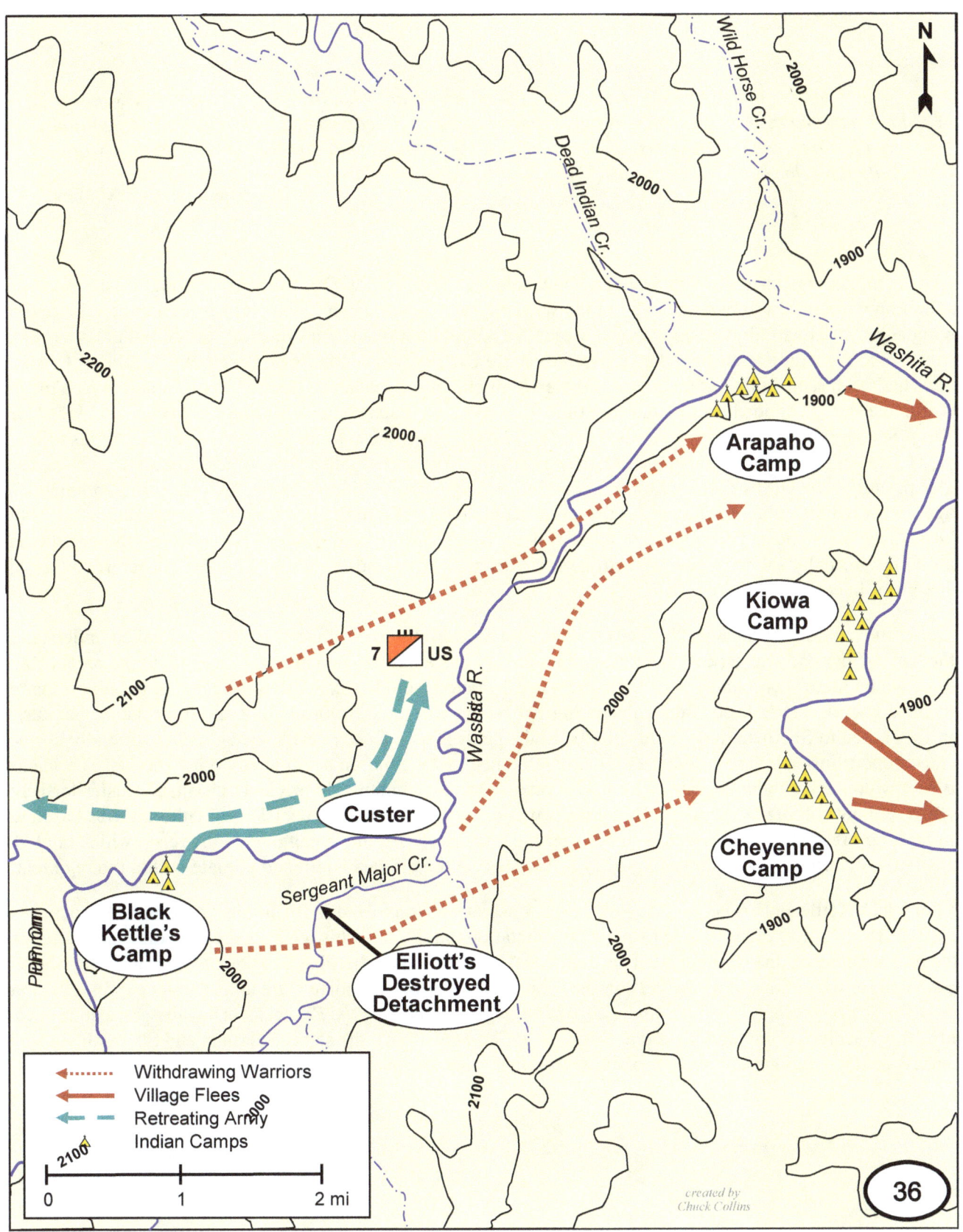

37. Retreat to Safety

"The column marched proudly in front of General Sheridan, who, as the officers rode by, saluting him, returned their formal courtesy by a graceful lifting of his cap and a pleased look of recognition from his eyes, which spoke his approbation in a language far more powerful than studied words could have done."[75]

— Lieutenant Edward Mathey

The command marched through the night and halted for a brief rest at 0200 the next morning. Custer sent West's battalion on without rest to find and support the wagon train. At sunrise on 28 November, Custer had the regiment moving again and finally linked up with the wagon train about 1000. After a brief rest, the command continued to the north, and sometime after noon they crossed over the Canadian River and made camp on Hackberry Creek. No Indians had been seen, and Custer allowed the men to pitch tents, unsaddle their tired mounts, and cook a meal. At the camp, Custer questioned his officers about the fight and then dispatched California Joe Milner and Jack Corbin to Camp Supply with Custer's report of the fight. On 29 November, the column marched another 22 miles following Boggy Creek to the confluence with Wolf Creek and camped about 10 miles short of Camp Supply. The next day, Custer proudly arrayed his column and marched into Camp Supply with Sheridan reviewing the command. The Osage scouts led the column followed by the white scouts with the Indian prisoners. The regimental band, playing *"Gary Owen"* came next. The balance of the regiment, with Cooke's sharpshooters in the lead, followed the band. The officers formally saluted Sheridan with their sabers as they passed in review. The general returned the salute with a lift of his cap.

After the parade, Sheridan and his staff interviewed each of the 7th's officers to obtain a detailed understanding of the battle. Sheridan was especially interested in any evidence that implicated the Cheyenne in the recent Kansas raids of which there was actually very little direct confirmation from Black Kettle's village. One troublesome topic must have been Custer's false claim of rescuing two white children. Unfortunately, the information had already been forwarded to Sherman and would soon be in the newspapers. Custer and Sheridan never officially corrected the false report; instead, they quietly never made reference to the children again in any other reports. Sheridan was also deeply concerned with the fate of Major Elliott and his detachment. He privately chastised Custer for leaving the field without solving the mystery. However, it was clear to most that the decision to withdraw was based upon sound military reasoning. Nevertheless, the matter quickly developed into a nagging controversy, which tainted the perceptions of Custer's leadership and greatly contributed to the divided command climate within the regiment.

For Black Kettle and his people, the fight at the Washita was tragic and sadly unfair.[76] As a man of peace, he had influenced the majority of his people to avoid confrontation, but a few of his rebellious young men had participated in the recent raids and, inadvertently, led the Army back to the village. Sheridan's policy of holding all the Cheyenne responsible for the actions of a few had cost as Thomas Murphy of the Indian Bureau of Affairs expressed, *"one of the best and truest friends the whites have ever had among the Indians of the Plains."*[77] The press soon compared the fight at the Washita to Chivington's brutal massacre at Sand Creek. All the same, Sherman and Sheridan vigorously defended Custer's actions and moved forward with their plans to continue the campaign.

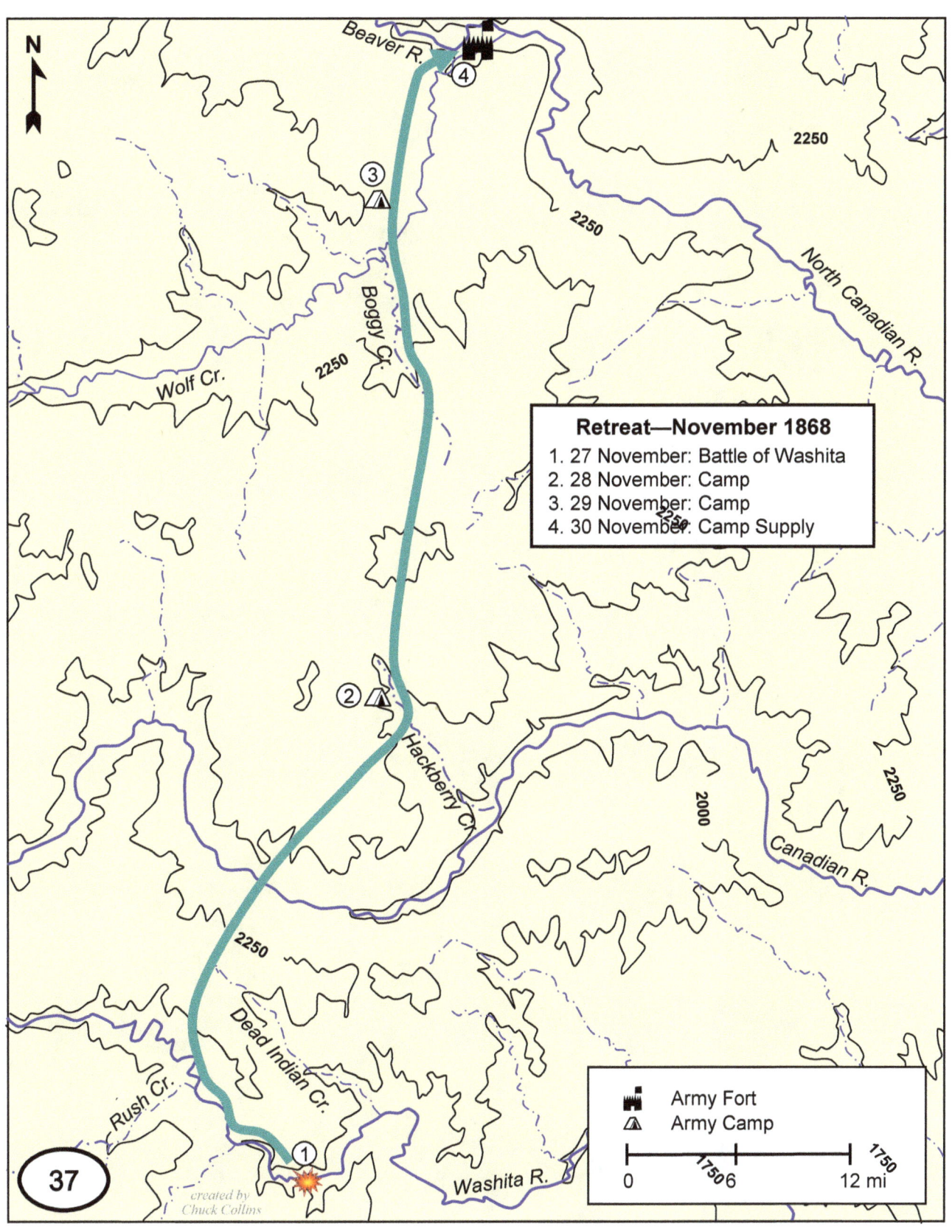

V. The Fight at Soldier Spring

38. Sheridan Continues the Campaign

"A few days were necessarily lost settling up and refitting the Kansas regiment after its rude experience in the Cimarron canyons. This through with, the expedition, supplied with 30 days' rations, moved out to the south on the 7th of December, under my personal command."[78]

– Major General Phillip H. Sheridan

Custer had his victory, but Sheridan's war against the Cheyenne continued. After demonstrating that winter campaigning on the Plains could be effective, Sheridan now believed, *"If we can get one or two more good blows there will (be) no more Indian trouble in my Department."*[79] He was anxious to follow up on Custer's success. However, the harsh conditions were tough on the Army's men and horses. The Kansas cavalry had lost most of their horses and now operated primarily as infantry, and Custer's soldiers needed rest and resupply. Sheridan allowed the 7th Cavalry only a few days rest then moved out on 7 December toward the Washita valley with the 1,500-man column (Custer's cavalry reinforced with the Kansas troops). On the second day of the march, a major blizzard swept down from the north, but still the command continued to push south. Sheridan reached the Washita valley on 10 December. The next day they found and buried the mutilated bodies of Elliott and his detachment. Sheridan also examined the sites of the other villages downriver from Black Kettle's village. They estimated the abandoned camps contained between 600 and 1,000 lodges. At one of the abandoned villages, they found the murdered bodies of kidnapped Clara Blinn and her 2-year-old son. Despite atrocious weather conditions, Sheridan still found an Indian trail and was able to resume the pursuit on 12 December. Ironically, the trail led Sheridan's column toward Fort Cobb. After the Washita fight, the majority of the Arapaho, Comanche, and Kiowa tribes viewed the winter campaign as a war solely against the Cheyenne. They had subsequently moved their villages to Fort Cobb asking Hazen for protection and rations. On 17 December, Sheridan happened upon a large Kiowa village which immediately surrendered. Sheridan accepted their surrender even though he strongly suspected they had participated in Custer's fight. Doubting the sincerity of the Kiowa people's expressed desire for peace, Sherman detained Chiefs Lone Wolf and Satanta as hostages. He then ordered their village to report to Fort Cobb. Over the next several days, the Kiowa failed to report to Fort Cobb, so Sheridan threatened to hang the hostages if their people did not obey. The threat had the desired effect, and finally, the majority of the Kiowa reported to the agency.

Nevertheless, many of the tribes continued to defy government orders bringing into play Sheridan's other columns whose role it was to hunt the holdouts down. Carr's Fort Lyon column had marched south on 2 December 1868 in the midst of a severe winter storm. Battling against terrain and weather, Carr's command did not arrive at the Canadian River until 28 December. He encountered no hostile Indians but probably helped drive the Indians into the area of Sheridan's third column under Evans. Evans' column departed Fort Bascom, New Mexico, on 18 November with six companies of the 3d Cavalry, one composite company from the 37th Infantry, and an artillery battery with four mountain howitzers, in all about 563 men. In early December, he established a base camp on the Canadian River near Monument Creek. On 15 December, he departed the Monument Creek Depot leaving behind a small security detachment, most of his wagons, and all his tents.[80] Two days later, about 18 miles west of the Antelope Hills, he discovered an Indian trail and followed it until he reached the North Fork of the Red River on 20 December.

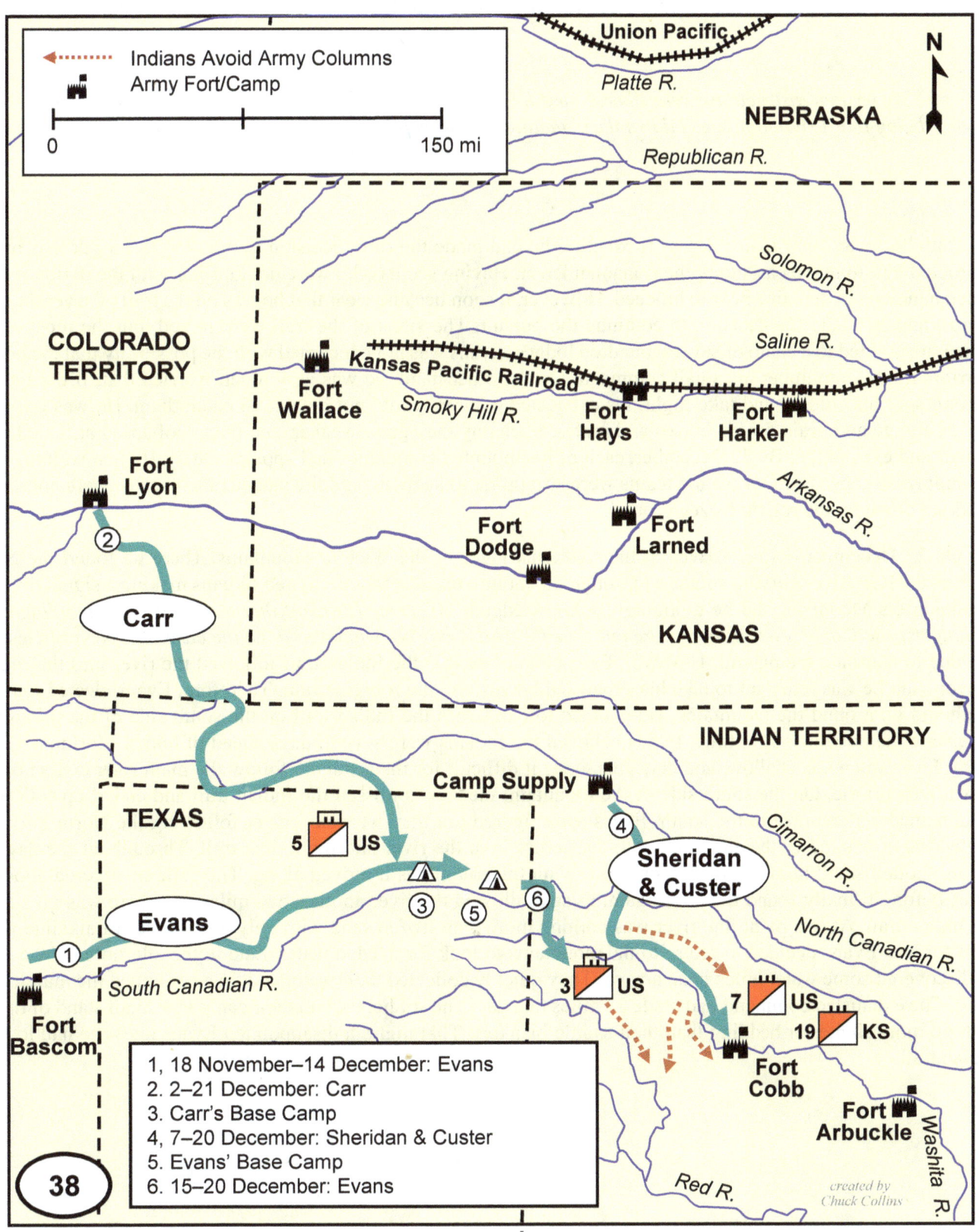

39. The North Fork of the Red River

"My written instructions were liberal, and left sufficient freedom of action, the general directions being that I should proceed down the Canadian as far as possible, and attack all Indians met."[81]
– Major Andrew Evans

Initially, Evans was undecided as to whether he had made the right decision to move to the south. His orders instructed him to move east along the Canadian River. Having scouts who were not familiar with the region was an added handicap in deciding how to proceed. However, it soon became clear that he was on the trail of several Indian camps, and he made the decision to continue the pursuit. The signs of the trail were mixed, but the most recent indicators pointed to a camp of several hundred lodges. Evans was not concerned with the possibility that the hostile warriors might outnumber his small command. On the other hand, he was very much worried that, if the Indians were to spot his column and take flight, his exhausted column would not be able to catch them. He was critically low on forage and grain for his horses and mules. Each day they grew weaker, and many collapsed and died from hunger and exhaustion. By 22 December, each of his mounted companies had approximately 10 men walking with the supply wagons. The four wagon teams were struggling to keep up, and the wagons themselves were constantly breaking down on the rough, frozen ground.

On 23 December, Evans arrived at the western fringes of the Wichita Mountains. There he found the North Fork of the Red River curving southeast through the mountains. His scouts spotted Indians making a signal fire near Headquarters Mountain, and he grudgingly acknowledged, *"it seemed evident that a surprise of any village was no longer practicable, even if there were one nearby, which was not supposed to be the case."*[82] Nevertheless, he decided to continue the pursuit. However, Evans could see that the Indian trail followed the river into the rugged canyon, and he was reluctant to take his exhausted horses into the rough terrain. Therefore, Evans elected to move south and go around the mountains. He planned to cut across the Indian trail on the south side of the mountains to resume the pursuit. At the time, Evans believed the Indians were several days ahead of him. Unfortunately, the North Fork was wide, shallow, and dry. This made it difficult for the scouts to follow the main river course on the vast frozen prairie. On the south side of the mountain, the scouts missed the Indian trail and ended up following an unnamed watercourse to the south. Evans soon figured out they were no longer following the North Fork and angled the command to the east hoping to cut across both the river and the Indian trail. Throughout the day, the scouts spotted small numbers of Indians shadowing the column as it moved along. The column covered about 12 miles before it finally found the river again. Evans followed the river another two miles, but there was no sign of the Indian trail. At this point, the river was nothing more than frozen sand with only a few holes of alkaline water unfit for use. Evans decided to return to the mountains to look for needed water. Late in the afternoon of the 24th, he discovered some water holes in an arroyo. They quickly collected their water and then continued the march until dark. The exhausted command had made 27 miles that day. The soldiers set up their camp in a small stand of timber with no more shelter or bedding than their saddle blankets. That night, a disappointed Evans knew he had lost the Indian trail.

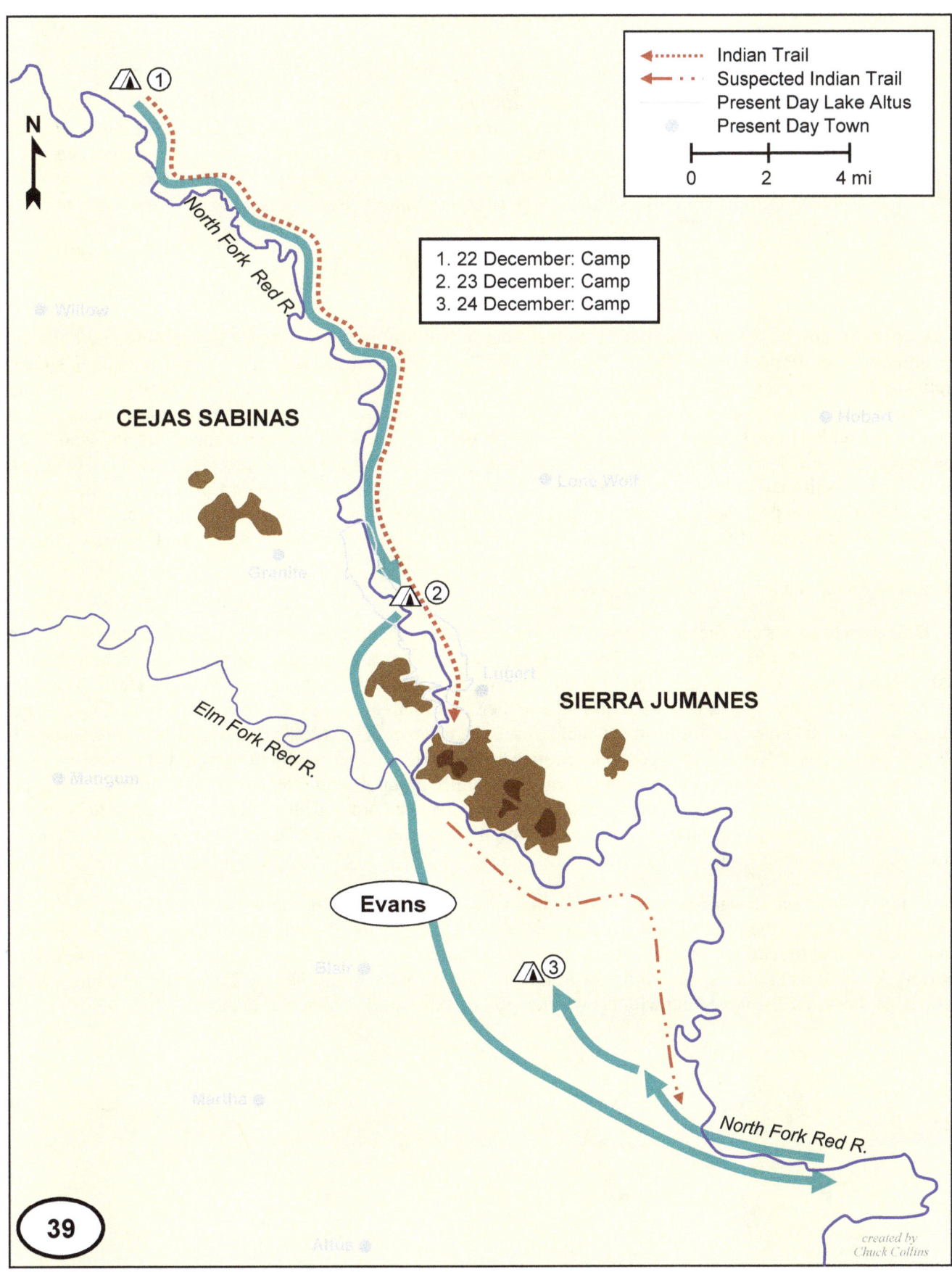

40. Christmas Morning Decision

"Determined no longer to neglect these individuals, who seemed to be watching us, I at once dispatched in pursuit of them Major Tarlton with his Company, which happened to be at the head of the column; and not supposing any force of the enemy near us, I proceeded up the stream with the remainder of the Command in search of a camp, my intention being, in view of the severity of the weather, the day being Christmas... to make a short march, resting upon the main trail, and to follow it all that night."[83]

– Major Andrew Evans

Christmas morning Evans resumed the hunt for the Indian trail in the midst of a biting wind and light snow. His situation was desperate; his soldiers were miserably cold, and their horses were dying. The column's meager supply of grain was exhausted, and there was no forage available on the frozen prairie. The cavalry companies now averaged about 30 men each with as many as 20 men per company now walking with the wagons having lost their horses. He decided to make camp early to reevaluate his options. Evans wanted to use the bluffs and woods along the river to provide shelter for his men. The determined major wanted to rest his command for the day and then resume the pursuit that night under the cover of darkness. As the column approached from the south, the scouts reported two Indians near the river. Evans ordered his lead company under Captain (Brevet Major) Elisha Tarlton to chase the Indians off. Evans continued with the remainder of the column to set up camp at the base of today's King Mountain. In camp, the soldiers removed the saddles from the horses, unpacked the mules, and turned out the animals to forage within the brush along the river.

Unknown to Evans and the unsuspecting Tarlton, there was a significant number of hostile Indians in the area. Near the east end of the mountains, hidden in a grove of trees, was a Comanche camp. Another five miles to the east, at the confluence of Elk Creek and the North Fork, was a Kiowa band led by Woman's Heart. The Kiowa had participated in the fight at Black Kettle's village then fled south after the battle of the Washita. The Comanche village of about 60 lodges was the band of Chief Horseback, a signer of the Medicine Lodge Treaty. Horseback, like the unfortunate Black Kettle, was a peace advocate who had tried unsuccessfully to prevent his band from raiding into Texas. It appears that he had moved his immediate family group to Fort Cobb to avoid hostilities. A war chief named Arrow Point was in charge at the village. The government had ordered all the Kiowa and Comanche to report to the Fort Cobb agency, and therefore, because Arrow Point's and Woman's Heart's people remained *"out,"* the Army classified them as hostile.

Arrow Point's scouts had spotted Evans' column on 23 December. His camp was well stocked with winter supplies and would have been difficult to move because of the weakened condition of his ponies. He, therefore, made the decision to remain concealed hoping the soldiers would pass on by. Evans' decision to circle back and the spotting of the Indian scouts shattered Arrow Point's plan to lie quiet. When he saw Tarlton's men coming toward the village, he hurriedly moved out with his warriors to buy time for the village to escape.

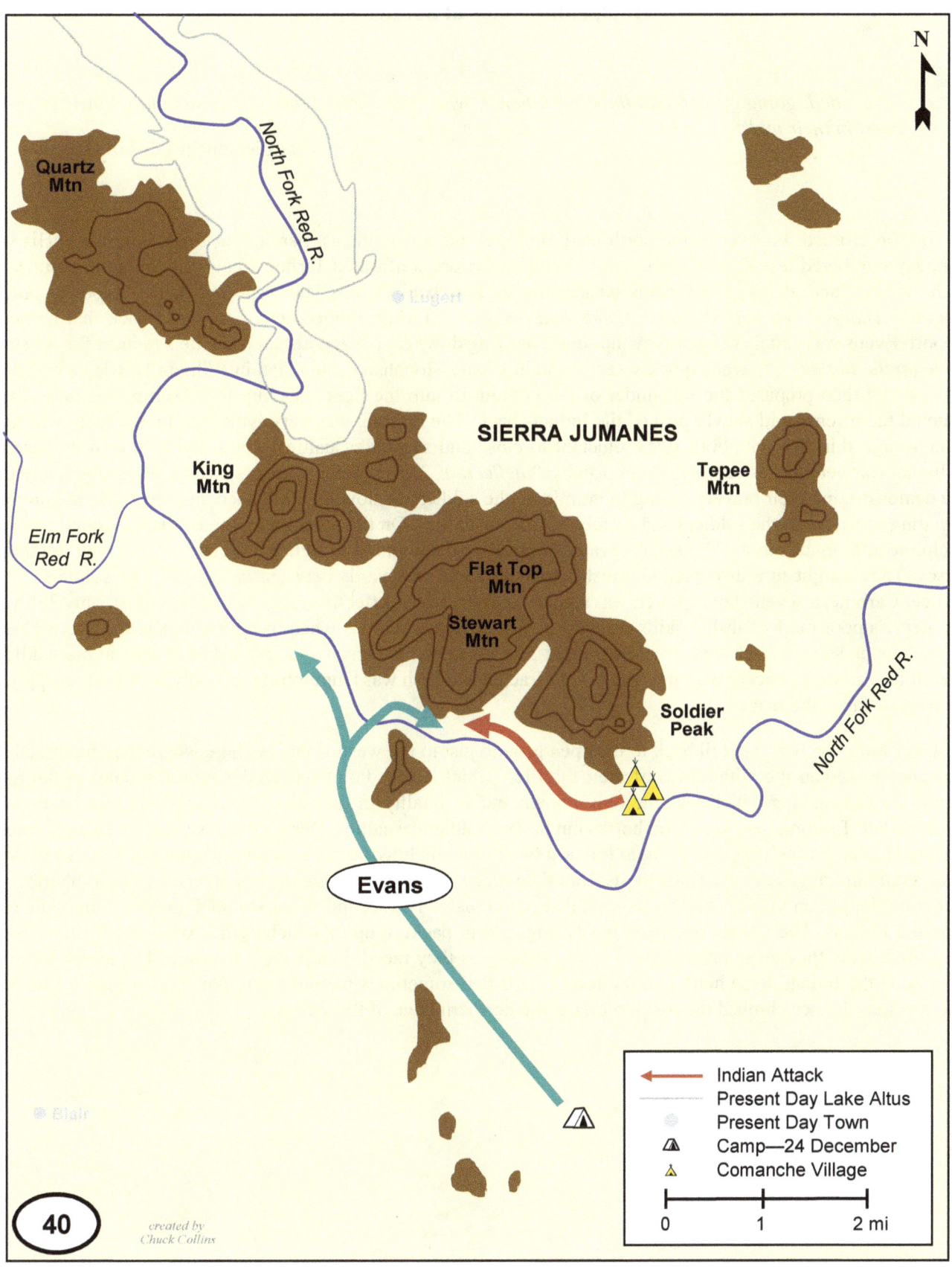

41. Opening Shots at Soldier Spring

"They fled, going off two and three on a horse, when two shells from a little mountain howitzer burst in their midst."[84]

– 1st Lieutenant Edward Hunter

Tarlton crossed the river to the north bank and then moved southeast paralleling the watercourse. His small company numbered less than 40 men. Arrow Point's warriors confronted Tarlton's company about two miles west of the village, and at first, the Indians pushed the soldiers back. Evans later reported that a *"superior party of Indians... charged him with the lance, rifles and pistols."*[85] Tarlton immediately sent word back that he needed support. Evans was caught off guard by the sound of firing downstream and his subordinate's request for assistance, *"to whip the Indians."*[86] Evans quickly sent Captain Deane Monahan's and Captain William Hawley's companies forward and then prepared the remainder of the column to join the fight. Leading three companies now, Tarlton resumed the offense and slowly pushed the Indians back. The fighting was very typical of most Indian war fights; a long-range skirmish with both sides reluctant to close and sustain casualties. These fights have been described by Indian war veterans as *"colorful"* but usually *"ineffectual."* The Indian warriors circled across the Army firing line demonstrating their bravery, trying to intimidate the soldiers to slow their advance, but always remaining wary of getting too close to the soldiers and thereby taking casualties. On the other hand, the soldiers' strength was their discipline and organization. The small cavalry companies dismounted to fight with every fourth man holding the horses. They fought in a dispersed skirmish line with about five yards between each man. The soldiers' 50 cal. Spencer Carbine, a seven-shot repeater, was a good weapon, but its effective range was, at the most, only 300 yards. The Army's poor marksmanship skills resulted in few enemy casualties when trying to engage the fleeting targets the Indians presented. Each trooper carried about 50 rounds on his person and another 50 rounds in his saddlebag. Therefore, Tarlton's concern with fighting in a protracted skirmish was ammunition; his only source of resupply was the wagons far to the rear.

Over time, the warriors fell back to the open ground just to the west of their village where they increased their resistance to screen the withdrawal of their families. Chief Arrow Point received a mortal wound in the mouth during the skirmishing which was the only known Indian fatality in the fight. The Comanche did have several ponies killed. Tarlton also lost several horses but had no soldier casualties. During this phase of the fight, Lieutenant Edward Hunter, Evans' adjutant, brought forward two mountain howitzers. He positioned the small guns just within their maximum range at under 1,000 yards from the village. Once in position, the howitzers fired two spherical case shots into the Indian village. The first shot failed to detonate. The second shot exploded, having a dramatic effect upon the Indians. The village had been busily engaged in packing up their belongings when the artillery rounds were fired. Now they abandoned most of their property as they raced, in a panic, to escape. The artillery fire also stampeded the Indian horse herd, and the last Indians fled sometimes mounted three or four to each horse. Many who lost their horses climbed the rocky bluffs at the northern edge of the village.

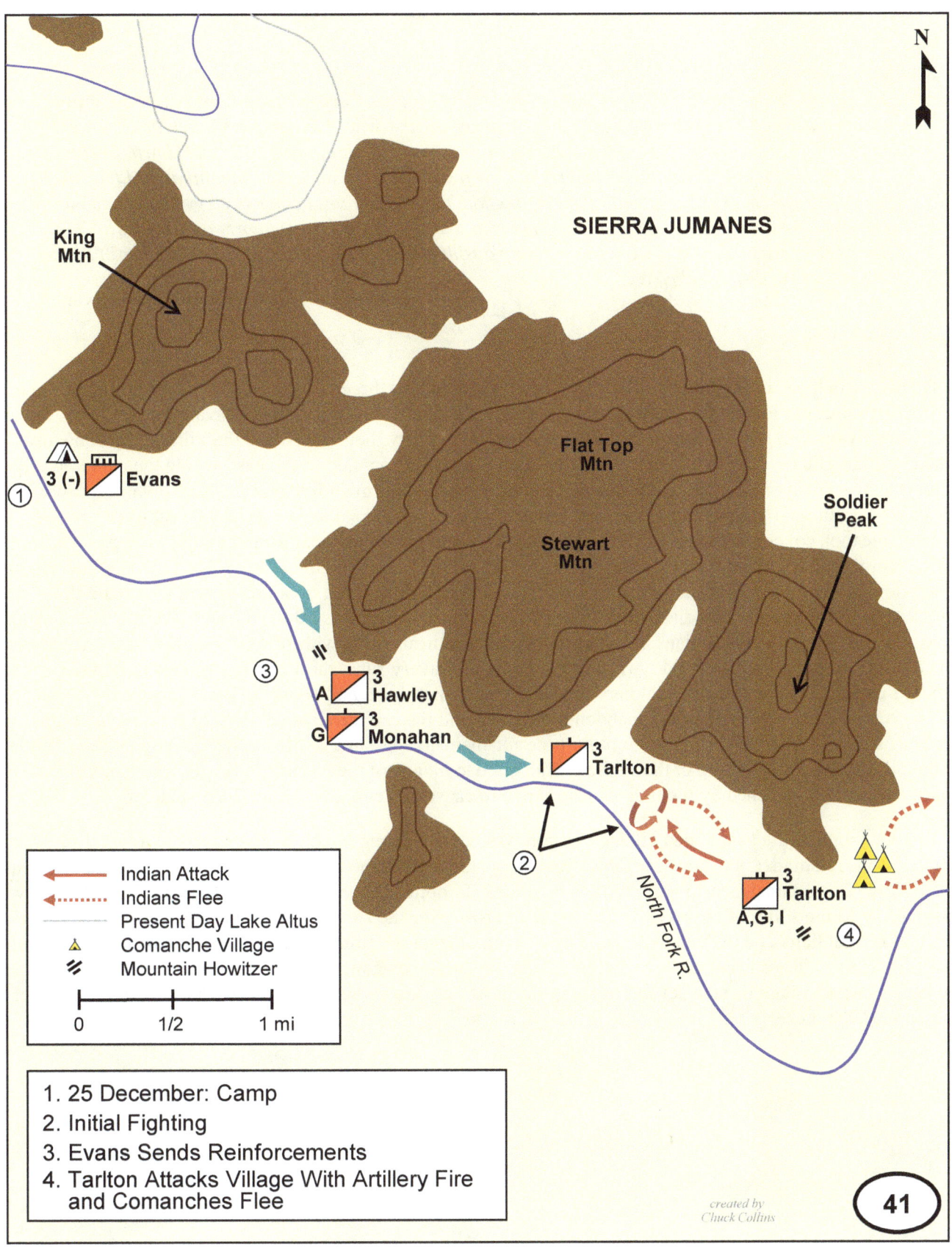

42. Major Tarlton Overruns the Village

"The party then advanced through and beyond the village, and drove the Indians out of the grove and over a ridge below it, the fight being kept up all the way. Lieutenant Hunter at once sent word back to me of their success, and was anxious to push the Indians still further down, but was overruled by Major Tarlton, who determined to await my arrival, in the meantime holding the ridge. This was an excellent position but for the fact that the Indians commenced getting up among the rocks above and on his left, annoying his men and picking off the supports of the guns... The Indians displayed their excellent horsemanship dashing round in circles, riding on the sides of their horses, waving their shields, &c."[87]

– Major Andrew Evans

Pleased with the success of the artillery fire, Tarlton ordered his three companies to conduct a mounted charge. Considering the condition of the 3d Cavalry's horses, it was probably not a thundering cavalry charge. Nevertheless, the cavalry's worn-out horses managed to find the strength to carry their riders into the village. Tarlton's troopers dashed into the village with pistols drawn and the Comanche warriors fled to the east. Inside the captured village, within the grove of trees, Tarlton dismounted his men, formed a skirmish line and pushed forward on foot to the high ground northeast of the village. The horse holders remained in the village to secure the captured property. The skirmish line took cover in a broken line of large granite rocks that extended out from the ridge. The position formed an arc from the high ground on the left to riverbank on the right. From behind the rocks, Tarlton's men engaged the warriors who had circled back to resume the fight. These Indians took up a position in a wooded draw about 300 yards to the soldiers' immediate front from which a small watercourse flowed down from Soldier Spring to the river. From the draw, the Indians harassed the soldiers' skirmish line with rifle fire. Occasionally, the warriors dashed out from their cover in bold bravery runs. In these bravery runs, the warriors demonstrated their courage by riding parallel to or toward the soldiers' line shaking their shields and shouting insults to the soldiers. These actions seemed to dare the soldiers to abandon their cover and resume the advance. However, the real purpose was to intimidate the soldiers and to procure more time for their fleeing families to escape. Throughout the animated fighting, the poor marksmanship of the soldiers who failed to hit any of the Indians, taking down no more than a few ponies, was equally matched by the Indians who failed to cause any casualties among the soldiers.

Having captured the abandoned village, Tarlton was content to remain on the defense and await the arrival of Evans with the remainder of the column. Nevertheless, he grew concerned when the Comanche received substantial reinforcements and threatened to surround his position. He noticed more warriors had joined the fight and were maneuvering to the south of the river. If they were to cross over the river behind him, they would pose a serious threat to his right flank and to the horse guards in the rear. Several warriors had also taken up positions on the bluffs above his line and were firing down onto his left flank. These newcomers to the fight were mostly Kiowa from Woman's Heart's village located several miles to the east. The Kiowa warriors had heard the canon fire and came to assist the Comanche.

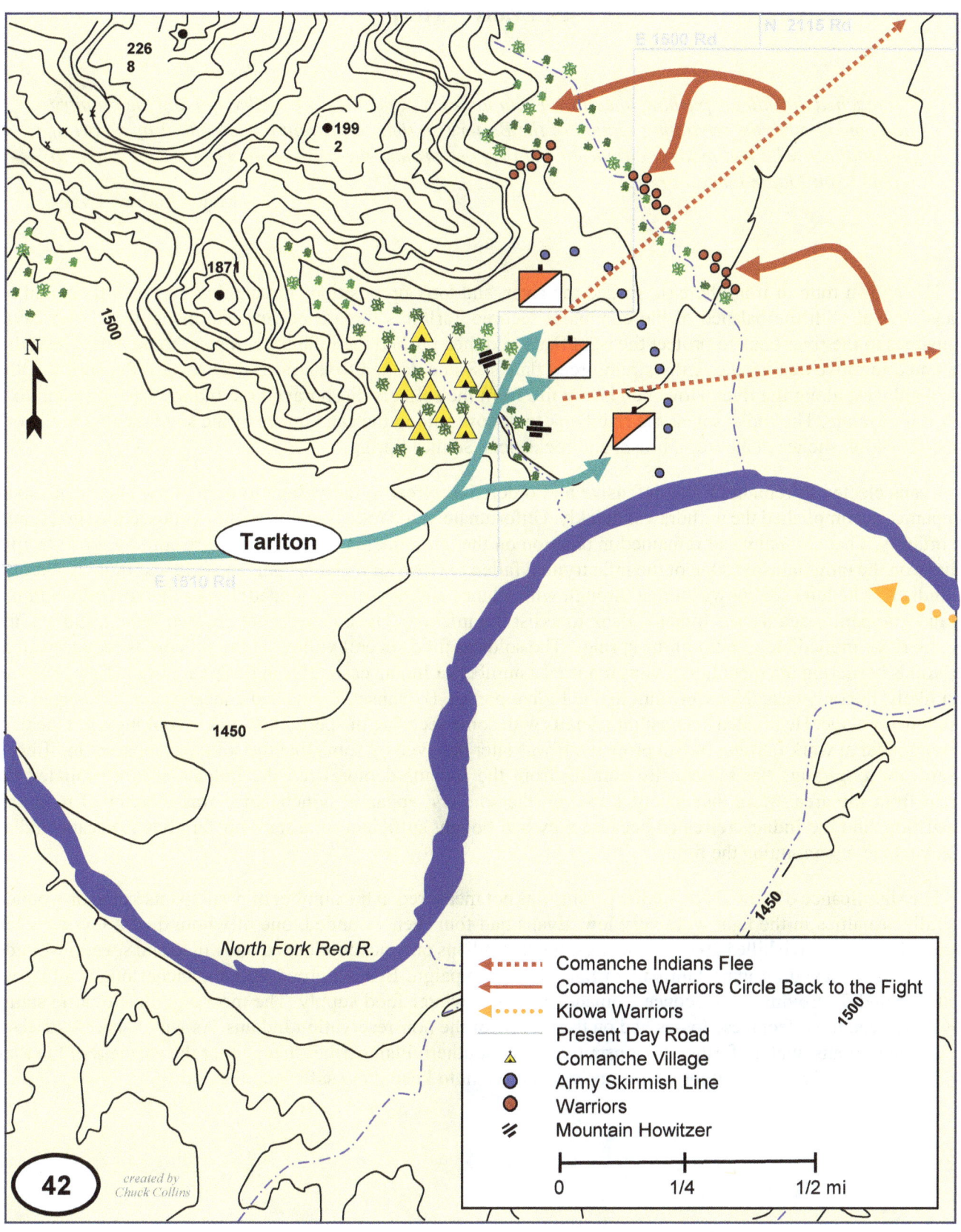

43. Evans' Victory

"I reached the village, pushing ahead with companies 'C' and 'D,' 3d Cavalry, leaving the Infantry to come up with the remaining section of the Battery, in time to prevent a dash into it by a part of the Indians, who had made a circuit for the purpose around the bend of the river on the right, to come in on Major Tarlton's rear."[88]

– Major Andrew Evans

The Kiowa rode in from the east, forded the river, and took up positions threatening Tarlton's flank and rear. Evans' arrival with the balance of the command secured Tarlton's threatened line. He maneuvered two cavalry companies to the river bank to protect the right flank and then pushed the infantry company to the left. The Indians attempted to move against the Army's reinforced flanks. Some dashed to the northwest toward the spring. Others rode southwest along the river. However, heavy fire from the soldiers discouraged the Indians causing them to fall back out of range. The Indians near the riverbank took cover along the sand dunes of the south bank. On the other flank, they took shelter in the trees, brush, and rocks near Soldier Spring.

Evans elected to remain on the defensive and ordered a retreat to the village to tighten his lines. The cavalry companies accomplished the withdrawal quickly. Unfortunately, the retreat of the cavalry exposed the right flank of the infantry. That company had remained in position on the left flank because of heavy fire coming down from the Indians on the mountainside. One of the infantrymen failed to close up with his comrades and was quickly cut off by the Indians. The lone soldier was thrust through with a lance and mortally wounded. Evans then maneuvered three cavalry companies against the Indians' flank to assist the infantry. The counterattack flushed several Indians from a rocky ridge immediately south of the springs. The soldiers fired several volleys at the Indians as they retreated to the woods bordering the mountain. Evans reported a number of Indian casualties in this phase of the fight, but, more than likely, the only casualties were among the Indian ponies. By sunset, Evans had concentrated all his men at the abandoned village. He divided his men into details with some securing the perimeter, others cooking a hot meal, and the remainder at work burning Indian property. It was later believed by some that the soldiers' apparent indifference toward the long-range harassment fire coming from the Indians demoralized the Indians and precipitated their retreat from the area. More than likely, however, the soldiers' apparent nonchalance was a factor of their sheer exhaustion, and the Indians retreated because they had bought sufficient time for their families to escape and saw no advantage in continuing the fight.

The significance of the fight at Soldier Spring was not measured in the number of participants killed or wounded. Overall, casualties in the fight were very low. Evans had four men wounded, one of whom died a few days later. Evans' claimed to have killed 20 to 25 warriors, but the Indians only acknowledged one killed and several wounded. Still, the fight played an important part in Sheridan's campaign. Evans burned 60 Comanche lodges along with capturing and destroying the Noconee Comanches' entire winter food supply. The most significant battle statistic may have been the effect these losses had on the morale of the non-reservation Indians. As with Custer's success at the Washita, Evans' victory further demonstrated to the Southern Plains tribes that neither the vastness of the Plains nor the harshest of winter weather conditions was sufficient to keep them safe from the Army.

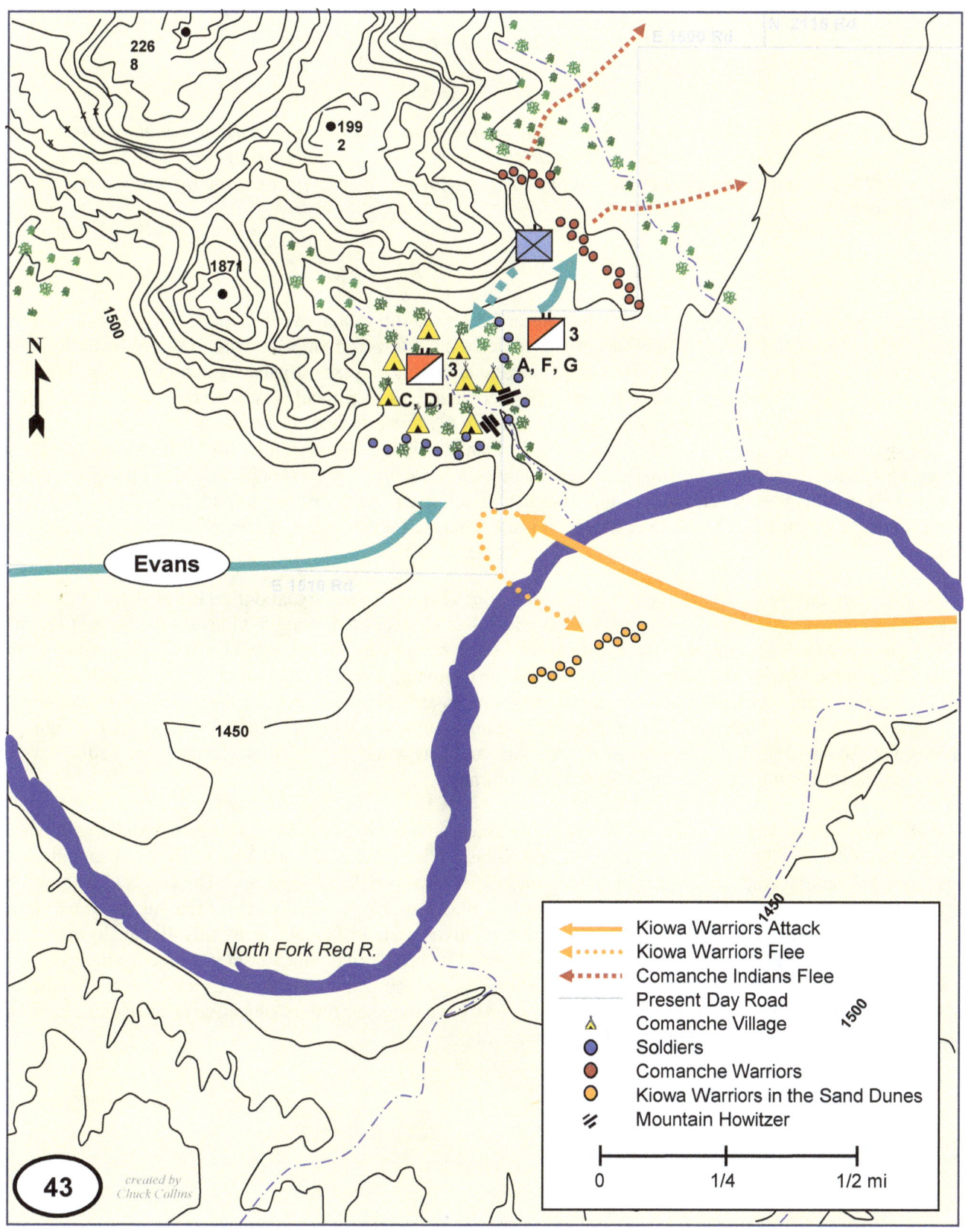

44. Sheridan's Campaign
26 December 1868 – 19 February 1869

"I regret that the Expedition should terminate with so little success, due mainly, no doubt, to errors of judgment upon my part. The hardships and privations of the campaign were cheerfully borne by the Officers and soldiers under me, and no lack of effort upon their part caused my failure in my plans."[89]

– Major Andrew Evans

The next morning, Evans determined the Indians had departed the area in two directions. Most had moved to the northeast toward Fort Cobb. They had reluctantly accepted the US government's demand to surrender to the agency. A few remained defiant and had gone west toward the Staked Plains of Texas. Evans wanted to continue the pursuit and follow the trails that led into Texas. However, he recognized his command was in no condition to continue the campaign, *"I did not think that our horses were in condition to pursue Indians behind with any success."*[90] He had captured significant food supplies for his men in the Comanche village, but very little for his horses and mules. The 150 bushels of corn captured in the village was, at the most, a few days' supplies for his animals. He had captured no horses to remount his men or reteam his supply wagons. Each day more of his horses and mules died. He therefore decided to move toward Fort Cobb to rest and refit his exhausted command and reestablish communication with Sheridan.

On 26 December 1868, he marched toward Fort Cobb. Then on 3 January, about 20 miles short of the fort, he met up with several wagonloads of supplies that Sheridan had sent forward along with orders for Evans to return to his base camp at Monument Creek.[91] By mid-February 1869, both Evans' column and Carr's columns had returned to their start points. Sheridan had prematurely decided the campaign was all but over. Daily, Indians were reporting into Fort Cobb to surrender, and he believed that Evans' victory at Soldier Spring was *"the final blow to the backbone of the Indian rebellion."*[92] In truth, it was only the Kiowa and Comanche who had moved to the agency in significant numbers. On the other hand, the majority of the Arapaho and Cheyenne refused to give up their nomadic ways and, instead, fled further to the west to escape Sheridan's columns.

With Sheridan's approval, Custer used Black Kettle's captive sister and Iron Shirt, a Kiowa-Apache, as emissaries to open talks with the Cheyenne and Arapaho. Little Robe, a Cheyenne chief, and Yellow Bear, an Arapaho chief, agreed to talk. Custer learned from them that their bands were impoverished and hungry. The chiefs also agreed their people were willing to consider coming in to the agency. Sheridan firmly declared that their surrender would only be accepted if they gave up their two remaining female captives. Late in January, with only 40 cavalrymen, Custer departed the newly established Fort Sill to bring in the hold outs. The two chiefs guided Custer's small column to the west. They found Little Raven's Arapaho village of 65 lodges camped on Mulberry Creek. Custer convinced the war-weary Arapaho to report to the agency. However, the Cheyenne, the primary objective of Sheridan's campaign, remained defiant and moved west into the Texas Panhandle.

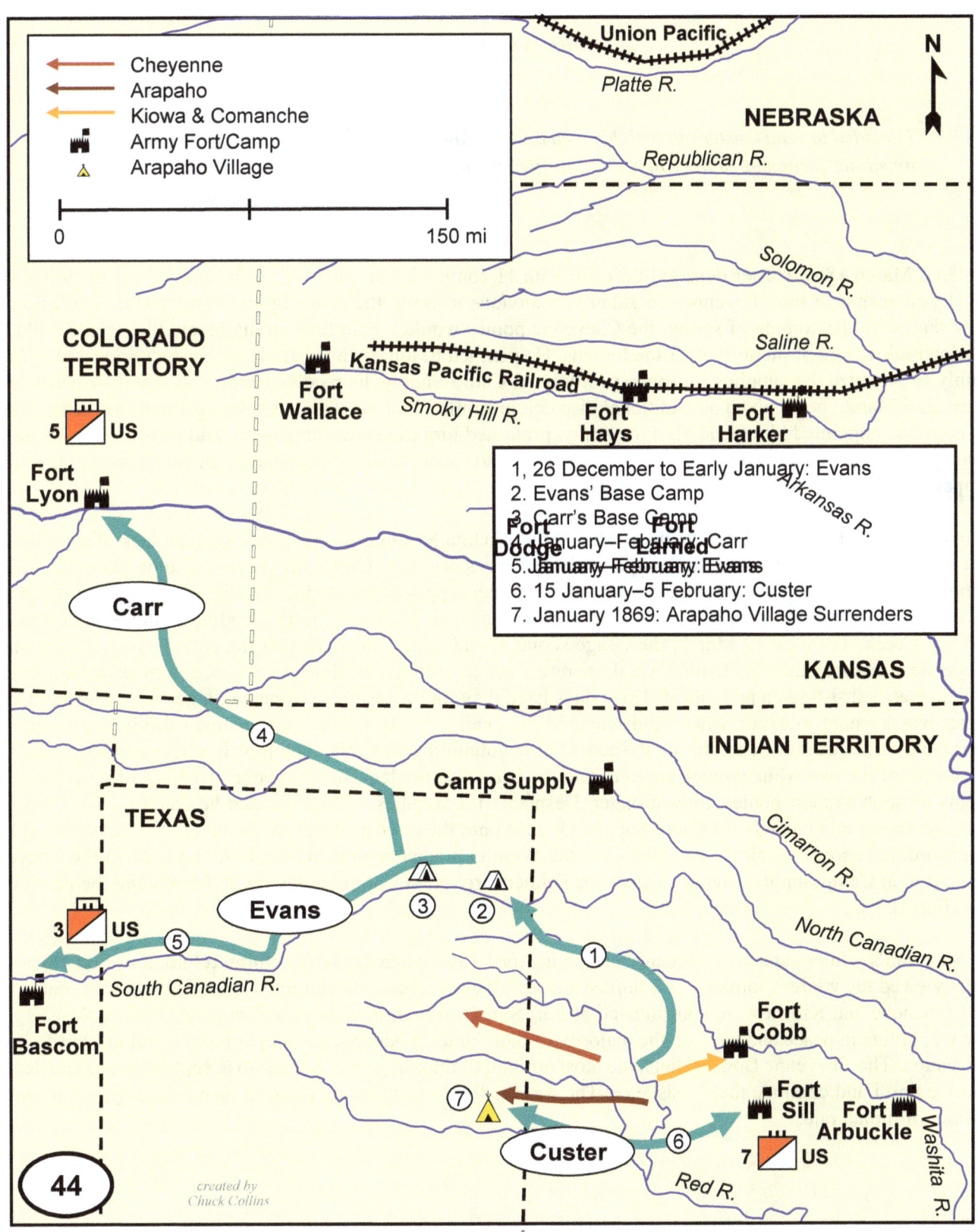

45. Custer Again
March to April 1869

"I decided to send Custer out with his own and the Kansas regiment, with directions to insist on the immediate surrender of the Cheyennes, or give them a sound thrashing."[93]

– Major General Phillip H. Sheridan

On 2 March 1869, Custer departed Fort Sill with 11 companies of the 7th Cavalry and the entire 19th Kansas Cavalry in search of the Cheyenne. Sheridan was anxious to bring the campaign to a successful conclusion. He knew that, with the coming of spring, the Cheyenne ponies would regain their strength, and the Army would lose its winter advantage of mobility over the Indians. He planned to join with Custer later, but first relocated to Camp Supply to organize the supplies for the expedition. At Camp Supply, he received orders to report to Washington. Then, on 6 March, he received an additional dispatch informing him that the newly inaugurated President Ulysses S. Grant had appointed him General of the Army, promoted him to lieutenant general, and directed him to assume command of the Division of the Missouri. It was now up to Custer to take command of the final phase of the winter campaign.

Custer moved west along the southern edge of the Wichita Mountains. The harsh weather, lack of supplies, and general poor condition of his horses hampered the column's progress. Custer divided his column at the North Fork of the Red River. He sent 400 men east to a newly establish supply depot on the Washita River and continued west with 800 of the strongest men and horses. On the Salt Fork, he discovered a trail leading to the northeast toward Gypsum Creek. Then, on 12 March, the Osage scouts found additional signs that the column was closing on the Cheyenne. Even so, Custer's situation was desperate. Each day more of his horses collapsed from exhaustion and his soldiers were subsisting on mule meat. Three days later, they found a large Cheyenne village on Sweetwater Creek. Custer was hesitant to attack when he discovered the camp contained two white women captives. He followed Sheridan's earlier example and, during the course of negotiations, took three chiefs as hostages and bargained both the release of the two white women captives and the band's surrender. The Cheyenne promised to report to Camp Supply as soon as their ponies grew stronger. Desperate for supplies, Custer decided he could not wait to escort them; he set out immediately for Camp Supply. He held onto the three hostages to encourage the Cheyenne to keep their word. He agreed to release the chiefs and the Washita prisoners, now held at Fort Hays, when the Cheyenne reported in at Camp Supply. Custer's exhausted soldiers arrived at Camp Supply on 28 March and then continued on to Fort Hays.

Sheridan's winter campaign officially closed in April 1869 when Custer's column returned to Fort Hays. The Army viewed the winter campaign as a limited success. Nevertheless, the victory was incomplete. The majority of the Comanche and Kiowa were consolidated at Fort Sill. However, the Cheyenne remained defiant. Most agreed they would live in peace and gave up the majority of their lands in Kansas, but they refused to submit to life on the reservation. The Cheyenne Dog Soldiers, the most militant of the Cheyenne, refused to accept the peace and decided to move north and continue their resistance. The Kansas frontier settlements braced themselves again for another summer of Indian raids.

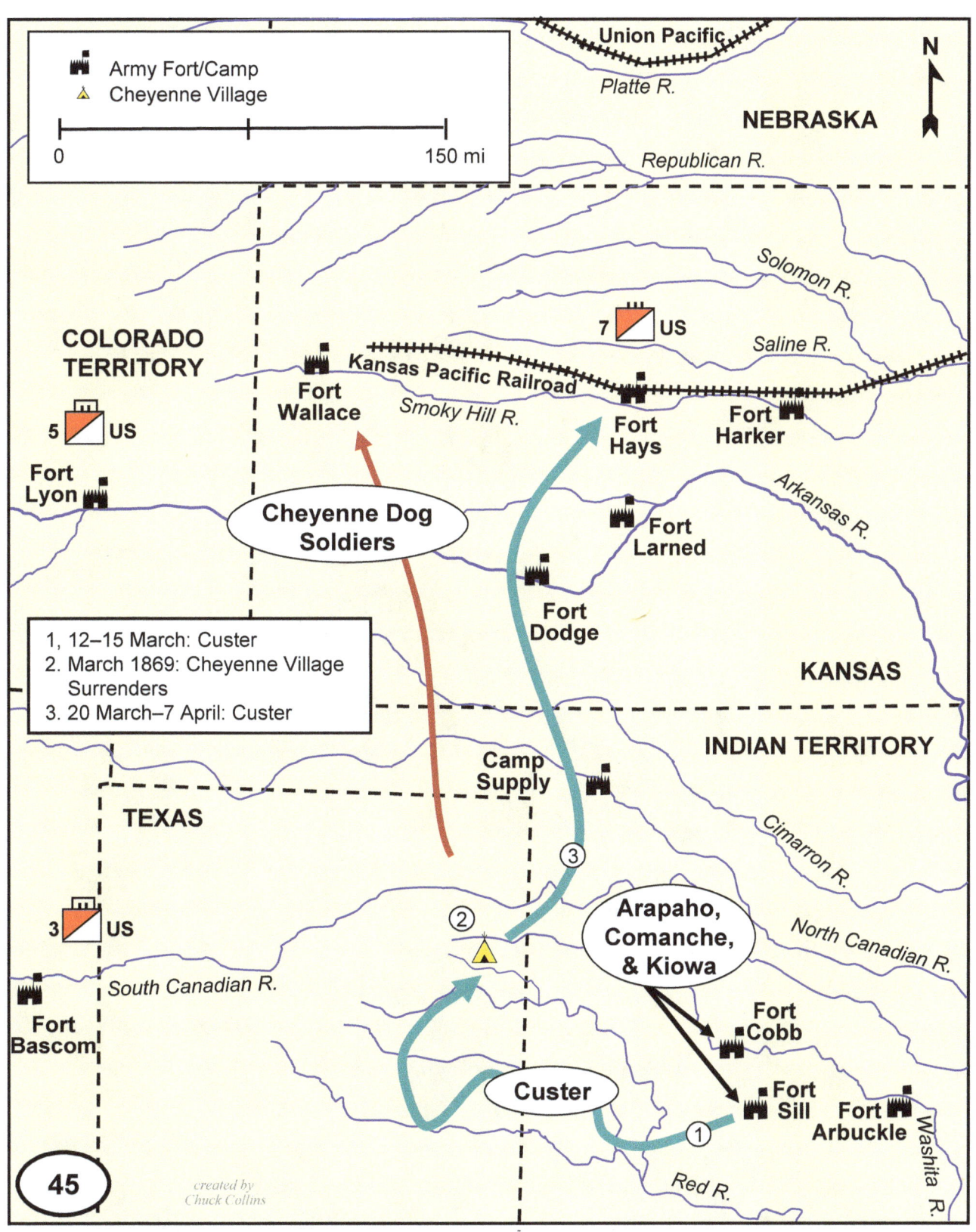

VI. The Republican River Expedition

46. Trouble on the Republican River

"Indications are that the Republican will again be occupied by Indians this summer, bands of Cheyennes and Sioux are reported in the country... the posts of Kearny and McPherson are necessary in view of the Republican still being a hunting ground for the Indians."[94]

– Brigadier General Nelson Sweitzer

By the spring of 1869, the Republican River Valley, a favorite hunting and camping ground for the Cheyenne, was now one of their last strongholds on the Southern Plains. A large band of Sioux had moved into the valley in the autumn of 1868. Then in the winter of 1868/69, the Cheyenne Dog Soldiers occupied land along the upper Republican River. The situation in Kansas, marked by the presence of the militant Dog Soldiers and the hostile Sioux in the region, threatened to be no different than the state of unrest that prompted Sheridan's winter campaign of 1868. Brevet Major General Christopher C. Augur, the commander of the Department of the Platte, determined that he lacked sufficient resources to counter the threat to north central Kansas and south-central Nebraska and requested reinforcements for his thinly manned department. Sheridan, now commanding all forces on the Plains as commander of the Division of Missouri,[95] transferred the 5th Cavalry from Fort Lyon, Colorado, to Fort McPherson, Nebraska, and directed them to patrol the region in response to the threat. On 26 April 1869, Carr departed Fort Lyon with the 5th Cavalry and headed for Nebraska. He passed through Sheridan, Kansas, in early May and then turned north toward Fort McPherson.

On 13 May, Carr's scouts discovered an Indian trail near Elephant Rock Crossing on Beaver Creek. Carr followed the trail and, that same day, engaged in a major skirmish with several hundred Indians. The Indians fought a hard rearguard action to screen their families' escape from a nearby village. The Indians had to abandon most of their camp paraphernalia during the fight, but they secured their families' safe escape. Carr had four men killed and three wounded. He reported the Indian casualties as 25 killed and 20 wounded. The next day, the soldiers burned a recently-deserted village. Carr reported the Indians as Sioux, but it had been a combined force of Sioux and Cheyenne warriors fighting on 13 May, and there had actually been both Sioux and Cheyenne villages in the area.

Carr followed the Sioux and Cheyenne trail northeast toward the Republican River. At the river, Carr issued three days' rations to his men and then sent most of his wagons to Fort McPherson. He then resumed his pursuit of the Indians. His head scout, Buffalo Bill Cody, stuck doggedly to the trail despite the Indians' repeated attempts to throw the soldiers off the trail. On 16 May, Carr's column arrived at Spring Creek where the advance guard was attacked by about 200 Sioux and Cheyenne warriors. The Indians gave up the fight when the rest of the column came to the rescue. Carr lost three soldiers killed and four wounded and reported no Indian casualties. The Indians fled to the south, moving back toward the Republican River, and Carr again resumed the pursuit. At the banks of the Republican River, he discovered the Indians had crossed to the south side and scattered in many directions. Carr recognized that his men and horses were exhausted after the long march from Fort Lyon and knew that he lacked sufficient supplies to continue the chase. He therefore decided to turn back to the north toward Fort McPherson. The command reached the Platte River on 18 May and then followed the river to Fort McPherson. Carr closed his column into the fort on 20 May and immediately began preparations to take to the field again.

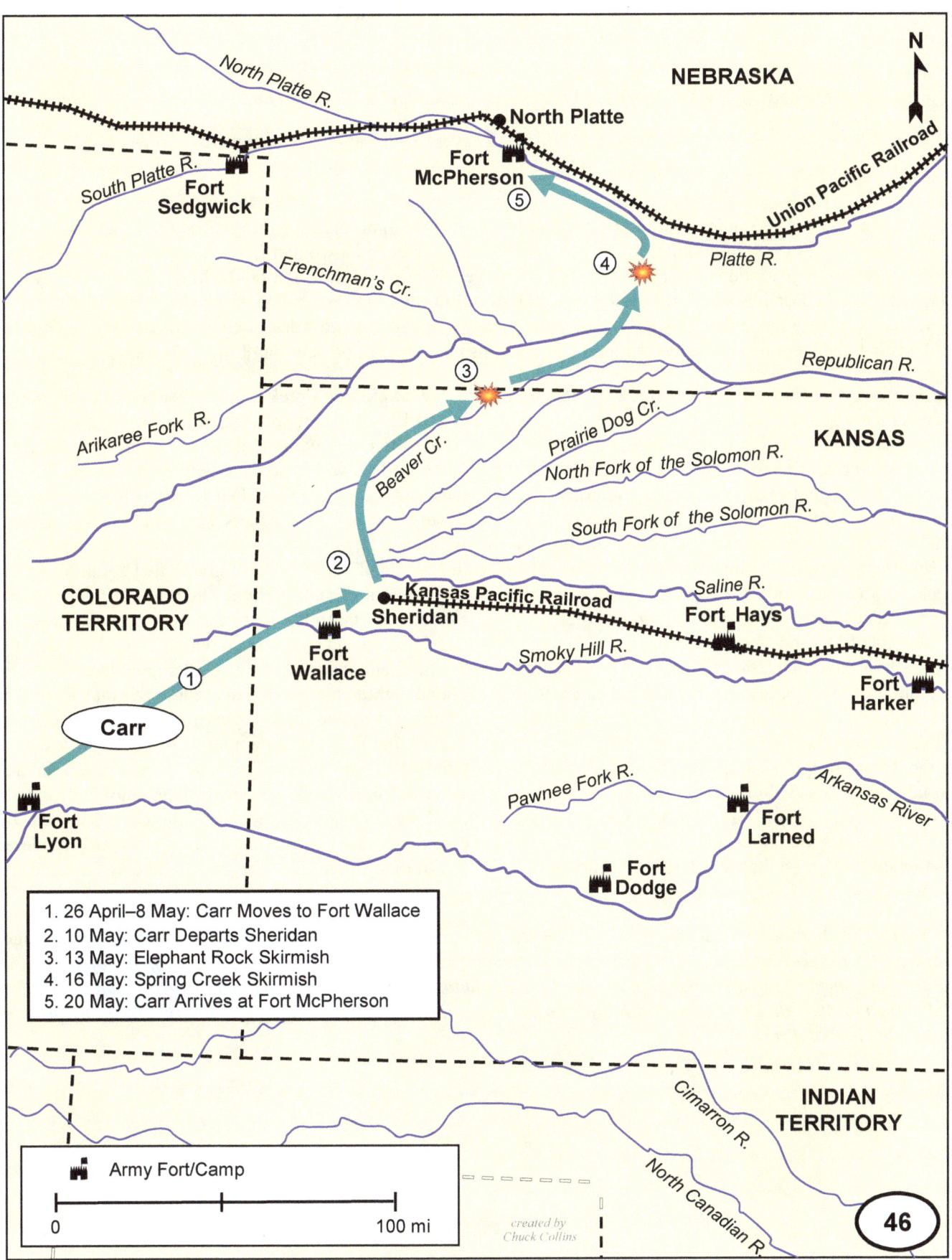

47. The Spillman Creek Raid

Indian Outrages - The Massacre of Thirteen Persons on Saline River – Murder of Nearly a Whole Family.[96]
– Leavenworth Times & Conservative, 29 June 1869

The Cheyenne Dog Soldiers were anxious for revenge after the fights at Elephant Rock and Spring Creek. On 21 May, they raided through Republic County, Kansas, killing six men and a woman. The Dog Soldiers killed several more people as they continued to raid along the river over the next week. Then on 28 May, about 30 Cheyenne attacked seven railroad hands near Fossil Creek Station killing two and wounding four. The raiders then tore up the track and succeeded in derailing a westbound train. Their largest and most destructive raid occurred on 30 May 1868 against the German and Danish emigrant settlements northwest of present-day Lincoln, Kansas.

That day, Tall Bull and about 60 Dog Soldiers rampaged down Spillman Creek killing 13 settlers and abducting two women and a baby. They first attacked John Alverson and Eli Zeigler who were driving a wagon up to an abandoned farm. The two farmers escaped into the brush along the creek while the Indians pillaged the wagon. The Cheyenne continued to the south and killed Eskild Lauritzen and his wife who were tending their garden. They also killed Otto Petersen who was the Lauritzens' houseguest. The Dog Soldiers then attacked the neighboring Christiansen home. The Christiansens were armed and ready and beat off the attackers with rifle fire. The Indians quickly moved on to easier targets. They continued downstream and happened upon Fred Meigheroff and George Weichell and George's wife, Maria, who were out inspecting the land. The three emigrants fled south along the creek for about two miles. They held the Indians off until they ran out of ammunition. Then the Cheyenne closed in and killed the two men and captured the 20-year-old Maria. Late that afternoon, the raiders approached the homestead of Mr. and Mrs. Noon. Staying with them was a Mr. Whalen and two women with their children. On the approach of the raiders, the Noons and Mr. Whalen escaped. The abandoned women also attempted to escape with their children. Mrs. Kline escaped into the Saline River with her daughter, but the Indians caught Susanna Alderdice and her four children. The Dog Soldiers shot the three young boys. Miraculously, four-year-old Willis survived even with five arrow and two bullet wounds. The Indians took Susanna and baby Alice captive then continued down the Saline River until they came upon two 14-year-old boys, Arthur Schmutz and John Strange. They killed John and mortally wounded Arthur. The Cheyenne camped that night on Bullfoot Creek. Ironically, Company G of the 7th Cavalry was camped only a few miles away but was unaware of the raids until the next day. On the 31 May, the 7th Cavalry pursued the raiders but soon lost the trail and gave up the chase. Unfortunately, Susanna's baby hindered the Indians' escape so they murdered the child on the third day of their flight. The Cheyenne held onto Susanna and Maria.

Fearing further Indian raids, the whole region from eastern Nebraska to Denver was in a state of panic. Augur decided he had too few forces to protect every settlement and determined, *"The only permanent safety to your frontier settlements, is to drive the Indians out of the Republican country... A command of cavalry will leave Fort McPherson on the 9th inst. Against all Indians in the Republican country. It will ... I think, relieve all the frontier settlements in that direction."[97]*

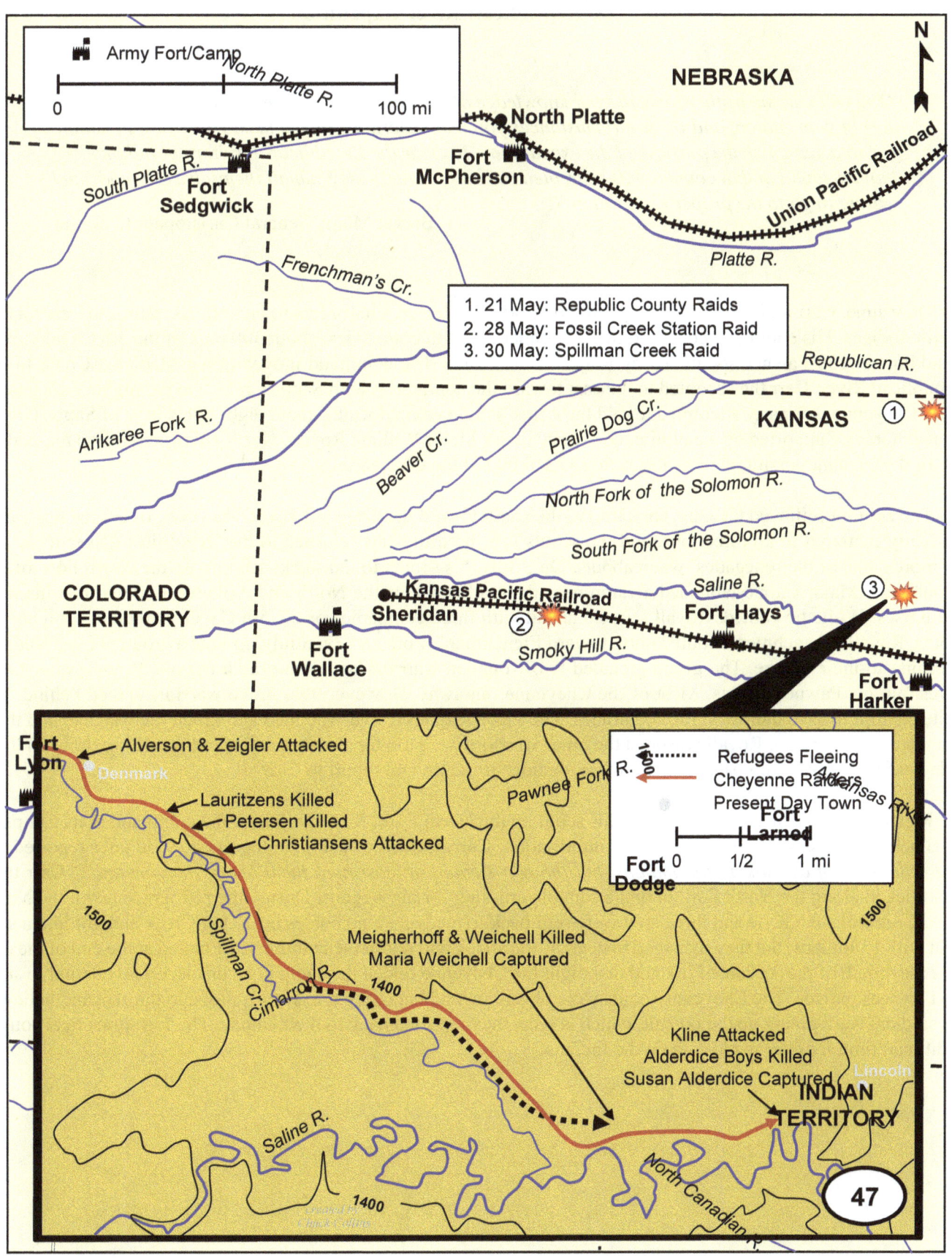

48. The Republican River Expedition

"You will take such other route as your knowledge of the country, the information you have acquired during your march, and other circumstances you may determine as the most promising to enable you to accomplish the purpose of the expedition, 'To clear the Republican Territory of Indians.' All Indians found in that country will be treated as hostile, unless they submit themselves as ready and willing to go to the proper reservation."[98]

– Brevet Major General Christopher C. Augur

On 9 June, Carr and his 5th Cavalry departed Fort McPherson with orders to clear the Republican Territory of hostile Indians. His command consisted of eight under-strength companies, about 300 men of the 5th Cavalry, plus an additional 150 Pawnee scouts led by Major Frank North. The command moved down Medicine Creek to the Republican River. Carr then scouted to the east toward the confluence with Sappa Creek. On the night of 15 June, a small Cheyenne war party attempted to raid the Army's night camp, located about eight miles west of Sappa Creek, to steal horses. Supported by a battalion of cavalry under Major William Royall, North's Pawnees drove the raiders off. In the ensuing pursuit, the Pawnee scouts killed two of the Cheyenne.

The column followed the Cheyenne trail to the south toward the Solomon River. However, over time the tracks gradually scattered in all directions, and the scouts lost the trail. Carr returned to the Republican River to search for more signs of the renegades' whereabouts. On 3 July, his scouts found tracks leading up the North Fork of the Republican. Major Carr established a camp near the confluence of the North and Arikaree Forks to rest his men and horses. While he waited, Royall scouted ahead with three companies of the 5th Cavalry and one company of scouts. Royall's detachment scouted north toward Frenchman's Fork and, on 6 July, spotted a group of Dog Soldiers returning to their village. The group included two wounded warriors on horse-drawn travois. Royall was unable to restrain his Pawnee Scouts. Most of the Cheyenne ran away. However, two brave warriors stayed behind in a futile attempt to save their wounded comrades. The Pawnee quickly overwhelmed and killed the warriors and their wounded. At this point, Royall reasoned the other warriors were too far ahead to catch and would surely warn their village of the Army's approach. He, therefore, decided to return and report to Carr.

Meanwhile, Carr had continued with his scout up the North Fork. Royall rejoined the command at its campsite on Black Trail Creek. With Royall's new information, Carr decided to continue the pursuit. He later reported, *"I had little hope of overtaking the Indians, but thought I could at least hunt them out of the country."*[99] Carr then backtracked along the North Fork to find a suitable crossing for his wagons. During the retrograde down the North Fork, Corporal John Kyle and three men were sent back to recover some horses near Dog Creek and got into a stiff fight with 13 Indians, but they managed to beat off the attack and rejoin the column. Carr halted at the end of the day near the mouth of the Arikaree Fork and that night the Cheyenne raided the camp in an unsuccessful attempt to steal the Pawnees' horses. The Cheyenne scouts were observing and harassing the Army's move to the east and believed the soldiers were giving up the pursuit, which is what they reported back to their camps. The fortuitous ruse bought additional time for Carr to close in on the Indians.

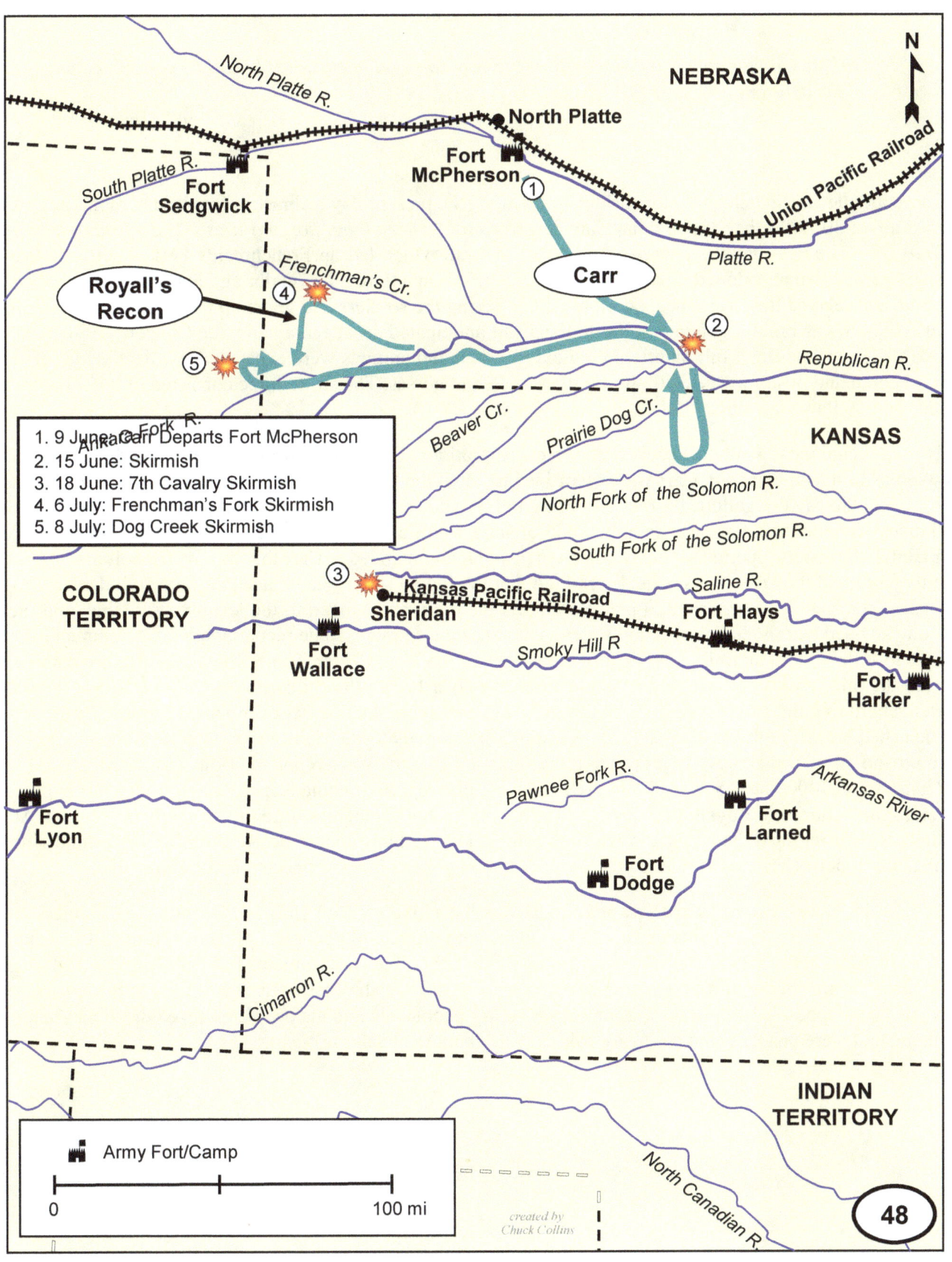

49. The Pursuit

"We will have a fight tomorrow sure. I hope we may come out victorious. I shall be careful for the sake of the dear ones at home."[100]

– Major Frank North

Carr continued his march on 9 July pushing north along the present-day Nebraska-Colorado border. The column marched about 30 miles that day in what Carr described as *"a very long, hot and tiresome day's march through Sandhills."*[101] The next day the command followed the trail which led up Frenchman's Fork. They marched 32 miles and passed two abandoned village sites then encamped on a third. The major and his scouts determined the Cheyenne had relaxed their vigilance, possibly still believing the soldiers had given up the chase. Carr recognized that his column was rapidly gaining on the Indians and anticipated an attack against the Cheyenne village might be possible. Even so, after a full month in the field, his men and animals were exhausted. He decided to leave his wagons behind and push forward with the strongest men and horses. The strike force consisted of 244 officers and soldiers, and 50 Pawnee scouts.

The command moved out on 11 July with three day's rations. The wagons were left behind with instructions to follow-on as best as they could. Carr was determined to catch the Cheyenne. Twice the scouts reported Indians to the front, and the cavalry galloped forward to bring the Indians to battle. Both times it proved to be no more than wild horses. Frenchman's Fork was mostly a bed of sand with no water available for the horses. Near the Platte River Bluffs, the scouts reported seeing two horsemen and recommended to Carr that he hide the column in a ravine while they scouted the area. The scouts determined that the Indian trail divided; a small, faint trail deviated to the right across the sand hills toward the Platte River, and the main trail moved to the left onto the table land. Scout Bill Cody advised that the Indians needed water as much as the soldiers, so he recommended the command should continue to follow the faint trail along the dry creek toward the Platte River. The soldiers resumed the pursuit and followed the faint trail. Carr gambled he could reach the river before the Indians. After several miles, the scouts reported a herd of animals in a valley far to the right and also spotted a number of mounted Indians far to the left. Carr detached Royall with two companies to examine the animals to the right and moved with the remainder of the command (four companies) toward where the mounted Indians were reported. Both groups moved out at a rapid gait. About 1400, the scouts leading Carr's main column reported seeing teepees to the front. Carr expected a fight and sent a courier to Royall directing him to send one of his companies to reinforce the main column. About this time, Royall rejoined the command with his companies. He had scouted nearly 20 miles and found nothing significant to report. Carr then continued the advance keeping the column concealed in the sand hills.

The distant camp spotted by the Pawnee scouts was the village of Tall Bull's Cheyenne Dog Soldiers along with some Sioux. The village contained about 84 lodges with around 400 people. Tall Bull and the other headmen had perhaps 100 to 160 fighting boys and men available to defend the encampment. Tall Bull had been moving his people west toward the South Platte and then planned to cross over the Platte River and join with the non-treaty Sioux. He had stopped at Summit Springs to rest his weary people. He and his people believed they had shaken off the pursuit and were unaware that the Army column was about to attack the camp.

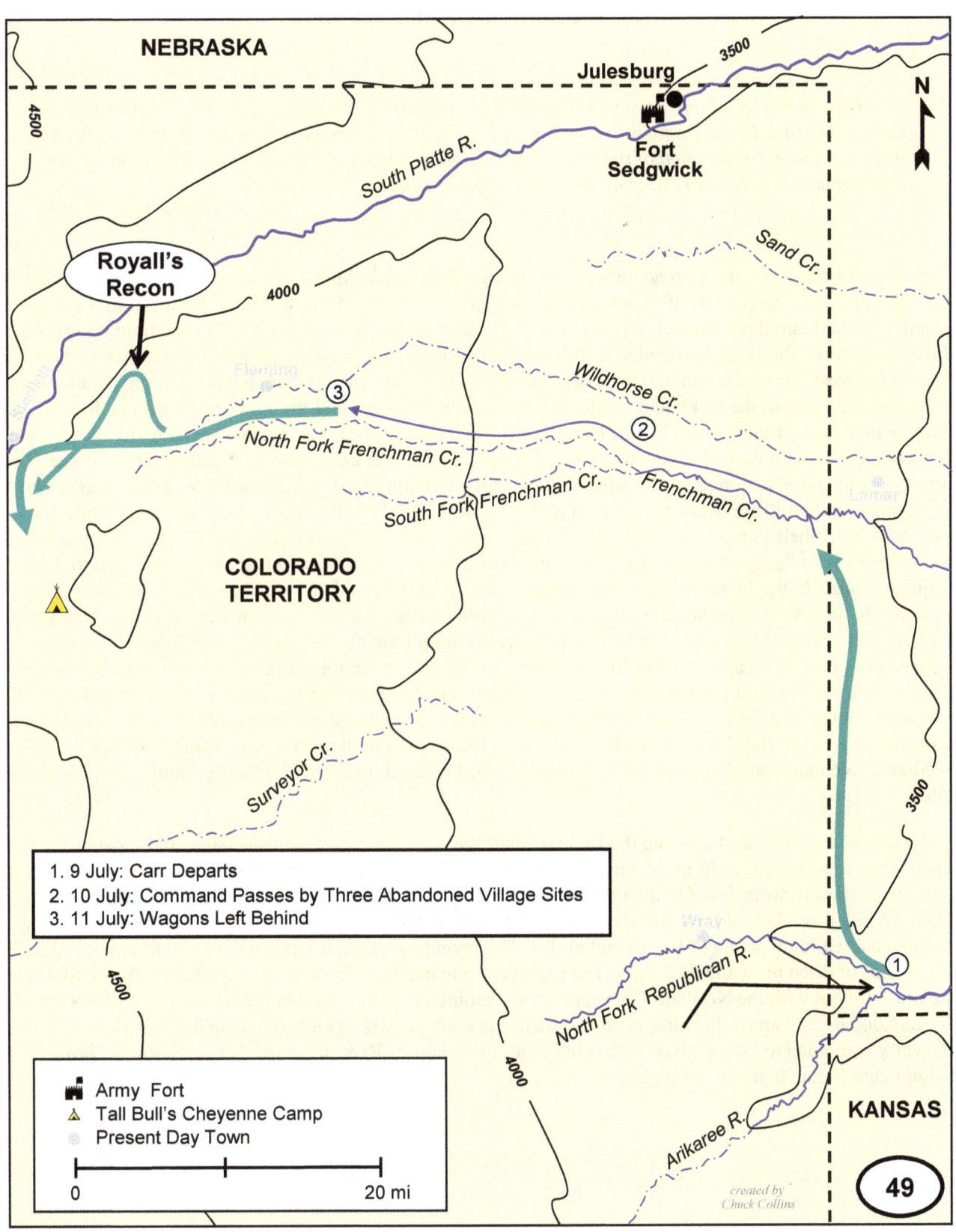

50. The Battle of Summit Springs

"We have, however, no pleasure in killing the poor miserable savages, but desire, in common with the whole army, by the performance of our duty, to deliver the settlers from the dangers to which they are exposed on account of the past mistaken policy, or rather want of policy, in Indian affairs; which renders it necessary to chastise them until they submit."[102]

— Major Eugene Carr

The column continued its approach toward the village until concealment was no longer possible. At that point, Major Carr briefed a hasty plan of attack. He had Major E.W. Crittenden's battalion form the first line with his companies arrayed into three parallel columns. Royall's battalion formed the second line. The time was about 1500, 11 July 1869, when the buglers sounded the charge. The attack was launched from the northwest and struck the village on the west, the north, and the east sides. The Cheyenne were caught completely by surprise, and their only avenue of escape was to the south and southeast. The cavalry troopers and the Pawnee scouts reached the village so quickly that most of the Indians had little time to get to their ponies. One company striking the west side of the village charged through capturing several hundred ponies. The center companies charged into the village. The left company was hindered by rough terrain which delayed their attempt to seal off the east side of the village. The delay allowed most of the village occupants to escape to the southeast. Despite being ill-prepared, the warriors fought bravely to protect their families, gaining time for the women and children to get away. The company commander on the village's west flank reported killing seven warriors who attempted to stop his unit's entrance into the village. Carr quickly brought up the second line and charged directly into the village. As the soldiers charged through the village, the Indians took vengeance on the two white women they had captured in Kansas. They killed Susanna Alderdice, and severely wounded Maria Weichell. In the initial attack, Tall Bull placed one of his wives and a daughter on a horse to escape and then bravely stayed behind in a vain attempt to rally those of his people who could not get away. Tall Bull, a few warriors, and several non-combatants took cover in a ravine near the village. The Pawnee scouts, hereditary enemies of the Cheyenne, played the major role in the attack on the ravine. Tall Bull was killed early in the fight. Soon after his death, his oldest wife climbed from the ravine with her daughter and surrendered. Eventually all those in the ravine were killed. The dead included Tall Bull's youngest wife and another daughter.

Carr detailed companies to pursue the fugitives, but the Army horses were exhausted, and most of the Indians escaped. Carr reported the fight as an *"undisputed success."* The results were significantly one-sided. The Army had one man slightly wounded. On the other hand, the Cheyenne and Sioux sustained significant casualties. Carr claimed 52 killed on the field. He did not record their sex or age; many were women and children. He captured 17 women and children, and 418 horses and mules. The inventory of other items captured and destroyed included 9,300 pounds of dried meat and 84 lodges. The fugitives were destitute for supplies and shelter. A few continued on to the north to join with the Northern Cheyenne, most rejoined their brethren in the south. The soldiers also found about a $1,000 in cash and gold coins, most of which was given to Mrs. Weichell to help her start her life anew. The 5th Cavalry continued to campaign between the Platte and Arkansas Rivers, but the fight at Summit Springs was the last significant Indian battle in the region.

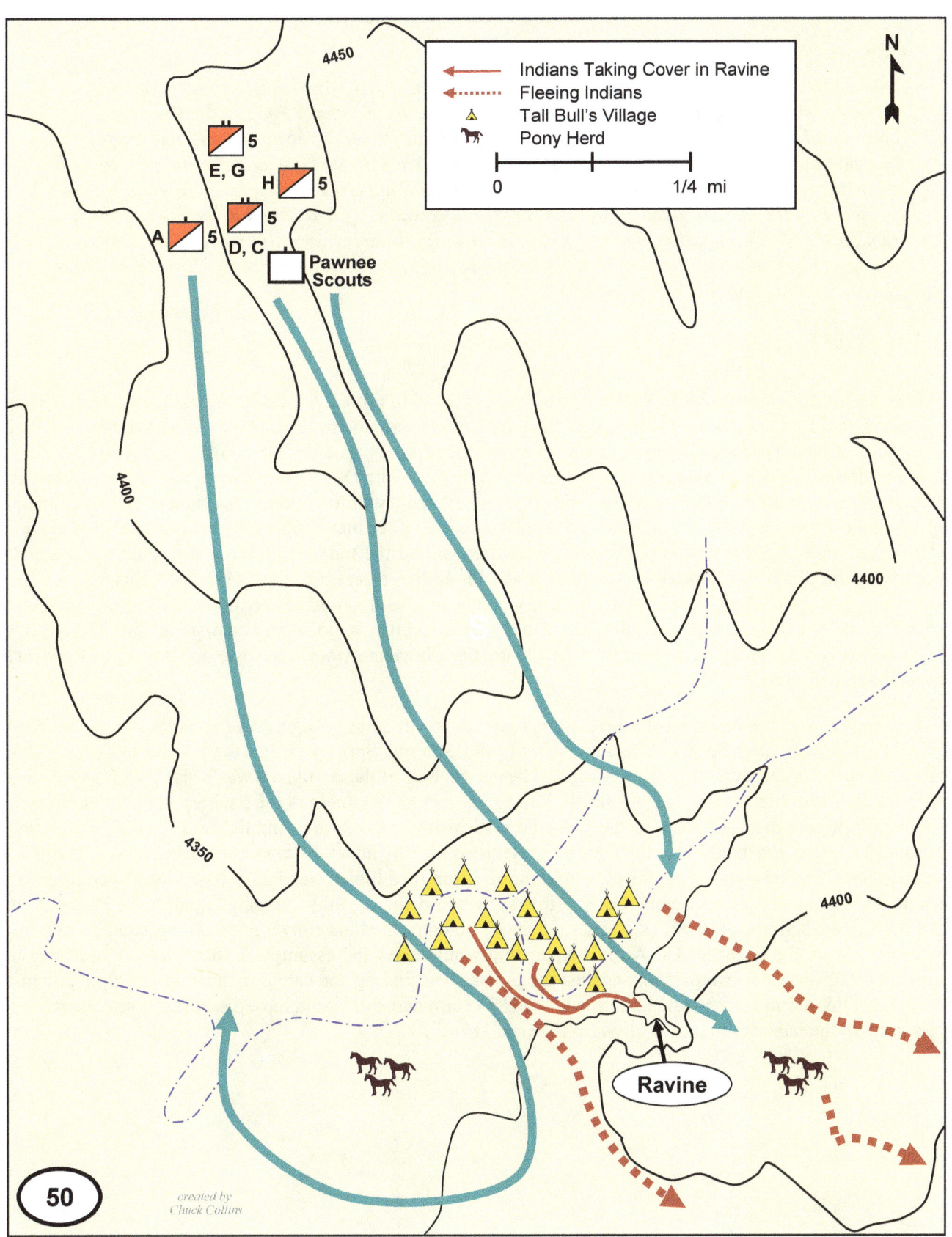

51. The End of the Cheyenne War

"Since those early days when Yellow Wolf, Medicine Snake, and Afraid of Beavers first led the Hair Rope People south of the Platte to capture wild horses, the Southern People [the Cheyenne] had considered the rich grasslands between Moon Shell [Platte] River on the north and Flint Arrowpoint [Arkansas] River on the south to be their own country. Then the ve'hó'e$_3$ came, killing the buffalo, then killing the People themselves, seizing more of the Southern People's lands as each summer passed. Finally only the great buffalo lands at the headwaters of Red Shield River, the Republican, remained. The Dog Soldiers had fought for them with all the bravery and power they possessed, trying to hold these last hunting grounds for the use of all the Southern People. Now those lands, too, were gone, seized by the ve'hó'e."[103]

— Father Peter John Powell

Sheridan initiated operations on the Southern Plains in 1868 to protect the emigrant trails, ensure the safety of the Kansas Pacific Railroad work crews and protect the Kansas settlements. The 1868 Winter Campaign fell short of the goal with many of the Cheyenne bands remaining defiant against the US Government. However, Carr's victory at Summit Springs attained the Army's desired objective. The Dog Soldiers were no longer a threat to the Southern Plains, and their defeat broke the other Cheyenne bands' will to continue resistance. The Cheyenne and other Southern Plains tribes reluctantly accepted an Executive Order that confined them to a small reservation in western Oklahoma. The campaigns of 1868 and 1869 had shifted the Indian frontier to the south and cleared the land between the Platte and Arkansas Rivers of a serious Indian threat. On the Southern Plains, the remaining area of instability was Texas. There the Kiowa and Comanche raided almost unceasingly. Over time, a number of Cheyenne joined in the unrest. Eventually this would lead to another major Army campaign, The Red River War of 1874. However, disregarding a few minor incidents, the Cheyenne wars were over for the settlers of Kansas, Nebraska, and Colorado.[104]

The Army had learned much from these campaigns. In the three most significant engagements – the Washita (November 1868), Soldier Spring (December 1868), and Summit Springs (July 1869) – the field commanders managed to surprise and overrun Indian villages. The destruction of these villages was a significant psychological blow to the Southern Plains tribes; they could no longer count on the vastness of the territory nor challenging winter conditions to protect them from the soldiers. At the tactical level, the Army established a formula for battlefield success: offensive action to maintain the initiative, relentless pursuit, attack from multiple directions to confuse and panic the enemy, and disciplined firepower to hold the undisciplined Indian warriors at bay. At the operational level, Sheridan had validated his experiment, proving the Army could successfully campaign against the Plains tribes in the winter despite serious logistical challenges. He had also confirmed his converging column strategy as a means to force an elusive foe to battle. The Army's leadership would carry the assumption forward to future campaigns that the major challenge in campaigning against the Indians was finding and catching them – not fighting them. For the most part, this assumption would hold true in the 1874 campaign but would have disastrous consequence for the 7th Cavalry on the banks of the Little Bighorn River in 1876.[105]

---

3 *Ve'ho'e* is the Cheyenne reference to all non-Indians in its generic sense. Here it refers specifically to the white man.

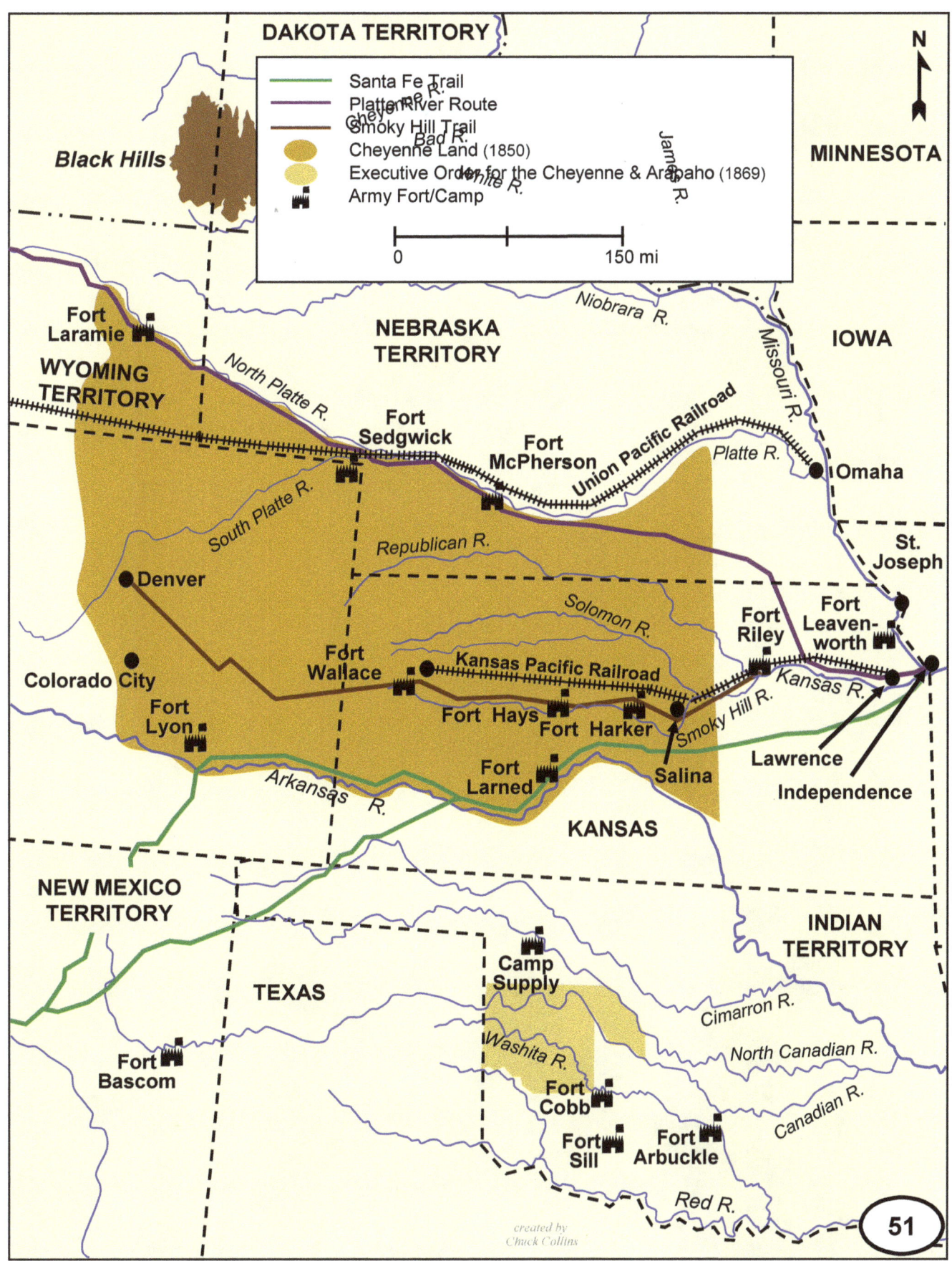

Appendix A
The 7th US Cavalry

"Instead of spa we'll drink down ale and pay the reckoning on the nail, for debt no man shall go to jail from Gary Owen in glory."[106] – *Gary Owen*, the unofficial marching song of the 7th Cavalry

Several regiments of cavalry and infantry, and detachments of artillery participated in Sheridan's Campaign against the Cheyenne. Nevertheless, an examination of the 7th US Cavalry provides an equitable look at the Army in 1868. The regiment was new, recently organized in 1866 at Fort Riley, Kansas. However, in its short history before the fight at the Washita River various detachments of the 7th had participated in a combination of 22 actions against the Indians, making the regiment a relatively experienced unit. The organization of the regiment was that of a typical post-Civil War cavalry regiment with 12 companies. It was authorized: a colonel, a lieutenant colonel, and three majors in addition to a staff consisting of an adjutant, a quartermaster, a commissary and a regimental surgeon with an assistant. The regimental staff also included: one sergeant-major, one quartermaster sergeant, one commissary sergeant, one saddler sergeant, a blacksmith, and two hospital stewards. However, like other regiments, the 7th lacked many of its key leaders in the field. Colonel Andrew J. Smith, the regimental colonel, was on extended leave of absence and allowed Lieutenant Colonel George Armstrong Custer to command the regiment in the field. Only one of the three authorized majors was present for duty. Major Alfred Gibbs was ill, and Major Joseph C. Tilford was on leave of absence. Only Major Joel Elliott was in the field with the regiment. Each of regiment's 12 companies was authorized 64 men. A captain commanded each company and was assisted by a first lieutenant and a second lieutenant. A full-strength company also had a first sergeant, a quartermaster sergeant, and a commissary sergeant. Other key personnel in the company included five sergeants, eight corporals, two teamsters, two farriers (blacksmiths), one saddler, one waggoner, and two musicians. During the 1868 campaign, the 7th's companies averaged 60 men each, which was very close to full strength in raw numbers. However, like the regimental staff the companies also lacked many of their key personnel. Most of the companies had only one or two of the three authorized officers and lacked many of the authorized sergeants. For the 1868 campaign, the 7th had 11 companies: A, B, C, D, E, F, G, H, I, K, and M. Company L was with the Fort Lyon column. Officially, the 11 available companies reported directly to Custer. The 7th Cavalry, as was common with other regiments in the post-Civil War Army, did not have permanent battalion organizations. However, like most field commanders, Custer formed temporary battalions to better coordinate the maneuvering of companies. A field battalion usually consisted of at least two companies, but it could have more. At the Washita fight, Custer organized the regiment into five battalions. Another key organization operating with the regiment was a detachment of scouts. At the Washita fight, Custer had several white and mixed-blood scouts, plus a group of Osage Indians. The Osages knew the country the regiment was operating in and more importantly, because of their frequent tribal clashes with the Cheyenne, they also had a good understanding of the Cheyenne culture.

The regiment's available strength for the campaign was 29 officers and about 845 enlisted men. Many of the 7th's officers had extensive military experience and had served with honor during the Civil War. However, like Custer, their experience against the Plains Indian was limited. A few of the officers were newly commissioned officers straight out of West Point or even commissioned directly from civilian life. The enlisted soldiers were much like the officers with respect to their experience against Plains Indians. The majority of the noncommissioned officers were seasoned veterans while those in the enlisted ranks ranged between experienced veterans and recent enlistees with little knowledge of the Army or its dealings in the West. The enlisted soldiers came from all walks of life. Some were former soldiers, even a few of which had been officers in the Confederate Army. Others came from diverse backgrounds and included a significant number who were foreign-born.

Like most Army units, the 7th was plagued by numerous desertions. The regiment had, therefore, acquired a large number of recruits prior to the campaign and had, in turn, conducted significant training of both men and horses to prepare for the campaign. The regimental training program included cavalry drill and placed particular emphasis on marksmanship. Custer especially emphasized accurate shooting and inspired competition by forming a special unit of 40 sharpshooters commanded by First Lieutenant William W. Cooke. These chosen men were referred to as the "Corps d'Elite" by the rest of regiment and were envied by all as the elite enjoyed the privilege of being exempted from guard duty.

The common soldier of the regiment was reasonably outfitted for a winter campaign. The field uniform consisted of flannel drawers, a pullover shirt, sky blue trousers and a dark blue, woolen sack coat. Each soldier also had a heavy greatcoat and leather boots. To further protect their feet, they had buffalo overshoes or other commercially made overshoes. The quartermaster also made available fur or woolen caps. Most soldiers also acquired mittens or gauntlets. Equipment included a leather saber belt with a pistol holster, percussion cap pouch, pistol cartridge box, carbine cartridge box, and a leather carbine sling. Weapons included a carbine, pistol, and saber. The issue carbine was the .50-caliber Model 1865 Spencer seven-shot-repeating carbine. The most common issue pistol was the .44-caliber Model 1860 Colt Army revolver six-shooter. Officers' clothing was usually somewhat higher quality except while on campaign when they tended to wear the same clothing and use the same equipment issued to the soldiers. Both officers and enlisted tended to supplement the issue clothing with privately purchased items such as flannel shirts and additional socks. Trooper John Ryan of the 7th Cavalry made the following observations about the soldiers' clothing during the Washita Campaign.

> *"Some lined their overcoats with woolen blankets, while others made leggings from pieces of condemned government canvas. Although in those days the cavalry overcoat was very warm about a man's body, while sitting in the saddle his legs were very cold. By lining the skirt of the coat they were made very comfortable as far down as the knees, and then the leggings, in addition to the long cavalry boots, kept the men pretty warm. The government also issued us buffalo overshoes, made from buffalo skin, with the fur side in, and buckled up in front. They were very warm, but clumsy. The gloves that were issued to the enlisted men were made of the same material as the socks, with a thumb and forefinger to each glove, and although they were clumsy they were warm."*[107]

Appendix B
Army Logistics

"Immediately after getting into camp, it was the custom, in the troop of which I was a member, to have a couple of men take buckets and get some water, while others got some wood. A fire was started, and in a short time, each man was given a cup of good strong black coffee. It was surprising how quickly they recovered from the fatigue of a hard day's march after getting their coffee."[108] – Private William G. Wilkinson.

Cavalry and infantry units required substantial logistics support on campaign. Sheridan and his commanders understood that the logistical challenges were even more significant in a winter campaign. In the frontier Army, most logistical requirements were handled at the regimental level. Normally, the officers assigned to manage logistical needs were detailed from the line companies and had no specialized training. In the 1868 Campaign, Custer appointed First Lieutenant Henry J. Nowlan as the acting commissary officer and First Lieutenant James M. Bell as the quartermaster. The commissary officer requisitioned and issued rations for the soldiers. The quartermaster's duties included submitting requisitions for all supplies and transport and accounting for regimental property. Other key responsibilities included acquiring animals and their forage and managing the regimental trains. Bell also acted as the regimental ordnance officer and was responsible for managing all the movement of the unit ammunition train.

In 1868, the Army generally hauled supplies by wagon trains while on campaign. The wagons tended to slow columns down and were vulnerable to raiding Indians if not protected. The Fort Dodge column had 400 wagons to support the expedition and for building a forward supply base. The regiment alone had two wagons for the staff, one for the band, two wagons for each company, and a supply wagon and seven ambulances for the Medical Department. A six-mule team, in the best season of the year and on good roads, could haul 4,000 pounds. In the 1868 campaign, they faced deep snow and frozen water courses, and roads were non-existent. Therefore, the loads probably weighed significantly less than the prescribed 4,000 pounds.

One of the most significant challenges was hauling sufficient food for the men and animals. The Army's prescribed daily individual ration for a soldier was 20 ounces of fresh or salt beef or 12 ounces of pork or bacon and 1 pound of hard bread. An additional company ration (every 100 men) consisted of: 15 pounds of beans or peas, 10 pounds of rice or hominy, 10 pounds of green coffee, 15 pounds of sugar, 4 quarts of vinegar, 3.75 pounds of salt, 4 ounces of pepper, 30 pounds of potatoes, and 1 quart of molasses. Horses and mules also required provision. Army horses were larger and stronger than Indian ponies, but without a regular diet of fodder and grain, the Army horses quickly broke down on campaign. The authorized ration for a horse was 14 pounds of hay and 12 pounds of grain. A mule's daily ration was 14 pounds of hay and 9 pounds of grain.

Since a six-mule wagon with driver required a daily ration of about 140 pounds, a major quandary for the logistician was that, even at maximum capacity a supply wagon could carry only enough provisions to merely sustain itself for 28 days. Realistically, neither man nor beast received the authorized ration on campaign; the challenge of supplying a column in the field was significant. The Army's solution was to establish forward supply bases near the campaign area and then send out mobile columns to track down the elusive foe. Even then, a cavalry column could carry only enough supplies on the horses to last a few days. If the column intended to stay in the field for even a week, it would still require dozens of the slow clumsy wagons to support the operation.[109]

Bibliography

Brill, Charles J. *Custer, Black Kettle, and the Fight on the Washita*. Norman, OK: University of Oklahoma Press, 1938.

Broome, Jeff. *Custer into the West*. El Segundo, CA: Upton and Sons Publishing, 2009.

Burkey, Blaine. *Custer Come At Once*. Woodston, KS: Western Books, 1976.

Chalfant, William Y. *Cheyennes and Horse Soldiers*. Norman, OK: University of Oklahoma Press, 1989.

———. *Hancock's War*. Norman: University of Oklahoma Press, 1989.

Collins, Charles D. *Atlas of the Sioux Wars, 2d Edition*. Fort Leavenworth, KS: Combat Studies Institute Press, 2006.

Cozzens, Peter, ed. *Eyewitnesses to the Indian Wars 1865-1890, Vol. 3, Conquering the Southern Plains*. Mechanicsburg, PA: Stackpole Books, 2003.

Custer, Elizabeth B. *Tenting on the Plains*. New York: Charles L. Webster and Co., 1889.

Custer, George A. *My Life on the Plains*. Lincoln, NE: University of Nebraska Press, 1966.

Evans, Colonel A. W. "Report of the Canadian River Expedition," *Chronicles of Oklahoma*, Volume 16, No. 3, (September 1938): 279-300.

Frazer, Robert W. *Forts of the West*. Norman, OK: University of Oklahoma Press, 1965.

Greene, Jerome A. *Washita*. Norman, OK: University of Oklahoma Press, 2004.

Grinnell, George. *The Cheyenne Indians*. New York: Cooper Square, 1923.

Hardorff, Richard G., ed. *Washita Memories*. Norman, OK: University of Oklahoma Press, 2008.

Hatch, Thom. *Black Kettle - The Cheyenne Chief Who Sought Peace But Found War*. Hoboken, NJ: Wiley & Sons, 2004.

Hoge, William M. "The Logistical System of the US Army During the Indian Wars, 1866-1889." Master thesis, Washington State University, 1968.

Hoig, Stan. *The Sand Creek Massacre*. Norman, OK: University of Oklahoma Press, 1961.

Jamieson, Perry D. *Crossing the Deadly Ground*. Tuscaloosa, AL: University of Alabama Press, 1994.

Johnson, Randy. *A Dispatch to Custer*. Missoula, MT: Mountain Press Publishing, 1999.

Jordan, David M. *Winfield Scott Hancock*. Indianapolis, IN: Indiana University Press, 1988.

Kennedy, W.J.D., ed. *On the Plains with Custer and Hancock: The Journal of Isaac Coates*. Boulder, CO: Johnson Books, 1997.

King, James T. *War Eagle, A Life of General Eugene A. Carr*. Lincoln, NE: University of Nebraska Press, 1963.

Kraft, Louis. *Custer and the Cheyenne*. El Segundo, CA: Upton and Sons Press, 1995.

Ladenheim, Jules C. *Custer's Thorn*. Westminster, MD: Heritage Books, 2007.

Leckie, William H. *The Military Conquest of the Southern Plains*. Norman, OK: University of Oklahoma Press, 1963.

Merington, Marguerite, ed. *The Custer Story, The Life and Intimate Letters of General George A. Custer and His Wife Elizabeth*. New York: The Devin-Adair Company, 1950.

Michno, Gregory. *Battle at Sand Creek, The Military Perspective*. El Segundo, CA: Upton and Sons, 2004.

———. *Encyclopedia of Indian Wars*. Missoula, MT: Mountain Press Publishing, 2003.

———. *Forgotten Fights*. Missoula, MT: Mountain Press Publishing, 2008.

Morris, Roy. *Sheridan: The Life and Wars of General Phil Sheridan*. New York: Crown Publishers, 1992.

Murray, Robert A. *The Army Moves West*. Fort Collins, CO: The Old Army Press, 1981.

Oliva, Leo E. *Fort Hays: Keeping Peace on the Plains*. Topeka, KS: Kansas State Historical Society, 1980.

———. *Fort Larned: Guardian of the Santa Fe Trail*. Topeka, KS: Kansas State Historical Society, 1982.

———. *Fort Dodge: Sentry of the Western Plains*. Topeka, KS: Kansas State Historical Society, 1998.

———. *Fort Wallace: Sentinel on the Smoky Hill Trail*. Topeka, KS: Kansas State Historical Society, 1998.

———. *Fort Harker: Defending the Journey West*. Topeka, KS: Kansas State Historical Society, 2000.

Powell, Father Peter John. *People of the Sacred Mountain*. San Francisco, CA: CA Harper and Row Publishers, 1979.

Rickey, Don. *Forty Miles a Day on Beans and Hay*. Norman, OK: University of Oklahoma Press, 1963.

Ryan, John. *Ten Years with Custer, A 7th Cavalryman's Memoirs*. Fort Collins, CO: Citizen Printing Inc., 2001.

Sheridan, Phillip H. *The Personal Memoirs of P.H. Sheridan.* New York: DA CAPO PRESS, 1992.

Stanley, Henry M. *My Early Travels and Adventures in America.* Lincoln, NE: University of Nebraska Press, 1982.

Spotts, David L. *Campaigning with Custer.* Lincoln, NE: University of Nebraska Press, 1988.

Sully, Langdon. *No Tears for the General.* Palo Alto, CA: American West Publishing, 1974.

Utley, Robert M. *Frontiersmen in Blue.* LincolnNE: University of Nebraska Press, 1967.

———. *Frontier Regulars.* Lincoln, NE: University of Nebraska Press, 1973.

———. *Life in Custer's Cavalry, Diaries and Letters of Albert and Jennie Barnitz 1867-1868.* Lincoln, NE: University of Nebraska Press, 1987.

Weingardt, Richard. *Sound the Charge.* Englewood, CO: Jacqueline Enterprises, Inc., 1978.

Werner, Fred. *The Beecher Island Battle.* Greeley, CO: Werner Publications, 1989.

Werner, Fred H. *The Summit Springs Battle.* Greeley, CO: Werner Publications, 1991.

About the Author

Mr. Charles D. Collins, Jr. is an assistant professor of history at Combat Studies Institute. He is the course author for numerous courses including: The Sioux Wars and Cheyenne Wars courses, and The Operation Anaconda Virtual Staff Ride. He received a B.A. in History from Southwest Missouri State University and an MMAS in History from the US Army Command and General Staff College. While on active duty, Mr. Collins served in various armor and cavalry assignments. He retired from the Army in 1996. Mr. Collins' published works include: *The Corps of Discovery: Staff Ride Handbook for the Lewis and Clark Expedition*, *The Atlas of the Sioux Wars, 2d Edition*, and numerous articles on a wide variety of military topics.

Notes

1. William H. Leckie, *The Military Conquest of the Southern Plains* (Norman, OK: University of Oklahoma Press, 1963), 6.
2. Peter G. Cozzens, ed., *Eyewitnesses to the Indian Wars 1865 -1890, Vol. 3: Conquering the Southern Plains* (Mechanicsburg, PA: Stackpole Books, 2003), xviii.
3. See George Grinnell, *The Cheyenne Indians* (New York: Cooper Square, 1923) for details on the Cheyenne.
4. See Robert W. Frazer, *Forts of the West* (Norman, OK: University of Oklahoma Press, 1965) for details on the forts of the West.
5. See William Y. Chalfant, *Cheyennes and Horse Soldiers* (Norman: University of Oklahoma Press, 1989) for additional detail on the 1857 campaign.
6. Gregory Michno, *Battle at Sand Creek*, The Military Perspective (El Segundo, CA: Upton and Sons, 2004), 96
7. Leckie, *The Military Conquest of the Southern Plains*, 22.
8. Robert M. Utley, *Frontiersmen in Blue* (Lincoln, NE: University of Nebraska Press, 1967), 294.
9. Stan Hoig, *The Sand Creek Massacre* (Norman, OK: University of Oklahoma Press, 1961), 168.
10. W.J.D. Kennedy, ed., *On the Plains with Custer and Hancock: The Journal of Isaac Coates*, (Boulder, CO: Johnson Books, 1997), 19-20. (Letter from Lt. General William T. Sherman to Major General Hancock, 14 March 1867)
11. Jeff Broome, *Custer into the West* (El Segundo, CA: Upton and Sons Press, 2009), 162. (14 March letter from Sherman to Hancock).
12. Henry M. Stanley, *My Early Travels and Adventures in America*, (Lincoln, NE: University of Nebraska Press, 1982), 10.
13. Broome, *Custer into the West*, 138-139. (excerpt from Hancock's Official Report of the 1867 Expedition)
14. Kennedy, *On the Plains With Custer and Hancock*, 58.
15. George A. Custer, *My Life on the Plains*, (Lincoln, NE: University of Nebraska Press, 1966), 44.
16. John Ryan, *Ten Years with Custer, A 7th Cavalryman's Memoirs*, (Fort Collins, CO: Citizen Printing Inc., 2001), 29-30.
17. Kennedy, *On the Plains With Custer and Hancock*, 72.
18. Custer, *My Life on the Plains*, 75.
19. William Y. Chalfant. *Hancock's War* (Norman, OK: University of Oklahoma Press, 1989), 204.
20. Kennedy, *On the Plains With Custer and Hancock*, 85.
21. Chalfant, *Hancock's War*, 224.
22. David M. Jordan, *Winfield Scott Hancock* (Indianapolis, IN: Indiana University Press, 1988), 195.
23. Robert M. Utley, *Frontier Regulars* (Lincoln, NE: University of Nebraska Press, 1973), 118.
24. Elizabeth Custer, *Tenting on the Plains* (New York: Charles L. Webster and Co., 1889), 571.
25. Marguerite Merington, ed., *The Custer Story, The Life and Intimate Letters of General George A. Custer and His Wife Elizabeth* (New York: The Devin-Adair Company, 1950), 199.
26. See Chalfant's *Hancock's War* for additional details on the skirmishes noted on Map 15 and Randy Johnson, *A Dispatch to Custer* (Missoula, MT: Mountain Press Publishing, 1999) for details on the tragedy of Lieutenant Lymon Kidder's death while carrying a dispatch to Custer.
27. Phillip H. Sheridan, *The Personal Memoirs of P.H. Sheridan* (New York: DA CAPO PRESS, 1992), 453.
28. Roy Morris, *Sheridan: The Life and Wars of General Phil Sheridan* (New York: Crown Publishers, 1992), 303.
29. Cozzens, *Conquering the Southern Plains*, 249. [Remembrances of Anthony C. Rallya, a soldier with I Company, 7th US Cavalry]
30. See Langdon Sully. *No Tears for the General* (Palo Alto, CA: American West Publishing, 1974) for details on General Sully.
31. Cozzens, *Conquering the Southern Plains*, 250-51.
32. Cozzens, *Conquering the Southern Plains*, 133.
33. Cozzens, *Conquering the Southern Plains*, 129. [Orders signed by Adjutant General Schuler Crosby to Brevet Colonel George Forsyth, dated 24 August 1869]
34. Fred Werner, *The Beecher Island Battle* (Greeley, CO: Werner Publications, 1989), 119. [Sigmund Shlesinger was born in Hungary in 1848. At age 15 he moved to New York and then went west the following year.]
35. Father Peter John Powell, *People of the Sacred Mountain* (San Francisco, CA: CA Harper and Row Publishers, 1979), 582.
36. Cozzens, *Conquering the Southern Plains*, 254. [An anonymous contribution from the Department of Missouri to the "Army and Navy Journal" 6, no. 13 (7 November 1868)].
37. See Gregory Michno, *Encyclopedia of Indian Wars* (Missoula, MT: Mountain Press Publishing, 2003) and Michno, *Forgotten Fights* (Missoula, MT: Mountain Press Publishing, 2008) for details on this and other small skirmishes in the American West.
38. Sheridan, *Memoirs*, 452-453.
39. Custer, *My Life on the Plains*, 276.
40. Custer, *My Life on the Plains*, 278.
41. Private David L. Spotts, *Campaigning with Custer* (Lincoln, NE: University of Nebraska Press, 1988), 60- 64.

42   Robert M. Utley, *Life in Custer's Cavalry, Diaries and Letters of Albert and Jennie Barnitz 1867-1868* (Lincoln, NE: University of Nebraska Press, 1987), 206 – 207.
43   Cozzens, *Conquering the Southern Plains*, 375.
44   Louis Kraft, *Custer and the Cheyenne*, (El Segundo, CA: Upton and Sons Press, 1995), 35. [Sheridan's 22 November 1868 orders to Custer].
45   Jerome A. Greene, *Washita* (Norman, OK: University of Oklahoma Press, 2004), 86.
46   Greene, *Washita*, 86.
47   Greene, *Washita*, 98-99.
48   Utley, *Life in Custer's Cavalry*, 215.
49   Custer, *My Life on the Plains*, 302-303.
50   Richard G. Hardorff, ed., *Washita Memories* (Norman, OK: University of Oklahoma Press, 2008), 206.
51   Utley, *Life in Custer's Cavalry*, 219-220.
52   Custer, *My Life on the Plains*, 322.
53   Hardorff, *Washita Memories*, 306-308. [Magpie, a nephew of Black Kettle, was a young man of about 16 at the time of attack. His father's lodge was on the west side of the village. Thompson's and Myers' failure to get into the assigned attack positions allowed Magpie and many others to escape the attack.]
54   Greene, *Washita*, 240 [reminiscences of Scout Ben Clark].
55   Utley, *Frontier Regulars*, 152.
56   Hardorff, *Washita Memories*, 325-326.
57   Custer, *My Life on the Plains*, 335-336.
58   Hardorff, *Washita Memories*, 332.
59   Hardorff, *Washita Memories*, 209.
60   Custer, *My Life on the Plains*, 338.
61   Jules C. Ladenheim, *Custer's Thorn* (Westminster, MD: Heritage Books, 2007), 99-100.
62   Hardorff, *Washita Memories*, 340.
63   Hardorff, *Washita Memories*, 147.
64   Custer, *My Life on the Plains*, 341 -343.
65   Hardorff, *Washita Memories*, 140-141.
66   Hardorff, *Washita Memories*, 140-141.
67   Hardorff, *Washita Memories*, 359.
68   The town of Cheyenne, Oklahoma, has greatly changed the landscape from what it would have looked like in 1868. To imagine the view in 1868 one must first remove all the man-made structures. There would also have been far fewer trees in the area. The ground would have been much more open with the trees and brush primarily concentrated along the watercourses. Today, Sergeant Major Creek flows due north into the Washita River. However, in 1868 it turned around the north side of Cheyenne and joined the Washita River much farther to the east.
69   Custer, *My Life on the Plains*, 344, 351.
70   Hardorff, *Washita Memories*, 143.
71   Hardorff, *Washita Memories*, 140-141.
72   Hardorff, *Washita Memories*, 178.
73   Custer, *My Life on the Plains*, 351.
74   Custer, *My Life on the Plains*, 372.
75   Cozzens, *Conquering the Southern Plains*, 365.
76   See Thom Hatch, *Black Kettle - The Cheyenne Chief Who Sought Peace But Found War* (Hoboken, NJ: Wiley & Sons, 2004) and Charles J. Brill, *Custer, Black Kettle, and the Fight on the Washita* (Norman, OK: University of Oklahoma Press, 1938) for details on Chief Black Kettle.
77   Hardorff, *Washita Memories*, 271.
77   Sheridan, *Memoirs*, 467.
79   Greene, *Washita*, 163.
80   Colonel A. W. Evans, "Report of the Canadian River Expedition," *Chronicles of Oklahoma* Volume 16, No. 3, September 1938. [Evans stated, "The organization of the Expedition embraced, beside, 13 Officers; 314 Mounted and 90 Infantry men; 42 Infantry men in the Battery; 9 scouts and guides; 33 citizen packers and teamsters; 112 pack mules; 5 horses and 27 mules in the Battery; and 328 Cavalry horses. Fifty (50) head of cattle were driven along. One (1) common tent, for the Hospital, was the only canvas permitted to be taken."]
81   Evans, Report.
82   Evans, Report.
83   Cozzens, *Conquering the Southern Plains*, 405. [Remembrances of Lieutenant Edward Hunter, adjutant of Evans' column]
84   Evans, Report.
85   Evans, Report.

86 Evans, Report.
87 Evans, Report.
88 Evans, Report.
89 Evans, Report..
90 Evans, Report.
91 Evans arrived at the Monument Creek Depot on 13 January 1869.
92 Greene, *Washita*, 177.
93 Sheridan, *Memoirs*, 477.
94 James T. King, *War Eagle, A Life of General Eugene A. Carr* (Lincoln, NE: University of Nebraska Press, 1963), 95. [Assistant Army Inspector General for the Department of the Platte report after touring frontier posts in the region.]
95 Map 16 of this atlas shows the Division of Missouri which includes the departments of Dakota, Platte, and Missouri.
96 *Leavenworth, Kansas Times & Conservative*, "INDIAN OUTRAGES; The Massacre of Thirteen Persons on Saline River--Murder of Nearly a Whole Family." 29 June 1869. Database online at http://query.nytimes.com/gst/abstract.html?res=9800EEDD103AEF34BC4E51DFB0668382679FDE (accessed 17 February 2010).
97 King, *War Eagle*, 100.
98 Richard Weingardt, *Sound the Charge* (Englewood, CO: Jacqueline Enterprises, Inc., 1978), 73. [From General Auger's published order to Major Eugene Carr.]
99 Fred H. Werner, *The Summit Springs Battle*, 62. [From Carr's official report of the Summit Springs Battle.]
100 Werner, *The Summit Springs Battle*, 80. [Excerpt from Major Frank North's diary.]
101 Werner, *The Summit Springs Battle*, 62. [From Carr's official report of the Summit Springs Battle.]
102 Werner, *The Summit Springs Battle*, 67. [From Carr's official report of the Summit Springs Battle.]
103 Powell, *Sacred Mountain*, 735.
104 The final fights in Kansas and Nebraska occurred when a band of Northern Cheyenne broke out of their agency in Oklahoma and tried to return to their home country in the north. The fugitive Cheyenne fought skirmishes with the Army at Punished Woman's Fork (near Scott City, Kansas) on 27 September 1878 and at Fort Robinson (near Crawford, Nebraska) on 9 January 1879.
105 See Combat Studies Institute's Atlas of the Sioux War, Second Edition.
106 Garry Owen was the unofficial marching song of the 7th Cavalry. Custer reportedly heard the song among his Irish troops and liked it. The tune was then played so often the 7th Cavalry became tied to it.
107 Ryan, *Ten Years with General Custer*, 47-48.
108 Don Rickey, *Forty Miles a Day on Beans and Hay* (Norman: University of Oklahoma Press, 1963), 245.
109 See - William M. Hoge, "The Logistical System of the US Army During the Indian Wars, 1866-1889" (Master thesis, Washington State University, 1968) and Robert A. Murray, The Army Moves West (Fort Collins: The Old Army Press, 1981) for details on Army logistics in the Indian Wars.